FREE RADICAL

FREE RADICAL

A Memoir

Vince Cable

Atlantic Books

LONDON

First published in hardback in Great Britain in 2009 by Atlantic Books,
an imprint of Grove Atlantic Ltd.

10 9 8 7 6 5 4 3 2 1

A CIP catalogue record for this book is available from the British Library.

The illustration credits on pp. vii–viii constitute an extension of this copyright page.

ISBN: 978 1 84887 046 8

Printed in Great Britain by the MPG Books Group

Atlantic Books
An imprint of Grove Atlantic Ltd
Ormond House
26–27 Boswell Street
London
WC1N 3JZ

Contents

Illustrations   vii

Preface   ix

1   Starting the Climb   1

2   You've Never Had It So Good   13

3   Ivory Towers   34

4   Olympia   53

5   Facing Mount Kenya   76

6   Red Clydeside   103

7   Latin Detours   135

8   A Passage to India   152

9   Big Oil   180

10   The Long March   202

11   Political Triumph and Personal Tragedy   232

12   New Millennium, New World   263

13   A Taste of Leadership   286

14   Fame, Fortune and Notoriety   297

15   Stormy Waters and Unfinished Business   318

Index   353

Illustrations

Baby Vince Cable, grandmother Annie Cable, and Mother Edith.

Aged around 7 with mother.

With younger brother, Keith, in Scarborough.

With adopted cousin, John.

Playing Macbeth, aged 17.

Father, Len and Vince Cable, aged around 12, on a visit to London.

Len Cable, testing concrete.

As President of the Cambridge Union, Summer Term, 1965.

Speaking in the Cambridge Union's 'No Confidence' motion, 1964.

Olympia Rebelo graduating from York University, 1966.

Olympia and her sister Amata preparing for the wedding, July 1968.

After the wedding on the steps of Nairobi's Catholic cathedral.

As Labour candidate for Hillhead, Glasgow, 1970.

With Shirley Williams, arriving at York Station, 1983.

With Olympia, celebrating election as MP for Twickenham, 1997.

With daughter Aida on her wedding day, 1999.

With Dee Doocey and a model of the 2012 Olympic site.
Photograph courtesy of Twickenham Liberal Democrats.

Abseiling for charity in Twickenham.
Photograph courtesy of Twickenham Liberal Democrats.

Promoting beekeeping at Chelsea Flower Show, May 2009.
Photograph courtesy of Claire Waring, Buzzwords Editorial.

Party leaders at the Cenotaph, Remembrance Sunday, 2007
© *Mark Cuthbert/UK Press/PA Images.*

With Nick Clegg.
Photograph courtesy of David Angell.

Wedding of son, Paul, to Agnesa Tothova, 1998.

With Rachel, in the House of Commons Chapel, 2004.

With family at home in Twickenham.

Unless otherwise credited, pictures are courtesy of Vince Cable.

Preface

Books by politicians about themselves risk adding an extra layer of self-indulgence to careers already characterized by a talent for self-advertisement. Prime ministers and party leaders can be excused for publishing their memoirs and diaries since, even if, as is often the case, they are excruciatingly dull and painfully self-justifying, they contribute to the historical record.

The point at which less elevated politicians have anything useful to add is a matter for conjecture. But the piles of autobiographies and biographies of long-forgotten ministers and political personalities on second-hand bookstalls at charity fairs suggests to me that many of them failed to appreciate that they were well below that point.

There are, however, occasionally politicians of the second rank who produce work of genuine interest. Alan Clark's wit, talent for racy gossip, and colourful sex life made for a fine book. I doubt that I could compete in any of those departments, however. A better model is Matthew Parris's *Chance Witness*, a well-written and painfully honest book which sought to understand and explain the motives and circumstances which make and break a political career. I do not share the sexual orientation which he struggled to come to terms with, but recognize the crucial interplay of public life and private relationships.

Before deciding to write this document I have tried to clarify in my mind my motives. My main purpose is a modest and personal one: to explain to my children and grandchildren where I, and therefore they, come from. If I thereby interest a wider audience, that is a bonus.

I make no claims to absolute historical accuracy. The central characters, Olympia and my parents, are not here to answer back, and my parents, in particular, may feel that I could have given them a better write-up. There are omissions too: secrets of the kind that all of us carry to the grave. But this is a reasonably honest account of what made and motivated one moderately successful politician.

Chapter 1

Starting the Climb

York was once an industrial city. The factories that supplied the country's railway carriages and fed its appetite for sweets have largely closed. They have joined the Roman ruins, Viking artefacts, and medieval walls and churches as monuments to a receding history.

I grew up when that history was still alive: breathing the delicious, all-pervasive smell of sugar, cocoa and vanilla; timing the day by the army of factory workers pedalling to and fro, announced by a swish of tyres and tinkling bells. My first home was a small terraced house close to the Terry's factory where my mother and our neighbours produced chocolates. Far from resembling a dark satanic mill, Terry's was built like a red-brick university, the dominating clock tower the main concession to the disciplines of factory life. The river flowed on one side, to the Archbishops' Palace; the green acres of Knavesmire racecourse stretched out on the other; but around the northern city approaches were the streets of workers' houses, which remain mostly untouched by the slum clearance or gentrification of the inner city.

Finsbury Street was one of them, populated by working-class families of long standing, or by young, ambitious and upwardly mobile workers like my parents, Len and Edith Cable, stepping on to the first rung of the housing ladder. My memories are sparse: the smell of drying clothes; the excitements of the street such as the horse and cart bringing sacks of coal, and the rag and bone man; the cruel cold of the outside lavatory. Some memories are more ambiguous, like the large metal bathtub in front of the coal fire, which may well have been for me, but possibly for the family, as it was when I needed later on to impress left-wing audiences with my proletarian origins.

It was the walks along the River Ouse which remain clearly etched in my mind. Stopping off at Rowntree Park, donated to the city by the bigger chocolate manufacturer, where a magical store dispensed an endless supply of ice creams and there was a large lake which sucked my toy boats into a miniature Sargasso Sea where they remained, becalmed, for ever. Past the Rowntree's baths, whose freezing waters deterred me from swimming until well into adulthood. Under the pulleys and winches and cranes that lifted jute sacks of grain and exotic-smelling fruit from barges into the warehouses, now luxury flats. To Lendal Bridge, looking across to the Tower where York's Jews had once been herded into a medieval holocaust, whose flames lit up many a childhood nightmare. Then, inland, past the Bar walls, dodging the arrows which rained down from the battlements. To the streets off Bishopthorpe Road: on one side rows of terraced houses with gaps of rubble left by German bombs; on the other, intact, Vine Street, where my mother's family, the Pinkneys, lived.

Their house was dominated by the spirit of my dead grandfather, a sportsman of distinction, who had once been a star of the breakaway professional Rugby League and a railway clerk. His life had been dominated by the First World War: captured in

1917 after battles in France, interned in a German prisoner-of-war camp, and returned home disabled by gas and ill-treatment in prison. He never worked again, but remained a brooding presence perpetuating hatred of the Germans, firm family discipline, and working-class respectability. My grandmother, Annie, boosted the family income as a charlady, but it was not enough and when my mother reached fourteen she was sent out to work, despite the protests of her teachers who had recognized her ability and creativity. The Pinkneys stayed clear of the pit of depravity inhabited by their rougher neighbours by means of hard work, temperance and voting Conservative. Grandmother made time after her early morning office-cleaning to distribute leaflets for the patriotic, Tory, Primrose League. My mother recalled that when she dated a young Irish socialist from down the street – one Bill Burke, later Labour leader of York City Council – she was beaten with a leather strap.

The Pinkneys were a warm, close family, populated by friendly aunts from the surrounding streets, who stuffed my mouth with chocolate from blue-paper packets: factory 'waste' from Terry's, which was a luxury not rationed by the little books which then defined our food intake. Much of the warmth came from my mother's sister Irene and her husband, Reg Mothersdill, a plasterer, whom I remember for his shining, brilliantined hair, endless chain of Woodbines, and tales of his war exploits escaping from sinking ships.

Unlike the Pinkneys, the Cables – my father, his brother and his father – had no direct experience of war. My father had been an 'essential worker', making and repairing aircraft in the village of Sherburn in Elmet, near York. His battles were against the stifling hierarchy of British class and educational privilege which had undervalued him from an early age.

His widowed mother – another Annie – lived in Layerthorpe, close to a notorious slum in which the family owned a grocer's shop. Their house was separated by a railway line from the mean streets that Joseph Rowntree had surveyed a century before, and, as its name implied, Glen Avenue was respectable enough – but not far enough away to escape the foul smell of the gasworks, which penetrated every nook and cranny.

Grandma's shop and, when he was alive, Grandfather Cable's income as a draper's assistant were enough to lift one foot out of the working class, but not both. My father's elder brother Reg was sent to a grammar school, then fee-paying, to prepare for a professional career, but there was not enough for my father, who was sent out to work as soon as possible. He recalled being sent around the streets shovelling manure from behind passing horses to earn a few pennies. But through aptitude and application he progressed to skilled work in the joiner's shop in Rowntree's factory, where his brother, after school, began a managerial career.

The resentments created by this sibling discrimination continued for many years, and family history as it was passed down to me was undoubtedly coloured by it. My mother – who sided with my father in this family feud, if not in much else – insisted that Grandma Cable was illiterate, though her copperplate handwriting suggests otherwise.

It was inevitable that, for a man of my father's intelligence, frustrated ambition and energy, the factory jobs and small terraced house were mere staging posts. And so it proved. One day, when I was just over four years old, a van came to carry away our furniture and I was carried, my feet dangling over the tailboard, to a new home.

*

The next step on our long social climb was Grantham Drive and a small, semi-detached house with a garden. My father, planning his next career move, was away at teacher-training college, which equipped him to impart his technical skills and not just practise them. My mother, at one bound, was promoted to the status of a middle-class housewife. And I started my own ascent of the educational Alps at the base camp of Poppleton Road Primary School.

In appearance and in reality, Poppleton Road Primary – still virtually unchanged in its century of existence – was an education factory, producing batches of children neatly sorted for the next, selective, stage of their manufacture. It towers on a hill above the low-lying river basin of the Ouse, rivalling the Minster in elevation, if not in architectural distinction.

I remember little of the early years beyond the smell of heaving, damp children on rainy days and the sordid mess of the toilets which dictated the rhythm and programme of my day, desperately holding on until I could get home without the humiliation of being caught short. There were memorable treats, like the boxes of red apples from kindly Canadians, sent to ease our post-war deprivation (I am not sure if the Canadians knew about our hoards of chocolates).

I struggled most of all with writing and never mastered the art of dipping the metal pen into the ink-pot and reproducing the required italicized print. I owned a pet spider who followed my pen round the page, leaving frequent blobs of black or blue. Until rescued many years later by the great Hungarian inventor László Bíró, I distressed teachers and parents alike by my lack of nib control.

But I clearly did something right. One hot summer day, the seven-year-olds were assembled in the playground and a roll call divided us into four lines. We knew that something momentous was afoot. As the clever goats gradually separated from the duller sheep, and even lesser species, we began to understand the choice was not random. I was relieved to be in the line assigned to Miss Whitfield, who always taught the top stream. Whether through astute judgement or self-justifying prophecy, the same group remained pretty much together in our respective schools for the next ten years or so. Our friendships with the other children became gradually attenuated.

Schooling acquired a new sense of purpose and direction: gaining more and more stars to add to the line snaking across the wall against my name, and achieving higher and higher ranking in the endless competition in 'mental' and 'mechanical' maths, composition and spelling, and the gamut of academic subjects that entered the curriculum. Praise at home followed praise at school, and I had plenty of encouragement to become a school swot.

Most swots had a hard time from their less academic contemporaries. Segregation by class did not provide protection in the playground or on the way home. I somehow survived that. I was tall and, also, in one fortuitous episode, acquired a fearsome and wholly unjustified reputation as a playground warrior. A small boy called Higginbottom demanded a fight at playtime and dozens of boys gathered round, chanting 'Blood! Blood!' His fists flailed wildly but they did not reach me on account of my having longer arms. Out of frustration he charged and I ducked from his blows. The duck, somehow, became a well-directed headbutt and soon the ground was fertilized with blood from his broken nose. I found myself carried around the playground in triumph and was never attacked again.

I was also rescued by reasonable competence in sport, achieved through endless games of street football and cricket, both played with tennis balls. I learned the importance of earning grudging, classless respect by heading a heavy ball or winning a tackle in the middle of the bog that passed for the school field, or being familiar with the weekly exploits of York City, thanks to my father who was a fan, and York's Rugby League team, with which I had an ancestral connection.

Along with books and ball games, like most children, I endured my share of terror and boredom. Both of these centred on God. My parents were God-fearing folk who attended the Baptist church for services twice a day with, for me, the added spiritual bonus of Sunday School. I heard it said that my father had studied to be a pastor and had attended a Bible college in Northern Ireland to this end, but there is no corroboration for this family story. Church was, nonetheless, a central pillar of their existence. Like most small boys, I understood little of what was going on and endlessly fidgeted with boredom, but was a dutiful little Christian, earning many heavenly credits by identifying obscure quotations from the lesser prophets.

One day, however, a serious religious schism occurred. We were late for a bus and I released a torrent of profane abuse learned in the school playground, but not understood. My father warned me that I would be punished and I was severely beaten when we returned home that evening. I felt a bitter sense of grievance and, for long afterwards, blamed God for the injustice of it. I also experienced nightmares centring on the figure of God in the religious painting hanging over my parents' bed, and screamed until it was removed. My apostasy must have been infectious, for the family stopped attending the Baptist church soon afterwards because of a bitter row the spiritual or personal origins of which were never explained to me.

The weekly cycle of boredom reached its climax with the ritual Sunday visit to Grandma Cable, for which I was required to be well scrubbed, seen, but not heard, and exceptionally well behaved. I suffered badly by comparison with my angelic cousin John, the adopted son of Uncle Reg and his wife Evie. I knew, however, that cousin John was not real, because I had helped to choose him from a book of orphans. The Cables had agreed that 'coloured and half-caste' children were unacceptable, and some of the other waifs and strays looked, even as toddlers, as if they were destined for a life of crime. In the middle of this unsavoury band of infants there was, however, a cherub with blue eyes and blond curly hair, lacking only wings. He duly became cousin John, the exemplar against which I was to be measured: his cleanliness advertised by a permanent smell of carbolic soap; his godliness undimmed, like mine, by doubt; and his heavenly voice untouched by late adolescence, remaining firmly stuck in the castrato range. He seemed, even as an infant, altogether too good to be true. He was. But the full scale of the ensuing disaster only became apparent after a couple of decades, when his hereditary Huntington's disease manifested itself.

My appetite for terror and my flight from boredom were both met in the fantasy world of films, radio and books which filled my childhood. Television did not arrive until my mid-teens. It was the vivid images from the weekly visit to the cinema that lingered in the imagination. My dreams and daydreams were long haunted by the early scenes from David Lean's *Great Expectations,* which my parents unwisely judged to be the best occasion for my cinematic baptism, aged six. The misty marshes of the Thames Estuary seemed uncannily like the familiar river-scape of the Ouse, and I could all too easily envisage a Magwitch-like convict emerging from the fog to snatch me. I progressed to the comfort zone of Westerns, where the good guys in the cavalry always managed to wipe out the Indians, and war films, where heroic Englishmen could be relied on to blast the Hun out of the skies or the seas. Some films had a profound influence: *Where No Vultures Fly*, which graphically captured the cruelty of ivory poachers in Kenya; Humphrey Bogart fighting off leeches in *The African Queen*, before a kamikaze attack on a German gunboat on Lake Victoria; and later, *Simba*, a horrifying depiction of Mau Mau oath-taking rituals and murders, also in Kenya. I had decided at an early age that, unlike my contemporaries, who were preparing to be train drivers, motor-racing drivers or spacemen, I would become a Big White Chief in Africa, ruling over the natives.

By the time I was eight, my father was on the move again to a bigger and better semi in New Lane, overlooking Holgate Park, near the rapidly expanding suburb of Acomb, our upward mobility underlined by the fact that our new neighbour was a bank manager. Our move was at least partly precipitated by our noisy neighbours, the Smithsons, who, these days, would probably have been in line for an ASBO. My father's main retaliatory weapon was to place our radio against their wall at full volume, covering it with blankets to dull the sound on our side. He failed. We moved.

For me the new home in New Lane sat in the middle of a vast adventure playground. Opposite were the woods of a park opening up to playgrounds and playing fields. The road itself led into a country lane lined with hedgerows, which led in turn to the wilds of Hob Moor. In the other direction was a disused windmill surrounded on three sides by a wilderness of scrub and trees, which were a perfect setting for Custer's last stand and for ambushing the

Sheriff of Nottingham. Though I understood nothing of economics at the time, the country lane and the wilderness were becoming prime sites in the post-war scramble for development land, and they gradually disappeared during my childhood. But these were the happiest years of my early life: friends (all boys), boundless space, and a freedom to roam that would be inconceivable today. It is tempting to romanticize the days before family cars, televisions and expensive toys, but even in the more protective and disciplinarian homes like mine there was a degree of trust – in neighbours, in strangers, in the safety of roads, and in the common sense of children and their instinct for self-preservation – which has largely gone. We somehow survived without protective helmets and without encountering predatory paedophiles or murderous gangs. Occasionally there was a really serious treat: a day in Leeds on the trams and trolleybuses; or a week in Scarborough or Filey, by train to a dreary boarding house and the hope that the weather would permit the use of buckets and spades. But it was treat enough to own the streets and the wide-open spaces.

A couple of years later, when I was ten, a series of events occurred in quick succession that radically reshaped our lives. My mother bore another child, Keith, and, like many unplanned, younger children, he was adored by his parents and elder brother. She succumbed, however, to what is now called post-natal depression but was then seen simply as a form of madness. She was taken to York's mental hospital – what my friends called the 'the loony bin' – and my brother was fostered for the best part of a year. The breakdown was not difficult to explain: her mother had just died; her sister, whom she loved dearly, had emigrated to Australia with my other Uncle Reg and my cousin Susan; her factory friends were no longer suitable company. Marriage had produced suffocating tedium and isolation, cooking and cleaning, serving three meals a day to a bad-tempered husband working off the slights and frustrations of the staff room in the technical college where he was now teaching, a clever but ungrateful son – and now a baby. Something also snapped in the relationship between my parents and I saw, or was aware of, violence for the first time (my brother, who witnessed episodes later in his childhood, recently reminded me of this, something I had managed to erase from my memory). When my mother returned from hospital she gradually put her mind together again with the help of adult education classes, but for the rest of my childhood and adolescence she was a damaged and diminished figure, usually found talking to herself in the kitchen.

Shortly after my mother's breakdown there was the eleven-plus. I had done well at school, but nothing was guaranteed. I was, moreover, becoming a vehicle for my father's frustrated ambitions. He might well be a mere craftsman amid the graduates in the technical college staff room, but his son was smarter than theirs. He was no fool, and understood long before Britain's educational establishment that intelligence was acquired, not innate. So I was set to work on practice IQ tests, as well as English and maths, progressing from initial bafflement to marvellous fluency. I passed easily enough, along with most of the top stream at Poppleton Road. But there were some casualties, like the pretty girl on the next desk, who collapsed sobbing when the results were announced in class and disappeared through the trapdoor of education into a secondary modern school. I never saw her again. That episode more than any other persuaded me that, although I was a beneficiary of it, there was something fundamentally wrong with the eleven-plus system of selection.

My father discovered, from his contacts in the education department, that not only had I passed but that I had gained the highest marks in the city. This entitled me not merely to a grammar school place but to compete for a single place at the cerebral Quaker public school, Bootham, or for one of five places at the posh and ancient St Peter's. I went for Bootham, my father having been advised that admission was a formality. Only an interview stood in the way – on my interests and my reading – with the distinguished head, Mr Green. I was extremely well prepared, with a compendious knowledge of the world's capital cities, Test match results, and the full sequence of English kings and queens. I was a well-travelled young man, having explored northern England with my friends, looking for rare train numbers in engine sheds, as far as Gorton in Manchester and Blaydon in Newcastle. I had read voraciously: the complete Biggles series of Captain W. E. Johns and two comics a week, which kept me fully up to speed with Dan Dare's battles with the Mekon and the fish-and-chip-eating running-track genius, Alf Tupper. It soon became clear, however, that Mr Green was neither excited nor impressed by this knowledge. He asked me to read a passage from Milton's *Paradise Lost*. I floundered, desperately trying to read, let alone interpret, this ancient gibberish. A few days later I received a letter confirming that I would not be going to Bootham but to Nunthorpe Grammar School. My father had, however, learned from this disaster and when he later repeated the eleven-plus success with my brother Keith, he was better prepared. Keith went to St Peter's, but detested the snobbery, underperformed, and always envied me my failure. Meantime, I flourished as a big fish in the smaller pool of a grammar school, along with my friends from Poppleton Road.

Chapter 2

You've Never Had It So Good

The 1950s saw my family firmly established in the lower reaches of the English middle class. And post-war prosperity brought a stream of new objects into the home: a vacuum cleaner, a washing machine, and eventually – and most reluctantly – a black-and-white TV, then a (shared) telephone and a Morris Minor. These purchases were all approached with great circumspection and we lagged behind the Joneses. My friends, whose fathers worked in the railway carriage works, and our poorer relatives were not sure whether to put this down to the Cables' snobbery or meanness, especially when I was reduced to knocking on their doors, asking plaintively to see *Billy Bunter* or *The Lone Ranger*. In truth, my parents were puritanical, never drank or gambled – my father's pipe being his only vice – and they resisted new-fangled acquisitions until abstinence put them at risk of ridicule.

In general, I added lustre to the family's achievements and upward mobility. Every prize-giving at Nunthorpe yielded another addition to our collection of encyclopedias and dictionaries. Occasionally, however, I brought shame. I discovered an air rifle and ammunition hidden in a bedroom cupboard. With my friend Duncan, our games of white game hunter were transformed once we discovered that we had the weaponry to hunt and terrorize the cats and dogs of New Lane. We progressed to being Second World War heroes directing sniper fire at Nazis hidden in the bedrooms of our neighbours. After local chatter disclosed a rash of broken windows and airgun pellets, someone traced the angle of fire back to my bedroom and, before long, a policeman appeared at the door. We were duly hauled off to York police station, but contrition, a blameless record, and my father's references to his influential connections in the city, got us off with a caution. This brush with the law was especially shocking to my parents, and also to me, since I had never previously shown much inclination towards criminality beyond such peccadilloes as pelting elderly people with snowballs. I was part of an orderly society in which we deferred even to such minor authority figures as park keepers and bus conductors, let alone the police.

With my mother relegated to baby-minding and household chores, my father superintended my teenage upbringing, and with rather closer attention after the episode with the gun. In many ways he was an exemplary father who kept me motivated at school but gave me space to play. He took me to London and regularly to football matches, including the 1955 cup semi-final when York almost achieved the impossible feat of beating Jackie Milburn's Newcastle at Hillsborough, having earlier disposed of Stanley Matthews's Blackpool.

He was a dominating personality, with great drive. He was also a bully who crushed weaker spirits, like my mother, but energized others, including many of his pupils. He was known at the college as Hitler, on account of his moustache and his reported ability to invest the teaching of even the most recondite corners of building science with the fervour of a mass rally. He married the skills of teaching and communication with those of a fine craftsman. His technical drawings were almost works of art, blending precision with elegant form and colour. Later, in retirement, he sketched with remarkable accuracy, and in detail, all of Britain's cathedrals. In the staff room, however, where he inhabited a twilight world somewhere between the graduate lecturers and the technicians, his confidence evaporated and he suffered years of indignity and real or imagined snubs.

He saw part of his parental duties as introducing me to political ideas and the art of debate. There was, however, little scope for reasoned debate, since his views had all the flexibility of the reinforced concrete he tested to destruction at work. He was unswervingly Conservative, his philosophy built on unquestioning loyalty to the monarchy, the army and the police, the sanctity of property, rewards for thrift and hard work, hanging and flogging for criminals, Britain's imperial glory, the innate superiority of white people, and the ingrained subversiveness of socialism and trade unionism. The last was particularly difficult to understand since at Rowntree's, and at his wartime aircraft factory, he had been a union shop steward and was apparently trusted by his workmates. Later in life he became President of his union, the National Association of Schoolmasters (NAS), compromising his hostility to collectivism because of the cause it served: fighting equal pay for women. Women were, he believed, steadily destroying the teaching profession, dragging down pay and undermining discipline at the chalk-face. Married women did not need full pay because they had husbands, and single women did not have a family to support. The NAS, a powerful union led by one Terry Casey, grew up around those doing battle with the feminist- and communist-dominated National Union of Teachers. The NAS eventually merged with a rival women's union to become the

NAS/UWT, and I suspect that it has buried the politically incorrect misogyny that inspired it and so attracted my father.

Trade unionism was but one of the perverse subtleties of his Toryism. He was also fiercely class-conscious and detested 'toffs' like York's MP, Sir Harry Hylton-Foster, who had once brushed aside a problem my father had brought to the constituency surgery, patronized him and addressed him as 'my good man'. Like the middle-class man in the John Cleese–Ronnie Barker–Ronnie Corbett sketch, my father looked down on the working class but also resented being looked down upon by his social superiors.

Eventually Nirvana arrived, courtesy of a grocer's daughter, Mrs Thatcher, and though he only lived to see three years of her earthly paradise he lived every minute like a Bolshevik revolutionary who has glimpsed the promised land. Even after a heart attack, aged seventy, he rushed out into the snow to deliver more Conservative leaflets, contracting the pneumonia that killed him. He died fulfilled and, though I did not altogether share his passion for Mrs Thatcher, I saw, then, what I loved in him.

My political education consisted of listening to rants directed against his many bêtes noires. Chief among these were the colonial upstarts who expressed their ingratitude to their mother country by demanding independence. India had been abandoned without a fight by the socialists, and now even the Conservatives were having to negotiate with uppity natives like Nkrumah and Makarios, while evil communists like Jomo Kenyatta lurked in the background. But it was the Arab upstart, Colonel Nasser, who brought him to paroxysms of rage. When the Suez crisis arrived he registered his anger at hearing Nasser's voice on the BBC by hurling shoes at the radio. He would calm down the following morning when our newspapers, the *Daily Mail* and

Sunday Express, provided what he regarded as a more balanced assessment than the unpatriotic BBC. Suez confirmed all my father's worst suspicions: Britain had been stabbed in the back by socialists and pacifists at home and the United Nations and the Americans overseas. Only the plucky Israelis emerged with any credit. For someone with anti-Semitic prejudices, my father had a strange infatuation with Israel and it was the only country he ever expressed any interest in visiting: the product, I think, of his Old Testament religion combined with relief that someone was giving the Arabs the thrashing they deserved.

Suez and the Hungarian uprising, both of which occurred around my thirteenth birthday, triggered in me a first stirring of interest in politics. I devoured the newspapers and numerous books on current affairs and began to see through the fallacies and factual inaccuracies of some of my father's arguments. I ventured to contradict him, which usually angered him further but occasionally prompted a bemused respect. I could even begin to see the limitations of my father's favourite tracts – like the dyspeptic column in the *Sunday Express* written by John Gordon, aka John Junor (the Richard Littlejohn of his day), exposing humbug and hypocrisy on the left – which, since he no longer went to church, had come to fill the gap left by the Sunday sermon.

Like most adolescents, I was emotionally and intellectually confused, very dependent on my parents, but increasingly rebellious, especially towards my father. I had two role models, both close friends, who in their different ways represented the zeitgeist of 1950s youth and sought to attract me into their respective orbits. One, Duncan, was my fellow delinquent in the airgun incident. He was a rebel without a cause. He was the only son of a quite elderly couple who had befriended me, taking me on their family holidays, which left me with an abiding love of Britain's fells and moors but bored Duncan to tears. He experimented, at an early age, with the joys of cigarettes (then the recreational drug of choice), sex, motorbikes, and the garb and companionship of Teddy boys. He left school at the first opportunity, without O levels, to earn money to finance his motorbike, which almost killed him in a horrific accident, and progressed rapidly to early marriage and parenthood, then early divorce. We gradually drifted apart, having only a passion for Elvis in common.

A bigger influence was rebel with a cause, David. David's father was a left-wing shop steward at the nearby carriage works, where many of our neighbours were employed. Specifically he was a Tribunite: the Tories were the Devil; Bevan was God; Gaitskell was Judas; and Michael Foot was the chief apostle of this sect. His son expounded this brand of true socialism with the same didactic, uncompromising certainty as my father showed in the opposite political direction. We had a third friend, John, whose father had a white-collar job and read the *Daily Telegraph*. Aged fourteen or fifteen, we wandered the streets of York in the evening, stopping for bags of scraps (bits of cooked batter) with salt and vinegar at the fish shop, while my two friends aimed ideological broadsides at each other and I tried to arbitrate a ceasefire. I already understood John's Conservatism, from home, but David introduced new concepts, like nationalization of the means of production, distribution and exchange, and the class struggle, which seemed to me of little relevance in a quiet, increasingly prosperous place like York, but which were announced with such conviction that it seemed churlish, as well as unwise, to contradict him.

David introduced me to more than socialism. He was a

genius with cars: by the time he was sixteen he had built his own fibreglass sports car, and took me to see future Formula One heroes like Jim Clark and Mike Hawthorn racing on the aerodromes around York. He was a fine artist, passionate about Impressionist and post-Impressionist art and, since I was his favourite captive audience, educated me in the works of Picasso, Klee, Modigliani and Dalí. Most remarkably, he was a womanizer of discernment and considerable experience. Despite his unprepossessing appearance – spotty face, horn-rimmed spectacles, hunched back and scruffy duffel coat – he pulled girls of, to me, remarkable beauty. When my friends and I doubted his sexual escapades, he would produce nude portraits of his latest girlfriend. He tried to introduce me to members of his harem, but while I could cope with socialism and Fauvism, women were altogether more alarming. David had what is now called charisma, and plenty of it.

Our friendship was put to its greatest test after he announced, shortly before the 1959 general election, that he was leaving Labour and joining the Communist Party. He was fed up with effete public schoolboys like Gaitskell undermining the Labour movement with social democratic treachery. There were revolutionary stirrings in the York working class, he announced, and it was time to fight the spread of false consciousness among the masses. When the general election was announced, the headmaster of Nunthorpe told us that the school would have its own. The aim, I think, was to let the upper-sixth practise their debating skills, but David put himself forward as the Communist candidate, citing me as one of his seconds. He produced dazzling posters, painted by himself, and agitated vigorously among Nunthorpe's lumpen proletariat in the lower forms. Nationalization and class war did not have much resonance as issues with grammar-school boys in a city with no history of industrial strife. But the burgeoning Campaign for Nuclear Disarmament did, and David skilfully promoted it.

The authorities panicked and it was announced that the Communist candidate had been disqualified for unspecified irregularities. I was secretly relieved, but David was outraged at this assault on democracy and civil liberties. He called for a school strike and civil disobedience. No one joined him on the picket line, where he shouted 'Scab' at the strike-breakers. I arrived head-down in the middle of a peloton of cyclists to avoid his gaze. His friends, including me, slipped away, and he reappeared a week later with a sick note. I voted for the Liberal. My friendship with David was never quite the same again. After A levels he went to art school, from which he claimed he was expelled for setting fire to the buildings during an 'industrial dispute'.

The 1959 election also proved a turning point for my mother. One day she broke down in tears and confessed to me – once I had pledged secrecy – that she had done something terrible. I thought initially that she had killed someone, but it transpired that she had defied my father's instruction to vote Conservative. In the privacy of the ballot box, she had supported that nice Mr Jo Grimond. From then on we formed a secret Liberal cell in the Cable household and she remained a supporter until she died.

Another liberal (and Liberal) influence was the Quakers. After the Baptists, I had wandered from one religious denomination to another, not so much in pursuit of spiritual nourishment as friendship. I spent several years with the Methodist chapel at the end of the lane where services were made tolerable by lusty singing of 'Onward, Christian Soldiers', 'Stand Up, Stand Up for Jesus' and 'There is a Green Hill Far Away'. The chapel organized Cubs, provided film shows after Sunday service, and asked little of us beyond signing a temperance pledge, breaches of which I have always associated with the fires of Hell and, perhaps for that reason, have broken only moderately and occasionally. One of my friends, however, lured me away to the Society of Friends when I was about eleven. I never warmed to the stillness of the Meeting as I did to Methodist hymns, and I never embraced pacifism, but I greatly liked the people, who were kindly, generous and compassionate, and made me welcome without testing my convictions. And while my father feared that I was being indoctrinated by liberal and left-wing ideas, he saw merit in my being involved with York's social and intellectual elite, including the Rowntree family, and I stayed with the Friends until I left for university.

My only problem with the Quakers was that I never saw God through the goodness and I worried seriously that, despite being a regular church attendee since my childhood (a somewhat more regular attendee than my God-fearing parents), I had never encountered anything that could be remotely described as a religious experience. Nor have I since. I decided at one point to visit each of the churches in York that I had not previously attended, looking for God, and went to the Mormons, Christadelphians, Jehovah's Witnesses, Presbyterians, Unitarians, and various shades of Anglicans. My market research suggested that the Methodists had the best hymns, the Anglicans the best churches, and the Quakers the nicest people and prettiest girls (from the Mount School). But the Almighty eluded me. I was left with a sense of the importance of the spiritual dimension of life, and I still have a yearning for Him and for whatever it is in

Christianity that provides me with such comfort and inspiration. But I struggled then, and always have, to get to grips with faith, as if I was trying to grab a particularly elusive bar of soap.

Politics was easier to understand and, warming to Liberalism, I market-tested this new political allegiance on my friends. The overwhelming consensus was that Liberals were a wasted vote. Conservatives complained that 'they let Labour in' and socialists that 'they let the Tories in'. Even my ill-formed political mind could grasp that while one or other proposition might be true, they could not both be true at the same time. Nineteenth-century history, taught in the O level curriculum, also led to the conclusion that Liberals were progressive and a Good Thing, while Conservatives – Disraeli excepted – were reactionary and a Bad Thing. That was broadly where I remained until midway through university.

Nineteen fifty-nine was a crucial year in other respects. It was time to choose A level subjects. I had begun to develop a certain flair in history essays thanks to an inspirational figure, 'Jimmy' Jewell. I was also discovering the delights of Thomas Hardy and Shakespeare and the war poets; and actually enjoyed translating Caesar's *Gallic Wars*. However, my father had a deep suspicion of 'arty-farty' subjects, a suspicion deepened by the fact that my mother, thanks to the adult college, now went around the house speculating about the nature of being, rather than attending to her domestic duties. In his sternly utilitarian view, there were serious choices to be made: did I intend to become an accountant, a lawyer, a teacher or a scientist? The last seemed the least of several evils and I embarked upon maths, physics and chemistry, in which I had shown competence but no great flair or passion.

As luck would have it, the choice proved less clear-cut than I had feared. Mr Jewell auditioned every two years for his Shakespeare production with the neighbouring girls' grammar school, Mill Mount, where his wife, Joyce, was the drama teacher. The play was his pride and joy, taken immensely seriously, with theatre critics summoned from as far as Hull. That year's play was *Macbeth*. I had no expectations beyond being a stagehand or spear-carrier, being shy, inarticulate and wholly untested. Moreover, I had offended Mr Jewell deeply by reproducing in a history essay some anti-Semitic diatribe I had picked up from my father, not appreciating that Mr Jewell was Jewish. He forgave that indiscretion, understanding, I think, where the nonsense had come from. He also found in my reading of the lines at the audition some dramatic quality that had escaped me and everyone else, and gave me the leading role.

A few months later I had mastered several hundred lines of blank verse, learned the rudiments of acting, and overcome my terror of speaking in public. Olivier, however, I was not, and on a disastrous first night I came on a scene early in Act Five to confront a group of baffled little boys advancing across the stage carrying branches: Birnam Wood in motion. The little boys took fright at a sixth-former with a false beard waving a sword at them and fled to the wings, and Shakespeare's tragedy dissolved into comic melodrama. By then, however, the dramatic tension had long since gone, not least because of the catcalls from the boys in the audience who had noticed that the backlighting revealed the three Mill Mount witches to be naked underneath their diaphanous gowns. Still, things got better after that, and I was credited with capturing some of the poetic quality of Shakespeare.

*

The play also introduced me to Lady Macbeth, who became my first love. Until that point I had been terrified of girls, and uncomfortable with women in general. My mother had become almost invisible after her breakdown, and the moments of tenderness I remembered from years before had been long since lost in the daily routine of a home dominated by the appetites of men and boys. My surviving grandmother, Grandma Cable, and I enjoyed a strong, mutual loathing. She had, in any event, been banished to an old folks' home where she claimed she was being detained against her will, constantly insisting that she was being robbed of all her money, and sitting with her stockings and knickers round her ankles, smelling of urine.

By our mid-teens, the barriers created by gender segregation at school had begun to break down. Relationships were measured on a primitive metric: Grade 1 was holding hands; Grade 2 was full-on kissing; at Grade 3 hands got inside bras; Grade 4 was heavy petting; and Grade 5 was intercourse and beyond. Conversation, let alone love, didn't enter into it. A few of my precocious friends had reached Grade 5 early on, or claimed to have, competing to be the school's Casanova and generating innumerable pregnancy scares around the city. Most of us, however, were clustered at the bottom of this ladder of sexual achievements and hadn't made Grade 1. I was generally thought to be pretty eligible, but underdeveloped, and received plenty of encouragement, including being paired off with a dark, flirtatious beauty called Carol. After two circuits of Hob Moor, where courtships occurred, I had not dared to utter a word or approached within a foot of her and she suggested I try someone else.

Audrey was a Grade 2 girl, the maximum allowed by her

Methodism, and she was my first real girlfriend. Apart from a mutual interest in physics and chemistry, however, conversation was sparse. We both resorted to bringing to our dates a checklist of talking points suggested by friends, but they were exhausted after a few minutes and the hours hung heavily. Another, more suitable and articulate, boy was found for her.

Lady Macbeth, Marion, had enormous eyes and a dazzling, wide smile but no chest, which made Shakespeare's allusions to her breast-feeding a source of considerable ribaldry among the more disrespectful juniors. Indeed, she suffered seriously from what is now called anorexia, though it was concealed beneath well-chosen, flowing garments. Our first date hit the buffers when she announced that she did not like to be touched by boys. Nonetheless, the relationship flourished and we became inseparable, talking endlessly on the streets or by phone about everything under the sun, including sex, albeit theoretically. We worked our way through the modern novel, concentrating on Lawrence. Marion saw herself as Miriam from *Sons and Lovers*, doomed to frigidity by a mysteriously unhappy upbringing, and urged me to find an Ursula before it was too late. *Lady Chatterley's Lover* had recently escaped censorship and we endlessly deconstructed it. Unfortunately, I carelessly left the copy at home, where it was found by my father who insisted that he, and my mother, should read it 'to find out what the fuss was all about'. To my amazement their reaction was restrained and good-humoured. While deploring the sexually explicit passages, which they obviously understood better than I, my father even ventured some perceptive comments on Lawrence's florid style and the thinness of the plot. This episode caused me to reassess my father, whom I had come to see in a monochromatic light as a bullying neo-Nazi. He had, in fact, a generous and tolerant side, as I should have more readily appreciated since, when I was old enough to drive, he allowed me to use his new car for my trysts with Marion.

Although we were very close, the relationship became a source of concern, as well as ridicule, among our friends. We became Darby and Joan. Marion was offered counselling by her earthier classmates. She decided on drastic action and after a holiday abroad announced that she had lost her virginity to a German. She reassured me that it had been an appalling experience which I had been spared. Shortly afterwards, she invited me to her bedroom and undressed. Whether it was my shyness or my shock at her emaciated body I am not sure, but nothing happened and we retreated into talk. Another attempt, equally ignominious, failed several months later, and we settled for platonic love. Marion arranged for me to go out with her friend, Gwyneth, an altogether less emotionally complicated, more physical and affectionate girl – so much so that I panicked and, unforgivably, fled while she was sitting her A levels.

When Marion and I met as students some years later, she explained that her problem had been that she was really a lesbian but had only just felt able to 'come out'. This seemed a plausible explanation, but its full accuracy was put into doubt when I met her mother while canvassing in the 1983 general election, who explained that Marion had emigrated to the USA, met a man half her age, and was now happily married with four children.

Somehow, amid this emotional turmoil and artistic distraction, I coped well with advanced calculus and the periodic table and was one of a small number of boys deemed by the head to be Oxbridge material. As such, I qualified for a grossly disproportionate amount of senior teachers' time. The head, Henry Moore, was anxious to push Nunthorpe from its status as a middling grammar school into the big league occupied by the direct grant and public schools which counted their Oxbridge entrants in double figures. A place at Oxbridge, or a highly prestigious red-brick institution like Imperial College, merited a half-day celebratory holiday for the school, so I did not lack encouragement.

Added motivation came from being appointed Head Boy ahead of an altogether more focused and disciplined rival. My appointment caused nervousness among the staff because my standards of dress and punctuality fell well below acceptable norms and the Head Boy had considerable devolved authority for imposing the school rules. Reflecting, no doubt, the changing mood of the times, standards of discipline were confusingly inconsistent. Some younger teachers opposed corporal punishment, but a few of the old lags relied heavily on canes and rubber tubing, sometimes administered with medieval sadism, for petty offences. I added to the moral confusion by zealously enforcing the rules that I agreed with and ignoring others. Noise levels rose alarmingly in break times, playground fights proliferated and the paper dart industry flourished, but smokers were not tolerated. There was not, then, a scientific basis for the smoking ban, but with a zealous gang of enforcers I tracked down every illicit smoker behind the toilets and bicycle sheds and in the surrounding streets and hauled them off to be given six of the best by the deputy head. This apart, I saw my rule as one of enlightened liberalism until, quite recently, I met an old boy with an altogether different perspective, who could, aged sixty, still recite the innumerable lines I had given him for some trifling misdemeanour.

Getting from Oxbridge potential to an Oxbridge place was

not, however, straightforward. The market for theatrical scientists with an interest in current affairs proved difficult to penetrate. I was turned down by innumerable Oxbridge colleges and other universities and ended up with offers of places at King's College, London, to read chemistry and Nottingham to study social administration. Someone then suggested Fitzwilliam House, Cambridge, now a serious academic college, but at that time known, like St Peter's at Oxford, as a college of last resort, mainly for rugger-buggers and other sporting hearties. True to stereotype, the senior tutor complimented me briefly on the quality of my physics entrance paper and then showed more interest than anyone before – or since – in my performance as first-team opening bat and wicketkeeper, occasional left-back for the soccer team, very occasional rugby player – both codes – and county trialist in school hockey. He wrote 'Blue?' on his notepad and I was admitted to read natural sciences.

The headmaster and Mr Jewell were delighted, though their investment in Oxbridge entrants proved unproductive because the school soon became an 11–16 mixed comprehensive and is now better known for its non-academic alumni like Steve McLaren, the former England football manager.

My father was over the moon. His investment had certainly paid off. I felt rather sorry for his colleagues at the technical college who now faced massive retaliation for two decades of humiliation by being endlessly reminded of his vicarious achievement: a son at university – and Cambridge, no less. Indeed, the family cup ran over: Dad achieved a long overdue promotion; we moved a big step up the ladder of social stratification by moving to a detached house in a quiet and respectable cul de sac in Dringhouses, near the racecourse; my brother Keith won an academic scholarship to a public school, St Peter's. The Conservatives then won a general election on the slogan 'You've Never Had It So Good'. It certainly appeared so for the Cable family.

For my mother, however, my success brought mixed blessings. Her pride was deep and genuine, but it meant exposure to new, clever people, who might mock her accent or disparage her lack of formal education. Upward social mobility and success energized my father, but my mother shrivelled. She had overcome her inhibitions to the extent of becoming a tourist guide at York Minster. But she nonetheless carried around the fear that some educational or social indiscretion would betray her humble origins, and she would dwell for weeks on the shame of a misplaced vowel in conversation with someone important. She was happiest away from people, producing art of high quality. The new detached house, moreover, presented a whole set of problems in itself, like neighbours who cared rather more for appearances than the socially mixed crowd down New Lane. In particular, a poisonous Conservative branch chair, Stella, who dripped venom with every phrase, acted as the custodian of local standards and mores. My father's growing expansiveness and my mother's introversion caused growing tension. Home was not a happy place, and I was relieved to escape.

The relief of escape was tempered by the fact that I had been admitted to an unfashionable college on false pretences to read a subject I was eager to ditch. Doubts were banished, however, during an idyllic three months spent guiding mountain hikers around the Welsh Black Mountains and Brecon Beacons.

This interlude proved to be my first real immersion in an adult world beyond that of parents, teachers and fellow students.

My job was to lead walks and climbs from our base at a Holiday Fellowship country house hotel. The HF had its origins in a movement developed around walking, healthy outdoor adventure and organized collective leisure, with evenings featuring Scottish country dancing, quizzes and record recitals. Meals always commenced with grace; alcohol and TV were strictly outlawed. The corrupting influence of the materialistic 1950s and the beginnings of the permissive 1960s were nonetheless becoming apparent, and the house parties I was required to lead were a combustible mixture of staid middle-aged couples and young bloods on the lookout for sex.

The house was managed by a terrifying man whose weepy, wilting wife and young horsey mistress occupied adjacent bedrooms. He patrolled the corridors at night, seeking out other people's vices. The other permanent presence, the 'Host', was there to organize social activities. Mine was a man called Derek, who strongly resembled the actor Donald Pleasance and had the same creepy, ingratiating voice. As I came to know him, he gradually revealed his politics. He was a dedicated Nazi, a firm believer in the Aryan master race, and kept Third Reich memorabilia in his suitcase. Despite being physically repulsive, he had the same charisma as my communist schoolfriend David and translated it effortlessly into sexual conquests. Every week he would assess the new female intake and draw up a shortlist and timetable for seduction. As far as I could establish from the bedroom traffic, he was invariably on target.

I sought refuge from these characters and from my social awkwardness in the mountains, where my energy and physique could prevail and I could daydream unhindered by real people. One exception was a pretty, shy nurse, Penny, from Manchester, whom I only really got to know as she was leaving, after which we exchanged poignant letters – she from the night desk of a cancer ward where she cared for the terminally ill – until the faint embers of our holiday romance finally burned out.

When I try now to come to a balanced assessment of my childhood and my parents, I am reminded of Chou En-lai's comment that two hundred years was too short a time to judge the impact of the French Revolution. But perhaps fifty years is long enough to reflect fairly on my upbringing without the intervening feelings of guilt, anger, revenge – and, finally, gratitude. There is now only one witness left, my brother, who is ten years younger and experienced different things at a different stage in our family life.

Something happened in childhood that cauterized my emotions. In contrast to the warmth of my own marriages and my strong parental feelings, I came to feel almost total indifference towards my parents. When they died, I felt a vague sense of sadness and guilt that there was nothing more: no tears. I met my father in hospital before he died and we had an awkward conversation about practical things before he told me that he had concluded his life and wished to meet his Maker. He was just seventy years old. As he talked, I understood for the first time the shape and meaning of his life's work. He was a fine, perhaps great, craftsman, with a genuine talent for communicating his skills. A generation of young people had learned from him. He had become President of the NAS not, as I imagined, to fight the good fight against the opposite sex but to promote vocational education, for which he had produced a national template. He had become President of York's Guild of Building, heir to those medieval geniuses who created the Minster. He had devoted his retirement not just to Mrs Thatcher but, as governor of a secondary modern which became a comprehensive school, to encouraging youngsters from underprivileged backgrounds to learn a trade. His tragedy was that of the country: the skills were no longer valued. The 'arty-farty' people had taken over: good with words and ideas but barely able to change a light bulb. I was one of them. And when I most needed words, I couldn't find any.

My mother survived more than twenty years of self-contained widowhood which my brother and I punctuated with dutiful visits. At the end there were a few months of unhappy confusion in a care home, and she died and was cremated far from her York home, in London. Her Christianity was deep and meaningful, and was mocked at her funeral by my having organized a locum priest whom she had never met and who struggled to remember her name.

Months later, Keith and I sought, in some way, to make amends and tidy up our past by mingling our mother's ashes with our father's in the grounds of York crematorium. It was a well-intentioned gesture but ambiguous: we both knew that they had merely coexisted. Today, couples like my parents would have split up, but in those days convention and household economics kept them together. In later life they developed an irritable companionship and mutual toleration and perhaps, even, rekindled some of their earlier affection.

For better or worse, they made me; and my good and bad traits originated with them. From my father I inherited his restless energy, drive, ambition and determination, some of his Gradgrindian prejudices against the idle and self-indulgent, and his weakness for the workaholic bottle. His dominating personality largely obliterated that of my mother, whose creativity and intelligence were kept well under lock and key when I might have appreciated them. Nonetheless, I have distant memories, as a young child, of a kind and gentle person, and my own family has, I hope, uncovered a little of that capacity in me.

For many years I blotted out my parents from my consciousness. Like many children, I learned how to shut my ears to the noise of rows and my eyes to what I didn't want to see. I created a walled garden of fantasy and reverie to hide in. The walls helped me through childhood and adolescence and the bitter estrangement from my parents that followed. I only came recently to understand that the defences I created were not on account of what my father and mother did to me – they were good parents, generous with their time and modest financial resources – but because of what they did to each other. Now that the wall has gone, I look back at them with more affection and gratitude.

Chapter 3

Ivory Towers

The Cambridge of the early 1960s was, at first sight, not greatly different from that of today, with the exception of a gross imbalance between men and women. Those with a discerning eye for class analysis could also see the university as I saw it, roughly divided into two: the privileged, lazy, effete products of traditional English public schools on the one hand; and the hard-working, undervalued, grammar-school boys on the make, like me, on the other.

I did, however, have one major advantage. In an institution as ferociously competitive as Cambridge was – and almost certainly still is – there is considerable merit in starting at the bottom, unburdened by high expectations. A 'NatSci' at Fitz from an obscure north-country grammar school and digs miles from the centre of town was as low as it was possible to get. My new college friends and I felt lucky to have scraped into the university at all, and were proud to ride around in our gowns and entertain awestruck relatives by walking them round the old colleges. We developed a camaraderie based on affected yobbishness, exaggerating our provincial accents and proletarian ancestry. Our main aim was to survive, which sounds more challenging than it was, since outright exam failure was extremely rare. (Two of my friends managed it, however, one succumbing to a breakdown, another departing bewildered and in tears back to Accrington.)

Fitzwilliam, after my first year, became a 'real' college with an adventurously designed new building and its sense of inferiority lifted. It provided me, also, with some new and rewarding friends. One was an Indian economist, Sarwar Lateef: unusually, a married student and, even more unusually, a Muslim married to a Hindu. He had enormous eyes and an infectious enthusiasm for his subject, economic development, and for India. More than anyone, he filled me with curiosity about India, which led to a vacation trip after my third year and a lifelong love affair with the country, professionally and personally.

Another was John Costello, a larger-than-life character who shared my involvement in the Union and, later, a twenty-first birthday party. He was a shameless exhibitionist, whose desperation for attention often took the form of loudly, and without provocation, insulting some hapless individual, chosen at random. His views were outrageously reactionary, from affectation as much as conviction; and in spite of, or because of, being one of Cambridge's few products of the comprehensive system, he was a fierce advocate of selective and fee-paying education. He introduced me to some equally bizarre characters, like an advertising genius, Robin Wight, and a Georgian prince, Michael Coward. His circle of friends also included a brilliant history student, Tom Glazer, who later worked with me on the Liberal magazine and, in the nicest way, tried to teach me how to write. As for Costello, he did little work and was almost certainly unemployable. But he developed a career as a freelance writer, produced the best-written account of Concorde, and moved on to traitors and spies. His colourful world of far-right politics, Soviet exiles and conspiracy theorists obtained him unprecedented access to KGB files at the fall of the Soviet Union. Before he could complete the culmination of his life's work he died suddenly on a transatlantic flight, leaving his friends and fans to speculate, as I am sure he would have wanted, that he was the victim of a KGB murder plot.

After an initial sulk, having failed to persuade the college authorities to let me switch to economics, I began to appreciate the privilege of being taught by some of the world's great scientists. Although the global centre of scientific gravity has firmly shifted to the USA, Cambridge in the early 1960s was a formidable place and our lecturers were pre-eminent in their fields. I disregarded tutorial advice and decided to enjoy science and chose the most exotic combination of new subjects I could assemble within the Tripos rules, including geology, the history and philosophy of science, experimental psychology, metallurgy, and chemistry, of only the last of which I had any previous knowledge. For the first and only time in my life I studied for the joy of it and discovered unexpected pleasures: the emerging science of plate tectonics and continental drift; a self-effacing genius called Cottrell who had changed the science of metallurgy; experimentally based explanations of the complex workings of the human mind; and theories that set out how new ideas were born and then destroyed.

This enthusiasm obviously communicated itself to the examiners since, to the amazement of the college authorities, and my friends, I finished just short of a first in the first-year exams. Unfortunately, I got carried away and, in the second year, recklessly added to an already overloaded portfolio with politics, drama, and an unhappy and passionate, albeit unconsummated, love affair with a Girton girl called Tanya. I lurched from false modesty to arrogant overconfidence and painfully discovered that political intrigue, memorizing lines from George Bernard Shaw, and late-night lovers' quarrels with Tanya were not the best mental preparation for learning the names and shapes of hundreds of fossils. I managed a respectable but undistinguished second in the Part One exams and was, thereafter, released to economics.

The relationship with Tanya cast a long shadow over this period. Cambridge undergraduate women were outnumbered by men by approximately ten to one. For those who were attractive, like her, there was constant attention from male suitors. Adjusting from the monastic life of A levels at academic girls' schools to this cornucopia of male choice and endless flattery was not easy. Immature, inexperienced men – like me – didn't help. This was the only seriously unhappy relationship I have ever had.

Even without such distractions, it was difficult in three eight-week terms to absorb all the intellectual excitement of the place. Outside our subject area, there was a ferment of debate around the nature of God. The Bishop of Woolwich had published his book *Honest to God*, questioning a large part of orthodox Christian teaching. Cambridge theologians responded in public lectures packed to overflowing with students. A civil war had broken out in English literature and many of us forsook the chemistry labs to listen to F. R. Leavis in full flow. A Marxist economic historian, Maurice Dobb, lectured to packed halls about the Soviet Union.

Not all the activity was so serious. This was an era of satire and inventive comedy and the Cambridge Footlights was building on the breakthrough achieved by *That Was the Week That Was* and, before that, the surreal humour of the Goons and the hilarious but dry, self-pitying, social drama of Tony Hancock.

Even in the self-regarding, narcissistic cocoon of undergraduate life we were also aware that this was a period of great political turbulence and excitement, unmatched since the rise of Fascism in the 1930s and not to be matched again until the global ideological upheavals at the end of the Cold War. Kennedy was in the White House and, in my first term, there was the Cuban missile crisis, with the genuine fear of nuclear annihilation. Macmillan had spoken in 1960 of the 'wind of change' in Africa, and the world of British imperial superiority and certainty was disappearing fast. There was a new debate as to whether Britain's destiny lay, instead, in Europe. The disintegration of empire, in turn, had triggered a new preoccupation with race. I had never met a black or Asian person until I arrived at Cambridge, but suddenly the politics of race was everywhere: apartheid and Mandela's Rivonia trial; a growing debate about non-white immigration which was changing the face of Britain for the first time in centuries; and a questioning of racial discrimination, formerly the natural order of things but now, suddenly, unacceptable.

The certainties of British politics – the apparently endless rule of the Conservatives and the hitherto irrelevant, impotent, socialist alternative – were starting to crumble and, with them, the self-confidence of the British Establishment. Nothing quite captured the spirit of the time, the sudden fracturing of old certainties, than the Profumo affair: a defence minister frolicking in a swimming pool at an aristocratic residence with a naked prostitute who happened simultaneously to be managing relationships with a Jamaican drug-dealer and a Russian spy.

Yet, although there was a growing irreverence for, and lack of deference towards, those who occupied exalted positions, today's cynicism and pessimism about politics and politicians had not yet arrived. Democratic politics mattered. Protest was passionate but innocent and good-humoured, as with the anti-apartheid banners that appeared between the spires of King's College, planted by rock climbers to the bafflement and annoyance of the college authorities. Even if I had not yet started to incubate serious political ambitions, it was difficult not to be caught up in the whirl.

The issue was: which party? For reasons already described, I was attracted to the Liberals, but they were not a major force. I was heavily influenced by the big national debate on entry into the Common Market, which was gathering momentum and passion. I knew nothing about Europe, beyond a short school trip to Germany, chiefly remembered for inedible food and a ride in a Mercedes at high speed on an autobahn, and I have never got to grips with modern languages. But for someone young, struggling to understand big political ideas, the arguments reached to the core of what the country's future was about: wallowing in the fading imperial past, which I now associated with the debacle at Suez and those resisting the rapid retreat from African colonies, or moving on to a project that seemed to combine practicality and idealism. The Conservatives seemed on the right side of this particular argument, despite my father's conviction that his party's leaders were compounding the treachery of decolonization by taking leave of their collective senses over Europe. What baffled me was the anti-colonial Labour Party whose leader talked nostalgically about a 'thousand years of British history'. A decisive intervention came from the Liberal leader, Jo Grimond, whose sharp wit and eloquence won over a lot of impressionable minds, including mine.

I decided to spend a few weeks sampling the alternatives by doing the rounds of the university political societies. The student Conservatives enjoyed much support, were professional, and, to my surprise, were not dominated by public school toffs but by people with backgrounds like mine. They seemed to be well connected, with weekly visits from cabinet ministers, some of them highly impressive, like the liberal-minded colonial secretary, Iain McLeod, the Education Secretary, Sir Edward Boyle, and the brilliant but rather spooky Enoch Powell, who had recently resigned from the government. Although individually the young Tory student politicians were pleasant and plausible, collectively they were repulsive. Their sycophancy towards visiting MPs and authority in general was flesh-creeping. They had an arrogant self-belief and self-importance based on the confidence (well placed as it turned out) that, at the age of twenty, they were already on a conveyor belt to political power. Whilst there was a liberal veneer, I knew, because I had seen it first-hand, that their activist base depended on the energies and prejudices of bigoted people like my father, whom they were only too happy to use. Many years later, when the Conservatives were in the wilderness, they started to wonder aloud why they were seen as a 'nasty party'. Back then, there was no such self-doubt, since the Conservatives were in power and, even if the cracks in their popularity were beginning to appear after a decade in office, the sense of being 'the natural party of government' was pervasive. The side of me that was ambitious and calculating – and also wanted to please my father – yearned to join them. Yet some rebellious, bloody-minded streak stopped me doing so.

The Labour Club was off-putting for different reasons. Unlike the Tories, who welcomed converts and new recruits, the young

Labour activists treated all newcomers with deep suspicion. One might be a 'careerist', or a Special Branch infiltrator. Activists were dressed up in donkey-jackets emblazoned with the name of a leading building contractor, designed to give the impression that they had come to Cambridge via a construction site, and there were earnest discussions about how best to show solidarity with the latest unofficial strike in the West Midlands car industry. Coming from a city where the workers never went on strike and many voted Conservative, despite the efforts of my friend David, this obsession with industrial militancy seemed to me remote from reality, let alone university life. And, since many of the militants had public school accents and had clearly never been near a factory, they were transparently phoney. Meetings were dominated by procedural wrangles about substantive motions and amendments which bored and bewildered me. There were coded references to different party factions which were lost on those of us who had not mastered the code. I struggled to see the connection between the ideas of Rosa Luxemburg and the Spartacist revolt on the one hand, and the mild economic downturn that Britain was experiencing in the early 1960s on the other. Unlike the Tories, the Labour Party itself clearly did not take the students very seriously, and none of the Labour student politicians were ever heard of again. I did not hesitate long before moving on.

This left the Liberals, who were, by contrast, friendly, welcoming, sensible and unpretentious. They signed me up. Though small in number, they were buoyed up by a recent by-election victory in Orpington which had, for the moment, stilled the ridicule of the bigger parties. The leading lights – Jo Grimond and Jeremy Thorpe – were clever, witty and devoid of the pomposity and self-importance that enveloped almost all Tory politicians, however liberal-minded. Unlike most leading Labour figures, they seemed to feel it was worth their time talking to us. The leading undergraduates, who included Alan (Lord) Watson and Chris Mason, later leader of the Lib Dems in Strathclyde, were good debaters and a match for their opposite numbers in quality, if not quantity. There was, moreover, a coherent and attractive set of beliefs, which Grimond articulated at national level: the Liberals were classless and had no bias towards organized labour or big business; they captured the growing concern over disappearing civil liberties; they had enlightened views on race, were internationalist in outlook, and offered an alternative vision of the future – in Europe – to Britain's fading and failing colonial role. I recognized too, in the belief in worker participation and share ownership, a model that seemed to work well in my native York. In practice, as in any party, there were ideological undercurrents, notably between those who advocated 'economic liberalism' – Grimond himself and Richard Wainwright, the Yorkshire MP who spoke on economic matters – and a group clustered around an Ipswich candidate, Manuela Sykes, who wanted to move to the left and also to associate the party with CND. But these were not, then, serious divisions.

The main problem with the Liberals was smallness. There were only six MPs, two of whom held their seats only because of local electoral pacts with Labour. Large parts of England, like York, had not had Liberal councillors or MPs for decades. The unfairness of the voting system was a plausible explanation and generated endless debates on the merits of different kinds of proportional representation, but this did not get us very far. I also discovered that small organizations attract people who feel more comfortable in small organizations, where they can shine and give expression to their idiosyncrasies. They clashed with people like me who were ambitious for the party (and ourselves). Jo Grimond held out a vision in which the rigidities of the British system were breaking down and tribal loyalties were dissolving, but this seemed to be happening on a geological timescale, and I, for one, was impatient.

One advantage of small organizations is that for ambitious and energetic people promotion can come rapidly. At the end of the first year, I was made editor of the Liberal Club magazine, *Scaffold*. I gave it an editorial and design makeover and printed vast numbers of copies, but paid little regard to the cost or the practical problems of marketing. After three editions, with mounting losses, the magazine had to be closed. Undeterred I went on to become the Club's President, committed to achieving rapid expansion of the membership. Since people more persuasive than I had failed to realize this objective through organic growth, I decided on an aggressive strategy of mergers and acquisitions. I looked around for other small political clubs, whose political outlook was close to the Liberals, to acquire or merge with. One was a liberal Conservative splinter group called PEST, and I wrote a pamphlet for them advocating a liberal approach to immigration (the co-author, David Wright, became British ambassador to Japan in due course). Its founder, however, was essentially a mainstream Tory who later became chairman of the 1922 Committee, Sir Michael Spicer, and he had no interest whatever in handing over his vehicle to me and the Liberals.

More promising was the Campaign for Democratic Socialism, founded by groups of young Labour Party social democrats, led by Dick Taverne and Bill Rodgers, which had an undergraduate offshoot. My own views, which were coalescing around the transatlantic social liberalism of J. K. Galbraith and the ideas of a new generation of Labour political thinkers like Anthony Crosland, found an echo there. However, my proposal for merger was treated with disdain by them and my Liberal members were outraged. I jumped before I was pushed. In retrospect, I perhaps deserved some credit for anticipating the Liberal/SDP merger by a couple of decades, though, in reality, I had been a reckless political neophyte who spread confusion among the Liberals and achieved nothing. I also overlooked a more patient political strategy being developed by another Cambridge contemporary, Bernard Greaves, which involved a long march through local government based on 'community politics'.

While this minor drama was being played out in the micro-politics of undergraduate life, there were big changes afoot nationally. Thirteen years of Conservative government were coming to an end ('thirteen wasted years' was the Labour campaign slogan). Now politically homeless, I fell quite easily into the embrace of Harold Wilson's Labour Party, whose pitch could well have been designed to appeal to people like me. Although supposedly from the left of the Labour Party, he did not use socialist jargon. His accent was reassuringly northern. He talked a lot about science and the untapped potential of the 'white heat of the technological revolution'. A clever, ex-grammar-school boy, he tapped not just into working-class solidarity but into a wider antipathy to the public school toffs who were supposedly running – and ruining – the country and perpetuating the rule of the 'old school tie'. In Cambridge there were plenty of loud, posh voices advertising this class, which aroused both envy and hostility among those of us who were not part of it. Wilson was widely accused of exaggerating his working-class roots with hints of attending school in bare feet; but for those of us who had grown up on the slippery slope between the lower middle class and the working class he was reassuring.

The Conservatives, unaccountably, chose a belted, chinless earl as their prime minister. While my Tory friends assured me that Sir Alec Douglas-Home was not as dim or amateurish as he appeared, he seemed to embody everything that was wrong with the country. It was not entirely clear what Wilson was for, but it was clear what he was against. And that was enough for many of us. I enthusiastically campaigned for Labour when the party turned Cambridge into a marginal seat in 1964, and then for Alex Lyon in 1966 when he broke the Tory hegemony in York.

The main forum for political debate was the Cambridge Union. It has become fashionable to decry the Union (as well as the Oxford and Scottish equivalents) for its pretentiousness and the juvenile banter that often passes for debate. The level of juvenile banter, it has to be said, is often not much higher in the House of Commons, on whose debating format the Union is based. It was, moreover, in the 1960s the training ground for a whole generation of national politicians, mainly Conservatives, who came to dominance in the eighties and nineties. Not merely politicians, but future QCs and judges too, experimented there with the adversarial system of debate. At its best, it brought out an ability to communicate with, and respond to, a live political audience. The House of Commons does that, unlike almost all legislatures in continental Europe and North America. The theatrical qualities and communication skills demanded of politicians in a television age are now somewhat different, but not wholly so. In any event, after hearing my first debate, I could see the outline of a ladder that I intended to climb.

The President in my first term was Brian Pollitt, son of the former UK Communist Party leader and a communist himself. He had a dominating presence, not entirely due to his being a mature student, and an intellectual clarity that shone among the muddled young minds. Although this was the height of the Cold War, the romanticism of the Cuban revolution, Khrushchev's denunciation of Stalinism, and the technocratic optimism of his Soviet Union created a climate in which revolutionary Marxism–Leninism was treated with some respect, even if in reality very little of the British electorate actually voted for it. Pollitt was also an example of the tendency of the Union to magnify people who were inconspicuous in other contexts; I later encountered him as an academic studying the Cuban economy in Glasgow, where he was happily anonymous.

His politics apart, Pollitt managed to pack out the place, which generated an often electric atmosphere. Perhaps I was unduly impressionable, but I have not, since, heard leading British politicians speak as well as Richard Crossman opposing the reunification of Germany, or Iain McLeod defending the winding-up of Britain's African empire. On such occasions, debates could generate real, sometimes alarming, passion. The debate on the Middle East, for example, pitted the university's mainly undergraduate Jewish students against mainly postgraduate Arabs and a few of their left-wing allies. The politics of the most recent atrocity would be played out much as it is today. It was the first time I saw raw political hatred publicly expressed, and there was ugliness too in the supercilious response of some of the neutrals, enjoying this cockfight between two Semitic tribes.

Pollitt excepted, the dominant personalities were mostly Conservatives. There was a batch of recent Presidents – Michael

Howard, Michael Tugendhat and Leon Brittan – who re-emerged from time to time. But the two future stars whom I saw at close quarters, and followed to the presidency, were Ken Clarke and Norman Lamont. Clarke, at that stage, had not developed the rounded political personality that later made him so formidable and likeable. His speeches were delivered too fast and seemed to have been scripted in Conservative Central Office. His term as President was generally deemed to be very dull, little more than a parade of B-list Tory celebs.

Norman Lamont, whom history has treated much less kindly, was – at least in that rarefied context – an impressive performer. He had grasped the obvious point which most of his contemporaries – and most politicians today – overlooked: that the quickest way to lose a live audience is to read from notes. His speeches were carefully researched and faithfully memorized, allowing improvisation with growing confidence. I copied his technique. Unlike his fellow Tories, most of whom seemed to have emerged immaculately conceived from the womb wearing blue rosettes and reciting the party line, he flirted with danger both politically and privately. The Cabinet minister who emerged from an off-licence with a black eye after meeting a left hook from a girlfriend's husband was recognizable even then. Since we were in the same college I got to know him a little. Even in the mid-1960s he was questioning the middle-way Butskellite, One Nation orthodoxy of the Tory leadership and, though he was a notoriously lazy economics student, he had a genuine passion for the subject and I recall a long conversation in which he vigorously defended the 1920s gold standard, a variant of which destroyed his career thirty years later.

Most of the other personalities and ex-Presidents disappeared

47

into semi-obscurity (though some, in judges' robes or top jobs in the BBC or business, have probably had more influence than the politicians). One memorable character, who is now known mainly in the world of academic sociology, was a diminutive Welshman called Christie Davies. He profited from a couple of simple but powerful insights. One was the power of humour. He collected jokes and manufactured others and demonstrated that telling one funny story was worth more than hours of dull worthiness. His other contribution was to recognize the power of accurate social observation: seeing the world as it is, rather than as we want it to be. He later combined these two into a magnum opus on the sociology of humour. As a student he specialized in the counter-intuitive: a Conservative who refused to observe dress codes; a campaigner against the admission of women to the Union who befriended radical feminists like Germaine Greer. Then a postgrad, he tutored me in my final year and taught me a lot. We met again, very recently, when he was emeritus professor at Reading.

The controversies of student life were mind-bogglingly petty and must have been incomprehensible to the outside world. Much outrage was generated by the 'oppression' of a group of pseudo-policemen called proctors who had the power to impose fines for not wearing gowns or climbing into the college late at night. There was a desperate rearguard action to keep women out of the Union and all-male colleges. The anti-feminist dam broke in the Union and threw up some talented women politicians, the best of whom, a beautiful left-wing firebrand called Sheena Mathieson who was Vice President in my term, subsequently opted out of political life. Another, Ann Mallalieu, who was the first woman to attain the presidency, became a Labour peer and champion of fox-hunting. I endeavoured to turn the Union into a broadly based student union on provincial university lines, which aroused as much hostility as my attempt to merge the Liberals and Social Democrats and was unceremoniously rejected. The inevitable then happened and a student union grew up in competition with the Union.

About the rest of my period in office, perhaps the less said the better. I was determined to avoid the experience of the previous summer term when Ken Clarke's boring speakers had emptied the place. I decided that the best way to get bums on seats in an exam term was to entertain or shock and lined up a succession of comedians and gangsters. Fortunately for my future reputation and the blood pressure of the Union clerk, Mr Ellwood, the Kray twins did not turn up after having accepted the invitation, though the self-styled leader of Britain's Black Power movement, Michael X, did. He was later hanged, in Trinidad, for a grisly murder. My concluding debate, 'Don't let the bastards grind you down', was an attempt to define my philosophy on life, and at least it attracted a good crowd and made the punters laugh. And I relished the brief celebrity status, being the object of gossip in the university newspaper and certain of attention at parties. One animated conversation with an attractive blonde proved more significant than I realized at the time. We met again thirty-six years later, both remembering the conversation, and are now happily married.

Although I allowed myself to be side-tracked, I did understand that the main purpose of being at university was to achieve a decent degree and, having been allowed to change courses, concentrated at the end on mastering the second half of the economics Tripos. As with natural sciences, the economics faculty saw itself as being at the centre of the known universe, which, at the time, it probably was. My contemporaries benefited from exposure to three Nobel Prize winners – Meade, Stone and Mirlees – and others, like Joan Robinson, Kahn and Kaldor, who probably ought to have been. Keynes was God and his apostles dominated the department. While we were all encouraged to bask in his reflected glory, there were two damaging consequences of the cult of Keynes. One was that the university increasingly lived in the past, ignoring the post-Keynesian challenges to macroeconomics and treating rival ideas being developed in Chicago by Friedman, Buchanan and others as the product of some kind of evil empire. A second was that economics became unhelpfully politicized. Keynes was a Liberal and, like other great thinkers, no doubt believed lots of different things during his lifetime. But at Cambridge he became an icon of the left – even, bizarrely, of the Marxist left. (A similar, if opposite, fate overtook Adam Smith, in whose name I later taught in Glasgow.) And while it inflated our own sense of importance to see our lecturers rushing back from London where they were building a five-year plan for the Labour government or administering price and wage controls, all of this proved to be a worthless cul-de-sac which did their (and Keynes's) reputations no good.

One of Keynes's most quoted aphorisms was that all men of affairs are the slaves of some defunct economist. If so, mine was James Meade. Meade was a former classicist of great modesty who would punctuate his lectures with apologies for being so boring. Actually he was, but he was also wise, and those who could stay with his meticulously logical verbal constructions achieved as good an understanding of theory as it was possible to get. He could reduce complex arguments to their simple essence, and his short book, *The Intelligent Radical's Guide to Economic Policy*, was one of the most sensible policy manuals I ever read: its main message being that while there are good reasons why governments should intervene in markets and in the flow of international trade, they should, in practice, do so sparingly.

While my more career-minded contemporaries immersed themselves in mathematical economics and econometrics, I opted, for reasons of both cowardice and curiosity, for more exotic and seemingly less demanding specialisms, which were, nonetheless, to have considerable impact later: development economics; a comparative study of China and India (a somewhat eccentric analysis provided by a Conservative historian who waxed lyrical about the British Raj and by Joan Robinson, whose visit to a Chinese collective farm led to a Maoist hagiography of outrageous naivety, apparent even to the students); and Soviet economic history (by the great, but somewhat partial, Maurice Dobb). As for most of my contemporaries, the question of whether communism – or socialist planning more generally – had been an economic success or failure was for me important and unresolved.

I decided one summer vacation to take a train trip to the eastern bloc to find out. Intourist tours did not, and were not designed to, provide unfettered access, but some was better than none, and the period between Stalin and Brezhnev was relaxed, especially in Hungary. There was a jarring contrast between the endless triumphalist visual and verbal propaganda and the modest (but not impoverished) standards of living; the celebration of spacemen and the crude technology employed on building sites; the trumpeting of universal solidarity and the racist behaviour we saw casually dished out to Asiatic soldiers; the official disdain for Western materialism and the endless requests in the streets of

Moscow to peel off our jeans in return for black-market roubles. I was to return, fascinated, to the Soviet Union the following year, en route to India on a far more ambitious journey.

This meandering between subjects, and continents, between politics and study, proved rewarding. I gained the first serious job I applied for, an Overseas Development Institute/Nuffield fellowship to work in the Kenyan Treasury, the professional experience of a lifetime.

I realized at the time, and even more later in life, that while I had arrived in Cambridge with something to prove and a sense of social and intellectual inadequacy, I emerged four years later with much greater self-confidence. Undergraduate life was a remarkably privileged existence. And unlike students today, I was free of debt, thanks to the help of a scholarship, free tuition and holiday jobs. As with the bitter-sweet triumph of the eleven-plus, I always felt a twinge of guilt that many of my childhood friends were not merely working for a living but, through their taxes, supporting me. But twinges of guilt are a weak counterpoint to the dominant themes of ambition and self-interest. A generation later I encouraged my three children to follow me to Cambridge, which they all did.

Chapter 4

Olympia

I first saw Olympia three years before I met her. With her glamorous *salwar kameez* and dazzling white smile beaming out from the front page of the *Yorkshire Evening Press*, she left a lasting impression. York University had just opened its doors and the first ever student to register happened to be a photogenic overseas student who had turned up a week early from East Africa.

Even if I had never met her and had not spent most of my life with her, that picture would still have been significant. It symbolized a fundamental change in the city. Until the opening of the university, York had been overwhelmingly monocultural. Leeds had a recognizable Jewish population, some black and mixed race, people including its (South African) football star Albert Johanneson, and a cosmopolitan university. Further west, in Bradford, Asians were appearing. Hull had some seamen from exotic places. In York, the nearest things to ethnic minorities were the Irish barmen and 'navvies' and the 'gypsies', a vague category referring both to the 'tinkers', who spread alarm and disapproval when they came round the doors selling from suitcases, and to dark-skinned people of unknown provenance. York had, I recall, one Chinese restaurant, around which swirled ugly rumours concerning the disappearance of pet dogs and cats.

The university brought both domestic and overseas students and, at about the same time, significant numbers of tourists to see the Minster and the medieval walls. Perhaps for the first time since the Roman occupation, the city centre had something of a cosmopolitan feel. But the visitors were not immigrants and, to this day, the city remains remarkably homogenous. Decades later, Olympia's appearance in a shop away from the central and university areas would silence the conversation and lead to nervous glances.

It was, perhaps, because the new population was transient that my parents felt at ease with it; indeed, it inflated my father's civic pride, and my mother discovered a new role in which she was valued, showing overseas visitors around the Minster. They often drove down to the new university to see the campus taking shape. Ironically, in view of what was to happen later, my father had saved the press cutting with Olympia's picture for me – as if to say, York is no longer the provincial backwater you thought it was.

I met Olympia, for real, in the unromantic rendezvous of a mental hospital, a Quaker home called The Retreat. Mental nursing was the most unwanted job on offer at York's employment exchange, and since I had two months to fill before leaving for Kenya I took the job. Once there, I drew the short straw of the geriatric ward, helping Alzheimer's patients to eat, wash and use the toilet, or changing their nappies. I developed a lifelong admiration for the full-time nursing staff who maintained their professionalism and good humour in this least glamorous corner of healthcare. I also developed a reputation for being kindly but careless, the latter a serious handicap for a job that required meticulous attention to drug dosages and sorting clothes from the laundry.

Our refuge was the staff room. One day a couple of Indian

nurses entered: one very pretty and languid, Nurse Naidoo; the other less pretty but more beautiful and fizzing with nervous energy, Nurse Rebelo. Both had acquired a reputation for aloofness, spurning romantic overtures from the male nurses. I found myself talking to Nurse Rebelo, who was puffing vigorously on a cigarette to calm her nerves after spending several hours with mentally disturbed children. She had flashing, restless eyes and within a few minutes I had been treated both to a wide-open smile and to a surge of anger which caused a mark on her cheek to stand out, the product of an unhappy chemistry experiment with sulphuric acid. What seemed to attract more than cursory interest in the scruffy young man in the staff room was a series of improbable coincidences. She was shortly to leave York for a postgraduate – DipEd – year at Cambridge, which I had just left, before going back to Nairobi, her home town, where I was now headed. I had, furthermore, remembered her picture in the local newspaper when she had first arrived. Intrigued, she somewhat nervously accepted the offer of a date.

My own romantic imagination was limited and one of my friends recommended an evening at the pictures. He had heard that there was an excellent war film at a cinema in a small town outside York, with a coffee house nearby. What he did not tell me was that the film was about nuclear war and our romantic evening involved reliving mass destruction and families being incinerated or, if they escaped, suffering a long, slow death from radioactive poisoning. I was numb with embarrassment at the time, and this was certainly not Olympia's idea of entertainment, let alone an aphrodisiac. But she seemed to find my personal and social clumsiness reassuring. I discovered later that she hadn't been out with a British boy before and her friends had helped her plan for all eventualities, with dire warnings about how to counter fast moves. A film on nuclear war was not a gambit they had anticipated.

I was given another chance. This time I opted for a summer evening drive and chat in one of the country pubs near the city. Olympia turned up for the date in a beautiful silk sari, her hair piled up to expose her long elegant neck, decorated by a filigree necklace. She was seemingly oblivious to the open-mouthed stares of the regulars in the Bull and Bush, who had just seen a fairy princess emerge through the haze of alcohol and cigarette smoke. In this improbable setting we began to piece together a knowledge and understanding of one another.

She was the third child, and oldest daughter, in a family of seven. Her father had come to Nairobi in the early 1940s from Portuguese Goa, like many Goans of his generation, finding work in clerical jobs in the British Empire and then bringing his young wife from Goa to start a family. Olympia was rooted in and devoted to her family and it defined her multiple identity, of which she was immensely proud. She was a Kenyan, and African, by birth and upbringing; an Indian by origin and identification; a Portuguese speaker (her first language, followed by English when she was eight); a Catholic; and a Brahmin, her family tracing its roots to the Kelkar, the land-owning sub-caste that had dominated her village, Verna, in Goa six hundred years ago, before the Portuguese occupation and conversion. One aspect of identity that she firmly repudiated was being a British subject, and I discovered that one of the easiest ways to ignite her quick and sharp temper was to suggest that there were political problems in the world for which British colonialism was not responsible.

Both her pride and prickliness derived in considerable

measure from her father. By dint of very hard work, long hours and thrift, he had supported and paid for an education for all his children, who, in due course, comprised two medical doctors, two academic doctors, a top barrister, a university dean, and a microbiologist turned business manager. He was clearly a very able and honest man who served his bank – now HSBC – way beyond the call of duty and for which he was poorly paid. He suffered the additional indignity of being 'managed' by some young public school dimwit who possessed superior rank and salary in order to preserve the racial hierarchy that colonial banking demanded. The family income had been crucially supplemented by Olympia's mother, a kindly, understated and accommodating lady who, when I met her, was managing a hotel with considerable efficiency. Earlier she had run an upmarket coffee bar in the town centre where, I was later told by an African friend, she insisted on serving black customers in contravention of the prevailing colour bar. A job, seven children and a difficult husband were more than enough for any woman, and Olympia spent a slice of her childhood helping to bring up her sisters and youngest brother.

Olympia herself had been brought up in this racially hierarchical and segmented society – not greatly dissimilar to Rhodesia, if not quite as ruthlessly stratified as South Africa. She was sent, as law and custom required, to 'Asian' schools, initially a Catholic school for Goans, and later with Hindus, Sikhs and Muslims until A levels. Her younger siblings were the first to be allowed into previously all-white schools.

There were also deep and divisive undercurrents in the Goan community, which numbered around twenty thousand at the time of independence in 1962. Attitudes towards the Portuguese varied from those who saw themselves culturally and racially as

Portuguese, to those, like Mr Rebelo, who were Indian and had opposed Portuguese rule. These divisions cut across families and were reinforced by the Portuguese embassy and a network of informers reporting back to agents of the Salazar dictatorship. The community was further divided by caste, and despite the best efforts of the Jesuits and centuries of Catholic teaching, the Church as well as the social clubs respected the lines drawn between 'good families' – Brahmins – at one end of the scale and Sudras – low-caste untouchables – at the other. One important difference, however, between Goans and other Indians was in their appreciation of Western musical culture, both classical and popular. Olympia was an accomplished pianist who had played Schubert duets with her sister Amata on Kenyan radio and had an eclectic taste ranging from Bach to Elvis.

Apart from her parents, Olympia had been shaped by several other strong characters. One of the more important was an Irish priest, Father Comerford. He had been headteacher at the Goan school, from which post he had been ousted following some feuding among the governors. Olympia, then aged fourteen, had led a protest march to the education department, which, on its return, had spun out of control, with some of the more hot-headed insurrectionists ransacking the school. In due course the rebels and the head were reinstated. Father Comerford was a charismatic figure, whom I met once before he was posted, as a Monsignor, to an important-sounding job in Rome. He was one of those priests who treated intelligent doubt with patience and respect, encouraged the brighter among his flock to develop their minds, and saw the potential of talented girls beyond child-rearing and the nunnery. Unfortunately, Olympia had also met the other kind, and it was the intellectual intolerance and the straying eyes and hands of less disciplined priests that drove her away from the Church. But she always considered herself a Catholic, and always lit a candle whenever we visited a place of worship. I suspect that the big-hearted Father Comerford would have approved of the fact that when she was dying she sought spiritual comfort from a happily married Anglican priest.

In her large extended family there was a range of saints and sinners, but one man stood out: a cousin, Pio Gama Pinto, whom she idolized as a man of high principle. Pinto was a communist who had thrown himself wholeheartedly into the African independence struggle and, according to Olympia, was responsible for caches of arms being delivered to the Mau Mau via a hut in the Rebelos' garden (no other member of the family, I should add, would vouch for this story). For someone to be above the petty feuding of Goan politics and contributing to the fight against the British colonial authorities was enough to win Olympia's enthusiastic support. Unfortunately he seriously annoyed someone in Kenyatta's circle and he was killed in mysterious circumstances.

When she excelled at A level and won a scholarship to study in the UK, an official in the education department thoughtfully recommended one of Britain's new universities, which would combine innovation and enthusiasm with the intimacy of a small, new student body. At York a few dozen students, initially, had the benefit of an exceptional array of British academic talent, including the vice chancellor, Eric James, a former head of Manchester Grammar School; Harry Ree, another noted educationalist and wartime French resistance hero; Alan Peacock, the liberal and Liberal economist, whose immense intellectual contribution was sadly neglected until later tapped into by Mrs Thatcher; and two history professors, Gwyn Williams, the Welsh

Marxist who inspired in Olympia an enthusiasm for Robespierre and Lenin, and Gerald Aylmer, who later moved to a chair at Oxford. Olympia revelled in this company and that of her friends, and I believe they valued her equally.

I was surprised to discover, however, that, apart from the lecturers, she knew few British people. Her closest friends were overseas students: Suan, the daughter of a Singaporean shipping magnate; Hun, a Malay Chinese, who died of cancer shortly before Olympia; and Maysoon, an Iraqi, who was last heard of in Baghdad in the early years of Saddam Hussein. Her one close English friend, Jenny, had suffered a nervous breakdown in her finals – frightened of failing to meet the expectations of her family – and Olympia had held her hand through the crisis, failing in the process to achieve the first-class degree her professors had expected of her. Outside the university, Olympia spent a year in digs with a homely and kindly working-class York family, whose unremitting diet of chips and endlessly boiled vegetables drove her to hunger and near-despair. One of Yorkshire's upper-class families offered hospitality at their country home in the vacations, the generosity of which was dimmed only by their insistence that she required lessons in the proper use of a knife and fork.

So the dates with the young Englishman were, I think, as much of a voyage of discovery for her as they were for me. We were both nervous and tentative and stuck to safe subjects like our families, the arts, religion and politics. Her politics, in particular, were unique and were not reflected in any party I have ever encountered: a mixture of revolutionary, anti-colonial fervour, socialistic disapproval of wealth and greed, strong support for academic competition and selection, and social conservatism with a particular disdain for the permissive lifestyle of the 'swinging sixties', of which we were then in the middle. She later supported me loyally in the Labour Party and the Liberal Democrats and tried, with some difficulty, to hold her combative, outgoing temperament in check for fear of perpetrating some terrible ideological faux pas.

We were becoming very close, but there was shyness, fear of rejection and, perhaps, fear of commitment too. Olympia warned me, in a roundabout way, that her destiny was already set. Her father had lined up a young man from a 'good family', the Ribieros, and would never accept dissent from his eldest daughter on matters as important as this. I also knew my parents well enough to realize that, for all Olympia's qualities, she would never be seen as a 'suitable girl': wrong colour, wrong religion. Much was left unsaid and much misunderstanding consequently arose. One last opportunity to say a proper goodbye was missed when we agreed to rendezvous in London before I departed for Kenya. We lost each other in the crowds around Piccadilly. Fate did not seem to be on our side.

There followed a year of eagerly awaited and affectionate, but restrained, weekly letters, which took us neither forwards nor back. I discovered that she had been pursued around Cambridge by a music student who fell madly in love with her and wrote quartets and sonatas in her honour. For my part, once established in Kenya, I struck up a relationship with an extraordinarily beautiful Kenyan African woman, Pamela Ogot, who was completing her degree at Nairobi University, though already an experienced teacher and several years older than her contemporaries. She had a figure to die for and a fine coppery black skin of the kind specific to the Nilotic tribes of western Kenya. She was a Luo, and from one of the tribe's leading families, a niece of the novelist Grace Ogot and, more distantly, a cousin of Tom Mboya, the planning minister, who, after Kenyatta, was the dominant personality in the post-independence government, until he was assassinated. Pamela was, however, a great deal more than a pretty face with a famous name. She was a woman of ambition and determination, becoming the first black teacher and then head of the leading girls' school in Kenya (Kenya High), head of the women's movement, and one of the leading lay figures in the Anglican church. She took her Christianity seriously, and it included a fierce attachment to premarital virginity. Despite my attempts to argue a contrary theological position, her knowledge of the scriptures defeated me. She was fiercely independent and brave, as she showed by taking her white boyfriend to her college functions at a time when racial sensitivities were still very sharp. We got on very well, but also parted amicably when Olympia returned to Nairobi.

I suspect it was the over-frequent references to Pamela in my letters, and to the musical Mr Talbot in hers, which made up our minds. When Olympia returned, we agreed to meet in parkland behind the Treasury, promptly set upon each other, and agreed to spend our lives together.

Hope, elation and love soon collided with the realities of family life. Olympia, I think, still harboured hopes that her father's heart would melt once he was confronted with the reality of his daughter's prospective love marriage, rather than the 'good' marriage he had planned. She was wrong. Her attempts to discuss the matter led to a shouting match and the warning that, if her nonsense continued, she would be expelled forever from the family home.

She suggested that I seek a meeting to put a formal request to him because it was the right thing to do: it might satisfy his sense of honour, and might persuade him to respond to me, rather than to an abstraction. The meeting took place at his bank, but while polite, it did not shift his position one iota. I received a long lecture on the promiscuity and general immorality of British people and the inevitability of our divorce. He made more specific inquiries about my family background and it was clear that the Cables and Pinkneys fell considerably short of the aristocratic status that might have redeemed the match. Mrs Rebelo took Olympia's side but was given short shrift.

The Cables, at this point, made their own contribution to the drama. I had written home telling them, in a matter-of-fact way, that Olympia and I were planning to get married. Since I was, by now, twenty-four years old and had lived away from home for several years, I assumed that they could trust my judgement but would appreciate their blessing and support. The reply, in which he stated that he was also speaking on my mother's and brother's behalf, was a parody of my father at his bigoted and snobbish worst. How could I be so naive as to imagine that mixed marriages could possibly work? What about the neighbours, especially the higher class of neighbour we now lived among in Dringhouses? An Asian girl? Then there was my brother, who had recently won a scholarship to a public school; how could he possibly be expected to explain to his socially refined classmates and teachers that there was a coloured woman in the family? Unless I had been afflicted by tropical fever my only possible motive was to humiliate him and undermine his two and a half decades of work towards social acceptance and civic respectability. I later discovered that he had been planning his own version of a dynastic marriage by introducing me to the daughter of York's leading building contractor and Tory grandee, a Shepherd. The bottom line was the same as Mr Rebelo's: drop this foolish idea or you will be expelled forever from the family home.

This letter added anger and further estrangement to an already combustible mix. Olympia was outraged and insulted and it confirmed her worst suspicions about British racism and hypocrisy (the latter because she had briefly met my parents in York, over a courteous if somewhat strained tea, and my father had expressed particular appreciation of her taste in classical music and her disciplinarian approach to teaching). The more immediate set of problems, however, related to her own father.

Mr Rebelo produced what he thought was a masterstroke. Since Olympia was committed, as a condition of her scholarship to the UK, to spending two years teaching for the Kenyan government, he managed to arrange for her posting to a remote school where she might, in the loneliness of internal exile, rethink her folly. The chosen school was run by nuns with a reputation for uncompromising moral rectitude and was located at a hamlet called Runyenjes, between Embu and Meru, on the slopes of Mount Kenya. Though remote, the school was not inaccessible, at least in dry weather, and could be reached after a long drive on a *murram* (dirt) road. He had seriously underestimated the capacity of star-crossed lovers to surmount obstacles of this kind and my VW made the journey most weekends, despite some hairy moments with mud and wild animals and, on one occasion, a late-night encounter with a gang of car-jackers.

Runyenjes was an earthly paradise. Every morning, the ice-tipped peak of Mount Kenya rose above the verdant green of the forest and the rich red soil of the terraced farms that stretched out beyond the school, and the air was fresh and clear. Contrary to expectations, and probably their rule-book, the nuns welcomed this fugitive Juliet and Romeo and soon turned me to practical advantage as postman and delivery boy. The girls had a thirst for knowledge despite coming to school with an array of handicaps, ranging from real hunger, poverty and lack of lighting for homework, to predatory adult males. Olympia's Cambridge O level class operated at a higher academic level than many she subsequently encountered in British comprehensives. The girls also understood the romantic drama in the life of the new teacher and she was touched by their support and that of the nuns.

In an ideal world, she would have stayed for a year at least and repaid the goodwill of the school. But she was conscious that the coming rainy season would make my visits impossible and she was anxious to be as close to her family as her father would permit. She managed to obtain a transfer to Kenya (Girls') High School in Nairobi. Kenya High was in the process of transition from an all-white segregated school to a multiracial one, predominantly of Asian girls and the daughters of the new Kenyan elite of ministers and senior officials. The staff was still largely inherited from the colonial days and some of them made little effort to hide their prejudices and their distaste for the 'collapse of standards'. There was one (Asian) non-white teacher and more with good qualifications were being sought.

There were two new recruits, Olympia and, as luck would have it, my friend Pamela Ogot. Olympia had no choice but to live in school accommodation since by this time she had been forbidden to return home – though she made many clandestine visits to see her mother, brothers and sisters, who, between them, bore the brunt of her father's anger. We had now become engaged and were planning to get married before I was due to leave Kenya in mid-1968. News of the clandestine visits and the engagement had, of course, reached the ears of Mr Rebelo and the Goan community, for which the embarrassment of one of its leading families provided endless gossip.

The growing alienation between Olympia and her father was, paradoxically, a result of their being so alike: proud and uncompromising, with unshakeable self-belief. This was a classic collision between an irresistible force and an immovable object. The confrontation reached its peak over our wedding, which Olympia decided should be in the Catholic cathedral: not so much as a statement of faith as a very public declaration of love and commitment. There was no question of a low-key, uncontroversial marriage in a distant parish or register office.

All of these tribulations had the effect of bringing us closer together, and while Olympia never lost her capacity for flying into a temper at regular intervals, it was always followed by a loving reconciliation. Our differences were few and quickly resolved. I insisted that she give up smoking, which she did, and I agreed, as a reciprocal commitment, to improve my rather slovenly habits in relation to bathing and dress.

We had the solid support of my friends: my best man, Trevor Sweetman, another Overseas Development Institute fellow, for whom I performed the same role when years later he married Reeti Sharma, a Bengali student at Wye College; Alan Doss, a UN official who now manages the peacekeeping force in the Congo and was on standby to give Olympia away if her brothers were prevented from coming; and Jill Wells, a university economist who let Olympia use her rooms to prepare for the wedding.

One of the many obstacles, however, was the priest, Father Whelan, an Irishman of the old school who made clear from the outset his distaste for unorthodox and cross-denominational marriages. I agreed to accept instruction from him and we had an amicable, if somewhat one-sided, relationship, in which I listened tactfully and with feigned enthusiasm to his uncompromising interpretation of Catholic marriage doctrine and his anecdotes about administering the last rites to large numbers of Kikuyus before they were dispatched by the hangman during the Mau Mau emergency. Our final session was, however, a disaster. Olympia joined us and made no attempt to emulate my diplomacy. She rose to his every provocation and told him that she had insisted on the cathedral ceremony to please her mother rather than out of respect for him or the Church. A full-frontal assault on the most powerful religious institution in the world was perhaps not the best preparation for a church wedding the next day and, although Olympia never apologized or expressed regret for anything she did, we both had a sense of apprehension about Father Whelan's revenge.

The Rebelo family was the other uncertainty. Her two brothers and sister, who were in the country at the time, expressed a determination to come to the wedding, although Mrs Rebelo decided to stay away so as to avoid too big a rift. The main worry was about loose cannons among the more distant relations. An uncle, Socorro, had a gun and threatened to come to the church to shoot us and redeem the family honour. Since he had served several years in jail for robbery, we could not entirely discount the risk. A few of my more muscular sporting friends were put on security alert.

In the event, the ceremony went as well as could have been

expected. The church was reasonably full, of both guests and curious Goans. Olympia's brothers and sister came and the assassin stayed away. Olympia was stunningly beautiful in a white silk sari and, with the help of a tailor, I managed to look creditably smart. Father Whelan's armoury of retaliatory weapons proved less than lethal. One was to stand down the choir we had requested and replace it with a group of tiny children who had not yet been taught to sing in tune. The other was to enliven our wedding service with a very long sermon on the evils of communism. After he had made his point, however, he even managed a bleak smile in the sacristy and, like many other people who clashed with Olympia, he could not resist admiring her fearless honesty and unquenchable spirit.

Despite two very alienated fathers and plenty of warnings that our marriage stood little chance of surviving, we left the church and reception happy and surrounded by supportive family and friends, and embarked on a brief but idyllic honeymoon in a hotel in the Aberdare Mountains and a longer break in Zanzibar. Zanzibar had recently experienced a communist and African, anti-Arab, revolution, and we were, I think, the only tourists on the island. We were followed around by a small army of sinister-looking, gun-toting secret police thugs in dark glasses, but even they could see our limited counter-revolutionary potential and left us to wander the deserted streets and enjoy each other's company.

We had one last adventure before we embarked on life together in Britain, where I had secured a post at Glasgow University. Most of our savings had been consumed paying off a bond to the Kenyan government on account of Olympia's failing to complete her obligation to teach, and so we decided to travel back over-land as far as possible, both to save money and to see more of Africa. I had lived rough for several months three years earlier, on an overland trip with Cambridge friends through the Soviet Union, Iran, Afghanistan, Pakistan and India, and felt reasonably comfortable with the prospect of tackling rural Ethiopia and the Sudanese desert, especially as Olympia was a tough and practical woman whom I had already dragged around some of the more god-forsaken corners of East Africa. Nothing, however, quite prepared us for the journey on country buses through the mountains of the Amharic and Tigray heartlands of Haile Selassie's Ethiopia: the squalor of the 'hotels' which were breeding colonies for fleas and cockroaches, the unremitting diet (*kinjara* and *wat*), and insane drivers who were in a hurry to embrace whatever afterlife their religion promised them.

We tried to appreciate the wonders of Abyssinian civilization and the character of a people who, uniquely, had seen off invading Europeans, but were immensely relieved to reach the Italian boulevards and *pensiones* of Eritrea. Khartoum in mid-summer in a cheap hotel followed by a train journey across the Nubian desert in third class were arguably even more challenging, but the Sudanese, once they had adjusted to the presence of a woman in the male sections of the train, were generous and courteous to a fault and we survived as far as the Nile steamer. Journeying through Egypt, and then Greece and Italy, was a return to romantic honeymoon mode – with the exception of a rough, deck-class crossing of the Mediterranean which coincided with Olympia's morning sickness, as she was now pregnant with our first son, Paul.

On the way to Glasgow, we called in at York to see my

parents, with whom I had not communicated since the letter of almost a year before. Nothing had changed. After a strained but polite cup of tea, my father continued as if he had been stopped in full flow months before. My mother sought to maintain the strained politeness of the conversation but was banished to the washing-up. My brother, now fifteen, was again invoked as the chief victim of my – now, our – misdeeds, but was dispatched to his homework, where he was a silent witness for the prosecution. My father had decided before we arrived that racial prejudice and rejection could be more palatable if presented in a tone of sweet reason, as if we could surely appreciate the pressure he was under from the unseen faces behind the lace curtains in White House Gardens. The failure of communication was absolute and it did not take long for the cumulative exhaustion of weeks of travelling to cause tempers to fray. We left amid shouting and recrimination, and if the neighbours had until then been unaware of the strange goings-on at No. 38, they were so no longer.

We had no further contact with my father and mother for six years. Together with Olympia's estrangement from her father, these events ensured that we started married life emotionally and practically dependent on each other, and this had the effect of helping us to thrive in adversity and to grow closer together. External events compounded this sense of being together against the world. While we had been marrying and travelling, the Kenyan Asian minority had become the centre of a triangular crisis involving Kenya, Britain and India. There was growing pressure on the Asian minority in Kenya from Africans seeking to occupy clerical jobs in government and make a start in small businesses – roles performed in Kenya almost entirely by the 200,000-strong

Asian minority. The Kenyatta administration made it clear that those Asians who had taken Kenyan citizenship – mainly the Ismaili community – were welcome, but those with British passports were a British responsibility. Growing numbers of Asians left for Britain, and as the exodus gathered momentum the British popular press had one of its periodic immigration panics, with wildly exaggerated numbers and rumours of the diseases, welfare dependency and criminality that the Asians were supposedly bringing with them.

The Callaghan government panicked, despite the information available to it that the total number of East African, let alone Kenyan, Asians was small; that many had no interest in coming to the UK; and that those that did had money, business and other skills. Callaghan threatened immigration controls. India refused to take any responsibility for British subjects, so large numbers of Asians who were well settled in Kenya and were not in any danger from Africanization fled for the airports before the UK controls could come into effect. The pictures of thousands of panicking Asians scrambling to get into the mother country before their UK passports became worthless created a hysterical environment in which Parliament pushed through legislation in record time, despite opposition from the Liberals and a handful of independent-minded Labour and Tory backbenchers.

These events had a direct bearing on people close to us. Mr Rebelo felt entirely vindicated in his conviction that I had dragged off his daughter to a deeply prejudiced country without honour or principles, and was determined henceforth that the family should rediscover its Indian roots. He proposed to return to Goa. My father was reinforced in his conviction that I had been conned into marrying one of these refugees who were so determined to live off the land of milk and honey (he started to reappraise his assessment several years later when a Tory government dealt with a similar crisis affecting Ugandan Asians in a much more rational and honourable way). Some of Olympia's relatives beat the UK ban; others, like much-loved Aunt Lyra, made it to Canada; but most stayed put, preparing for an eventual move to India. Olympia and I were angry and unsettled and I put some of my energies when I arrived in the UK into writing articles, including a Fabian pamphlet which, together with David Steel's book *No Entry*, provides, I think, a good account of this rather sordid episode in British political history. I came close to leaving the Labour Party which I had only recently identified with, but was talked out of it by Maurice Miller, a Glasgow MP, who put himself at the head of opposition to the 1968 Immigration Bill, seeing a close analogy with the way his Jewish forebears had been treated when they had fled to the UK from the Russian pogroms.

Olympia and I settled down to life in Glasgow with first one baby, Paul, and then another, Aida. We were a contented, loving family and, while we made some good Glaswegian friends, we must have seemed to them and others rather precious and narcissistic in our little self-sufficient cocoon. Olympia faithfully sent a weekly letter to her mother in Nairobi, and later in Goa, and kept in touch with her family through sisters studying in Southampton and Oxford and a brother, Celso, who came to Alloa for training in brewing technology. I re-established contact with my brother Keith, who came to study in Dundee rather than at Oxbridge, which my father regarded as a failure directly attributable to the upheaval and indiscipline that I had generated at home. The cold war separating us from our fathers continued, however, and seemed likely to continue indefinitely.

Cracks in the ice appeared only gradually. Mr Rebelo occasionally expressed curiosity about his daughter and grandchildren, and surprise that we had not realized his prediction of marital collapse. He faced rebellions, too, on other fronts. Amata, Olympia's sister, hoped to marry a Hindu, Manu, whom she had met while studying medicine in Delhi. Aurelio, the eldest son, had an English girlfriend, Jill. And, the ultimate horror, another daughter, Selina, planned to marry her black boyfriend, Harry (now professor of sociology at South Bank University). Selina's relationship aroused the deepest Indian prejudices about race, colour and caste, which were all the more difficult to handle and to express because they could not be channelled into a politically acceptable rant like the denunciation of British colonialism and imperialism. Although Olympia and I were blamed for starting the rot, we were no longer outcasts-in-chief. When Olympia's second brother restored family honour by marrying a suitable upper-caste Goan girl, Judy, at the Catholic church in Verna, we were invited as guests. Mr Rebelo took me aside and invited me to share his evening walks down to his paddy fields and coconut grove and my status as son-in-law was established. Although Olympia was never entirely forgiven for laying waste to her father's marital plans for his children, she regained her status in his affections and acted as a catalyst for the rehabilitation of the rest of the family, which was gradually reunited.

My own father put out peace feelers at about the same time. We had confounded his predictions, too, by staying together, and he had heard favourable reports of our academic progress and of the grandchildren. And as with Olympia's family, a greater marital disaster helped him achieve a better sense of proportion. My brother Keith made a young woman student pregnant in Dundee.

Susan Papp had fled as a child from the Russian tanks in Hungary and had later been reunited with her parents in Scotland. To reach university was a great achievement and one that now threatened to fall apart. My father urged my brother to walk away. We took the opposite view. Keith took our advice rather than his father's and married Susan. The marriage was not a great success but, despite an eventual divorce, Susan and Keith remained friends and my nephew Harvey, after a turbulent and rebellious young adulthood, has settled into a serious career and a family of his own.

Now with two estranged sons, my father was forced to rethink his priorities. On one level he had achieved a great deal. He had risen to become national President of the NAS and President of York's Guild of Building. On his retirement these achievements were properly honoured in the local press. He sang in the Minster choir with his fine baritone voice, and had achieved some recognition among the local Conservatives. But he faced a lonely old age, locked into a relationship of loveless mutual dependence with my mother. She had survived a series of operations for bowel cancer, but whatever spark had once fired her had long since gone.

They came to see us in Glasgow on their way to a holiday in Scotland and all the earlier rancour had disappeared. They invited our children to stay with them and my father became devoted to them. Slowly, a friendship developed between my father and Olympia. It gradually dawned on him that, colour apart, he had far more in common with his Asian daughter-in-law than with his sons or his wife. They shared the same passion for beautiful music, the same withering contempt for the decline in discipline and academic standards in education, the same uncompromising commitment to hard work, thrift and demanding professional standards. He came to see Olympia as his closest friend and shared confidences about his early life and private anxieties that he had never shared with anyone else, including my mother. There was a certain irony in a man, one of whose central beliefs was the need for women to know their subordinate, domestic place in society, finding consolation in his advanced years in two strong women: Olympia and Mrs Thatcher.

I doubt whether Olympia would ever have blinked first in the confrontation with our two fathers. But when they did, it gave her great satisfaction to return to a central place in the network of interlocking families. Family life mattered to her more than anything else: primarily her own children and husband, but also more widely. She frequently quarrelled with one or other of her brothers and sisters, as she did with me, but it was quarrelling underpinned by caring and love. More than anyone I have ever met, she strove to achieve integrity and understanding, not just in the public domain, but in private relationships too.

Chapter 5

Facing Mount Kenya

Two years before marrying Olympia and the family dramas that ensued, I had stepped on to an aeroplane for the first time, little appreciating what lay in store for me in Kenya. I remember Nairobi, four years after independence, as a tropical Woking or Basingstoke: neat, new, well manicured, unpretentious, suburban and provincial, differing from its English equivalents mainly in the jacaranda and bougainvillea blossoms, the red laterite soil, and the brown and black faces of passers-by. When I returned four decades later to see Olympia's eldest brother and his family, the Rebelos' remaining link with Kenya, Nairobi was a mega-city with twice the population of Paris.

The country now had a population of forty million, four times bigger than when I left, and most of the increment had gone to the cities, especially the capital. The segregated tidiness inherited from colonialism had become a messy melting-pot. Kenya had also become a laboratory for some of the pathologies of development: the slums bigger and more squalid, the inequalities more extreme, the corruption grosser than elsewhere. But the country has survived and grown in a way that my more pessimistic contemporaries never believed possible. The different races, tribes and religions have more or less coexisted. The army has stayed

in the barracks. A robust, if flawed, universal democracy has survived – though the events following the stolen Kibaki election of
January 2008, including some brutal ethnic cleansing in parts
of the country, cast some doubt on that optimistic assessment.
For all its anarchic and corrupt excesses, Kenya's model of capitalist development, underpinned by the entrepreneurialism of
small-scale peasant farming, has served the country better than a
lot of African alternatives and the enclave economy, settler-based,
that preceded it.

I arrived in 1966 with a mixture of high expectations and
preconceived prejudices. I had travelled quite widely, but had
never set foot in Africa. Olympia was the only Kenyan I had ever
met and hers was the only direct account of Kenya's colonial history that I had heard, featuring the semi-apartheid of society, the
theft of land by the white settlers, and the British atrocities at
Hola Camp. I had rejected my father's alternative view of history
and his expressions of dismay and outrage when he discovered I was leaving Britain to work for the evil genius who had
fomented the Mau Mau. I had read my way voraciously through
a pile of African histories and political tracts and had been most
impressed, and perplexed, by Kenyatta's tribal anthropology,
Facing Mount Kenya, which he had written in the early 1930s as a
postgraduate at the LSE. I was also fiercely determined to be bored
by animals, as a reaction to the popular understanding of Kenya
as a game park whose people were a rather dull backcloth to the
lions and elephants.

The job I was recruited to do was, at least initially, somewhat
less glamorous than I had supposed: a finance officer in the
Treasury was there to fill a gap in the post-colonial civil service
until African graduates had completed their training. I was one of

six British economics graduates recruited to work for sub-Saharan African governments by the Overseas Development Institute and its founder and director William Clark. William had been one of the leading foreign affairs journalists of his generation and made his name by resigning as Foreign Office press officer over Suez. He was larger than life, and somewhat camp, with an unparalleled talent for name-dropping which rarely descended below the level of heads of state or the royal family. The ODI fellows were his chosen people: the brightest and the best, who would populate the upper reaches of development decision-making in years to come. This particular dimension of his vision has been realized. But what William saw as a temporary, self-liquidating scheme to ease the transition from colonialism has proved to be a permanent arrangement to meet growing manpower gaps in numerous failing governments in Africa, the Caribbean and the Pacific.

It was an earlier ODI fellow who took me in hand in Nairobi and helped me to settle in his cottage in the heart of the Karura Forest, the last expanse of virgin jungle near the city. Terry Libby had boundless energy and enthusiasm and radiated positive thinking. He was the son of a general, more socially and politically conservative than me, but his good humour and organizational skills sustained our joint household. The organization took in a Kenyan servant, Mubia, later joined by a friend. Terry felt entirely at ease with servants and managed the relationship in a professional but caring way. I felt, however, deeply uncomfortable with the whole idea, which I associated with upper-class decadence, but lacked the courage or conviction to reject it. I could also see that making Mubia unemployed would be deeply inhumane to him and his family, whom he saw infrequently but who depended on his modest income. Mubia was also highly competent and hard-working and seemed to see nothing undignified about his labour for the two *wazungu*. My own relationship with the two men oscillated between overfamiliarity and cold detachment, and I felt especially uncomfortable when African friends came to stay. But when Terry left Kenya, the 'houseboys' moved with me and then worked for a succession of ODI fellows. I later discovered that, by saving a high proportion of his pay, Mubia had been able to become a modest landowner and successful farmer in his village near Nyeri and to put his growing band of children through school.

The cottage in the forest also provided a vivid and somewhat alarming immersion into the physical realities of Africa. The nocturnal sounds of wild animals and the distant rhythm of music and dancing in the nearest villages were occasionally augmented by mysterious footfalls: curious villagers, perhaps, or, it was rumoured, a gang of outlaws. When the rains came the forest roads became impassable and on several occasions I had to abandon my VW and walk. Those night walks, alone, through the forest, in torrential rain, still inhabit my bad dreams.

These exciting extramural activities sustained me through the initial months of life in the Treasury when I was learning how to be useful. I was wedged awkwardly between an earlier generation of colonial civil servants who saw me as an instrument for perpetuating British good administrative practice, and the young African inheritors of the system, most of whom, with varying degrees of impatience, regarded white faces as a symbol of the past from which they were seeking to escape. In my two years there, the administrative centre of gravity shifted decisively from white to black.

The permanent secretary throughout this period was a Kikuyu, John Michuki. He never showed any hint of racial preferment, was impeccably professional, fair, competent and honest, and provided the leadership that was absent from our ministers: the finance minister, Mr Gichuru, who was permanently ill or drunk; and his deputy, Mr Okello-Odongo, who was sidelined by Kenyatta as a communist subversive before disappearing into preventive detention. Michuki resurfaced four decades later as a key minister in the present Kibaki government with a reputation for tribal partiality, thuggishness and corruption, qualities that were wholly absent from his younger persona.

Under him was my immediate boss, a formidable woman called Joan Tyrrell with a fearsome reputation for rigorous standards, workaholism and not suffering fools gladly. She had learned her trade in the colonial administration of Nigeria and was now in overall charge of the government's capital development budget and of negotiations with aid donors. Thanks to her as much as anyone, new roads, water supplies, agricultural credit, tourist lodges and small-scale industries multiplied rapidly in post-independence Kenya. After initially regarding me as a particularly hopeless case, useful only for feeding parking meters and carrying files, she discovered, during a long absence, that I could cope, and we developed some rapport. Unfortunately, her habit of bawling out dimmer colleagues, with a splendid indifference to colour or rank, caught up with her and she was encouraged to retire early. My next boss was another bright young Kikuyu civil servant, Joe Kibe, whose kindly, jocular manner disguised a tough and ruthless operator who, like Michuki, returned in later life to a position of power in the Kibaki administration. Although we got on well, he made it clear that the era of white expatriate civil servants in the Treasury was over and I was, before I left, required to train an African replacement. My designated successor was to be an unfortunate choice: a seemingly very stupid but cunning young man called Arap Ngeny, who was from a tribe of nomadic pastoralists, the Nandi, and was promoted in the interests of ethnic balance. His one claim to fame was kinship with the then vice president, and future president, Daniel arap Moi, who eventually made him governor of the central bank. There he oversaw large-scale looting of the government's finances.

The person who had most influence on me was neither British nor Kenyan but a Swedish economist called Kurt Savosnik, working, courtesy of the Ford Foundation, in the planning ministry. There was predictable tension between the Treasury, which controlled the sinews of financial power but whose officers had a narrow, bean-counting approach to economics, and the planning ministry, which occupied the political and intellectual high ground but had no direct control of how money was actually spent. Interdepartmental conflict was reinforced by a key tribal and personal fault-line in the government. The finance minister, Gichuru, though hopeless and an alcoholic, was a long-standing political ally and fellow tribesman of the president. The planning minister, Tom Mboya, was a Luo, the most glamorous figure in the Cabinet and a source of much envy on account of his brains, good looks and communication skills. How much planning he actually did is debatable, and my friends on his staff reported a large and steady procession of beautiful women of all colours and creeds to his office, who would emerge, dishevelled, some time later.

Nonetheless, he added status to the art of economic planning, which was then considered essential to the achievement of economic growth. Indeed, much time and consultancy money was spent compiling vast documents based on the supposed economic achievements of Nehru's India, Harold Wilson's Britain, and de Gaulle's France (by then, the USSR and China were no longer considered suitable role models for Kenya). Earnest American, Indian and Scandinavian professors laboured to produce National Plans which were then studiously ignored by ministers, my Treasury colleagues, visiting aid donors and foreign investors, and, indeed, anyone who mattered. Savosnik had been recruited from Sweden at considerable cost to 'plan' industry, but instead of spending his years in Kenya playing charades, had decided to try to introduce discipline and genuine economic rigour into how decisions were actually made, for which he needed an accomplice in the Treasury: me.

Savosnik had been one of the brightest economists of his generation: one of several Swedes who contributed generously to the construction of trade theory. He was fiercely honest to the point of bluntness, which meant that he lived dangerously in a world where tact and political correctness were strongly recommended for expatriates. But he lacked totally the air of effortless racial superiority that even well-intentioned Westerners would often exude, and African ministers appeared to like him. He was the son of Jewish refugees from the Nazi Holocaust who had escaped to Sweden. Far from feeling a sense of gratitude, however, Savosnik detested the smug moral superiority of Swedes who, he had discovered at school, often harboured ideas about Aryan purity not greatly different from those of the Germans across the Baltic Sea. He endeared himself to his acolytes, like me, for a different reason. He was a widower whose late wife had been crippled and in Kenya, in his forties, had just discovered conjugal bliss with an attractive French lady. Our morning meetings would start with a review of the stock exchange and world commodity prices followed by a graphic and detailed account of his sexual exploits of the previous night.

The particular project he embarked upon, and for which he enlisted my help, was to open up the opaque process by which the government granted licences, import quotas, hidden subsidies and tax reliefs to large numbers of mainly foreign businessmen who came to Kenya to help the government 'promote industrialization'. Many of the projects, on closer inspection, turned out to be wealth-subtracting, though the glamorous vision of pulp and paper mills, steel factories, car-assembly units and textile plants was seductive to African decision-makers anxious to wean Kenya away from the imperialist past of, as they saw it, 'hewing wood and drawing water'. It was also becoming clear that corruption was beginning to percolate into government in a serious way. One of the president's closest associates, Paul Ngei, had recently been criticized in a public inquiry into a scandal involving the Maize Marketing Board. But the most egregious abuses centred on trade and industry, where the minister, Dr Ciano, was universally dubbed Mr Ten Per Cent. The problem did not stop at Ciano. The businessmen promoting the contaminated deals usually included in their visits courtesy calls on the president, and it was increasingly believed that the fish was rotting from the head down, rather than from the guts in the middle. Savosnik believed, and persuaded me, that it was irresponsible and immoral to look the other way and play games with economic models while foolish and ruinously expensive, and often corrupt, projects were being allowed through unquestioned.

The problem was how to communicate dissent without appearing directly to challenge not only some very powerful figures in the government but the whole concept of modernity. To an economic liberal like Savosnik it was obvious that systems of licensing and government permits would generate 'rent-seeking activities' (i.e. corruption), but in an intellectual climate in which it was still necessary to pay lip service to 'planning' and 'socialism', the defence of markets and competition was not likely to find a ready audience. We did, however, have allies. My permanent secretary, John Michuki, was, at least at that stage of his career, a puritanical stickler for due process. There were plenty of other African officials who subsisted on low salaries, had not yet been faced with overwhelming temptation, and could be relied upon to reinforce any serious questioning. Indeed, there were some fine, idealistic young civil servants who could see the danger signs only a few years after independence. Prominent among them was Robert Ouko, permanent secretary at the ministry of works, whose department presented considerable opportunity for graft, and who was killed in mysterious circumstances some years later for opposing the excesses of President Moi.

Where malpractice could be identified, Savosnik was smart enough to point the finger at the white or brown bribers rather than the black bribee. Adam Smith's unsentimental warning from two centuries earlier that all businessmen were potentially engaged in a conspiracy against the public found an African echo.

My modest role was to help him develop a simple methodology for evaluating projects at world, rather than local, prices: an idea that, in a more sophisticated form, later became a standard economic tool. Savosnik taught me in addition to analyse the balance sheets of companies that had solicited government protection and favours in order to identify suspicious 'black holes'. We then had a sound basis for warning our superiors of questionable activities and, to a surprising and encouraging extent, our advice was acted upon. I also had access, as a Treasury official, to parts of the government that he could not reach. I sat on the boards of state corporations, notably those dispensing credit to the industrial and tourist sectors. Bizarrely, John Michuki also placed me on a sensitive committee determining the pace of commercial Africanization (in effect, the replacement of Asian licence-holders by Africans). Since the role of the Treasury representative was to urge caution in the interests of the economy, it was all too preditcable that there would be a backlash. Had I been a senior African official I would, I am sure, have taken umbrage at an Englishman in his mid-twenties seeking to block progress, however sensible the objections. One powerful permanent secretary, Kenneth Matiba, who later became a leading figure in the opposition to Moi's rule, recommended that I be deported, but I was defended by Michuki and the head of the civil service and allowed to continue.

These personal excitements were rare and, in retrospect, I have undoubtedly exaggerated their importance. But I did have a ringside seat, and occasionally a small acting role, in the big dramas being played out at the time: the debate on commercial Africanization, which led, in 1968, to the exodus of Kenyan Asians; the break-up of the East African Union; the 1967 UK devaluation, which was seen as a massive breach of trust by a sterling-holding government; and the pushing through of a land reform programme under which white settlers were bought out and replaced by African smallholders. The last of these was Kenyatta's master stroke and it prevented Kenya going the way of Zimbabwe, an achievement somewhat diminished, later, by the greed for land of Kenya's new black elite.

The main role of a Treasury official was to say 'no'. But it was occasionally possible, and wise, to be more positive. One major project, with long-lasting consequences, for which I could claim considerable credit – or blame – involved a new road to the far north where the Turkana nomadic pastoralists lived precariously in the semi-desert around Lake Rudolf. President Kenyatta had spent several years of his detention there during the emergency and made a commitment to lifting the Turkana from their abject poverty. Various rather bizarre ideas were put forward, including an oil refinery, notwithstanding the absence in the region of any oil or any market for its products. The president made clear his displeasure at the Treasury's blocking tactics and I saw the opportunity to earn some brownie points by promoting one of the more sensible options: to build a road to Lake Rudolf, thus enabling the Turkana to diversify their economy by fishing and exporting dried fish to the fish-eating regions of Kenya and Uganda. After a feasibility study showed genuine promise, an official visit was agreed and I made a perilous journey by jeep with an assistant minister and the chief roads engineer along the proposed route. There were, for me, some eye-opening discoveries along the route, including a sophisticated system of gravity-fed irrigation on the slopes of the Rift Valley, developed by the Elgeyo Marakwet people in pre-colonial times. I was also bitten by an insect on my elbow, which later turned seriously septic. According to Olympia, I barely survived. But the upshot of the expedition was a decision to build the road. I was responsible for mobilizing Norwegian aid for the project and, to my amazement, the money was pledged and the road duly materialized shortly after I had left the country. Regrettably, my colleagues and I disregarded the advice of an anthropologist that the project ran the risk of destabilizing the delicately balanced relationship between the Turkana and their inhospitable environment. Years later, he was proved right. The Turkana, not understanding or liking fishing, invested all their profits in more cattle, leading to serious overgrazing. The project was subsequently often cited in the manuals of development disasters; my defence is that I probably stopped others that would have been worse.

The best of the expatriate staff I worked with were among the most impressive people I have ever met, though there was a large amount of dross: the UN 'experts' and miscellaneous consultants who cost a fortune, lived the lifestyle of princes, and contributed little or nothing. My role models, Savosnik and Joan Tyrrell, were like canaries down a mine: they could detect a bad smell before it became dangerous. The smells were the bad aid projects and the crooked businessmen, and far too often they spread undetected until great damage was done. One of the best books about Africa in the 1960s, *False Start in Africa* by the French agronomist René Dumont, describes how (if I may switch analogies) a rapacious plague of locusts descended on the green shoots of development that appeared at the time of independence. The most visible signs of their visitation were the snowploughs 'donated' to Guinea, the billion-dollar hulks of rusting steel left behind by 'investors' in Nigeria, the new hospitals without doctors or medicines, and the Olympic-standard sports facilities almost everywhere. But most of the exploitation and waste was more subtle, which is why the smell-detectors were useful.

Typical 'turnkey' projects were promoted by machinery salesmen offering generous credit terms and, as a major 'concession' to Kenya, giving a large slice of the equity to the host government, supposedly in the interests of 'localization' and public ownership.

Their aim was to shift risk on to the Kenyan government and to make a killing by padding out the costs of the equipment or an associated management and consultancy agreement. Issues of risk transference are, of course, universal and lie behind the contemporary controversy over private financial initiative (PFI) contracts in the UK. For Kenyan ministers, however, it was counter-intuitive to decline such 'generosity', and the crooks with whom we negotiated were adept at playing to a nationalistic gallery. It was often the case that the best projects came from local Asian businessmen moving from trading to manufacturing with second-hand equipment, or the traditional multinationals who were there for the long haul. But this was not a message ministers wanted to hear and, too often, snake-oil salesmen with generous presents and impressive visiting cards were able to get through the government's defences.

Aid donors, too, were adept at passing off mercenary and self-interested schemes as acts of saintly generosity. One of my main responsibilities was unscrambling the tangled finances of a Russian-built hospital in Kisumu negotiated by the Russian sympathizer Mr Okello Odongo, before President Kenyatta had him locked up. The running of the hospital was to be financed by sales of surplus sugar that Russia had acquired from Fidel Castro. Unfortunately, Kenya had, by now, its own surplus of sugar, grown near Kisumu, so the sugar was declined and the hospital remained empty. I came to appreciate the urbane charms and gold teeth of the Russian ambassador and the culinary skills of his pretty wife, and eventually the Russians stumped up some real money.

The Americans were worse. Much of their aid was in the form of local cash generated by the sale of US wheat surpluses, which did serious damage to the local grain market. We declined it, much to the irritation of the US embassy, which was now in the ascendancy on the Kenyan front of the Cold War. I particularly enraged the embassy by ignoring their elaborate, bureaucratic financial reporting requirements, and on one occasion was carpeted by the minister for putting at risk the comradely relationship developing with the Americans. There were some dreadful financial deals dressed up as 'aid' offered, inter alia, by the French, Italians, Israelis, Japanese, Danes and even the blessed United Nations. There was some really valuable assistance too, from Holland, Sweden, Germany, the soft loan arm of the World Bank, and also from the British. The skill, which I was just beginning to acquire when I left, was to know when to say 'yes' and when to say 'no'.

I cannot say, in all honesty, that I made a major, or even a positive, contribution to the development of Kenya. But Kenya made a massive contribution to mine. Simply learning how to navigate a way through the minefield of racial sensitivities was an education in itself. I learned much, too, from watching politicians in action, albeit in a rather different environment from Westminster. Kenyatta himself was a towering figure. Yet, unlike Mandela, who has become a latter-day saint and an iconic, inspirational figure far beyond South Africa, Kenyatta is now seen as a diminished, tribalistic and tarnished character. Like Mandela, however, he was a father to his country, suffered many years of imprisonment, showed forgiveness and magnanimity towards the settler farmers and the colonial power on his release, displayed a pragmatic understanding of the need for a mixed economy, and prevented a slide into racial and tribal strife. But human failings, greed and acquisitiveness, undid his reputation and opened the way to the rampant kleptocracy of Daniel carap Moi. When I served in Kenyatta's government, his reputation was still largely intact and '*Mzee*' enjoyed genuine respect and popular support. This could be seen at his mass rallies, some of which I attended out of curiosity. He was a mesmerizing orator in Swahili (though laboured in English). I had only a rudimentary grasp of the language but I was gripped by his wonderful, deep, rich voice, flowing cadences and rapport with the crowds.

His close entourage of ministers was altogether less impressive. Almost all had acquired top-of-the-range Mercedes (the 'Wabenzi'), large stomachs, sizeable land holdings and personal fortunes. The only white member of the government, Bruce Mackenzie, the agriculture minister, competed well on all these counts (he was, it later emerged, also an MI6 agent, before he died in an air crash). As civil servants, we were, of course, party to the gossip about our political masters, and it was mostly very unflattering. There were some exceptions: Tom Mboya, who was assassinated shortly after I left Kenya; Ronald Ngala, who died later in a suspicious car accident; and Mwai Kibaki, who frequently deputized for our Mr Gichuru.

Kibaki was clever, incisive, conscientious. Unlike most ministers, he did not owe his place to the 'independence struggle' or to close tribal links with Kenyatta; he was a Kikuyu, but from a different, Nyeri, clan. He had taught economics at Makerere University in Uganda and was the only minister to be not only economically literate but able to engage with technically complex development issues. The four decades that elapsed before he became president seem to have knocked the physical and moral stuffing out of him. Perhaps the most damning indictment of Kenyatta's rule is that the genuinely talented among the next generation were corrupted (like

Kibaki and Michuki) or killed (like Mboya, Ngala and Ouku) while the mediocrities accumulated wealth and power. Just as Lenin will be forever tainted by creating the conditions under which Stalin could succeed him, Kenyatta paved the way for Moi.

While I was in Kenya, Moi took his first decisive steps up the ladder to the presidency when the half-Masai, half-Goan vice president, Joe Murumbi, died. Moi succeeded him and presented himself as a simple farmer and former schoolteacher with undemanding tastes and Christian virtues, including large numbers of children. He had been chosen to provide balance, coming from one of the pastoralist tribes of the Rift Valley, like the Masai and Turkana, and having been a leader of the pre-independence opposition party (KADU) which had brought together the smaller tribes that feared domination by the Kituya and Luo. He was already showing his mettle by leading the charge against the breakaway Kenya People's Union. Its leader, Oginga Odinga, was a proponent of a kind of populist African Marxism that would have been as disastrous in Kenya as in Nkrumah's Ghana, Mengistu's Ethiopia or Mugabe's Zimbabwe. But it had potential appeal, not just to Odinga's Luo but to the growing numbers of impoverished Kenyans of all tribes who were not experiencing the fruits of independence and liked the KPU's 'free things' policy (free education, free land, free food, and, it was sometimes suggested, free beer and free women). Kenyatta and Moi did not want to take the risk of losing an election: Odinga and his associates, including Olullo-Odongo, were locked up. A general election took place on a single-party basis, with competing candidates from the government party, KANU. Half of the MPs lost their seats, which suggested to optimists that there was a real democracy at work and to pessimists that the government was desperately unpopular. For all Kenyatta's faults and Moi's even greater venality and thuggery, this semi-democracy was allowed to continue and, in due course, KANU was voted out of power.

What disfigured Kenyatta's administration most, and Moi's even more, was corruption. The process by which corruption entered and rapidly took over a group of hitherto honest people alarmed and fascinated me. Colleagues who had been absolutely fastidious in declaring gifts and living within their means would, according to the rumour factory, suddenly be 'on the take' and luxury cars beyond the reach of their civil service or ministerial salaries would appear. In some cases there would be pressure from acquisitive wives or from extended families to pay for school and college fees and health care. Widespread reports that powerful people, from the president down, were accepting, then demanding, gifts, and were apparently immune from investigation, let alone prosecution, were hardly an incentive to behave well. I guess that, for many, once a psychological threshold had been breached, succumbing to temptation became much easier. I noticed, too, the unalloyed cynicism of many overseas, including British, businessmen, who did little to hide their belief that bribery was a necessary – indeed, entirely defensible and proper – way of conducting business with foreign governments. (The British government's reaction to BAe Systems' allegedly corrupt dealings with Saudi Arabia suggests that little has changed for the better.) Corruption became a self-reinforcing process, and clumsy attempts to regulate and plan the economy rather than let markets operate freely created yet more opportunities.

The debates in the press, and outside, about corruption overlapped with a broader argument about the strategy for development. In 1967 Tanzania embarked on a fundamentally different path, '*Ujamaa*', stressing 'self-reliance', socialism and cooperation, rather than engagement with Western capital and free enterprise as in Kenya. The Tanzanian model did not work well and arguably further impoverished Tanzania, not least because it destroyed incentives for peasant farmers. But this was not known at the time, and President Nyerere's simplicity and transparent honesty provided an attractive counterpoint to the Kenyan theme of acquisitiveness and rampant greed. With the possible exception of Botswana, Africa has yet to produce a model that works and combines the best of both approaches.

Exposure to these debates and to the reality of development on the ground clarified, for me, a set of fundamental ideas that I carried through subsequent decades and different roles: the importance of a genuinely competitive, liberal model of capitalism (as opposed to 'crony capitalism'); property rights and security for entrepreneurs, particularly small farmers; government doing a few essential things well – such as policing, education (especially primary education), basic healthcare, water, roads, agricultural extension and research, and the regulation of basic utilities – rather than lots of things badly and corruptly; openness to trade and foreign investment; an aggressive approach to the removal of racial and other barriers restricting opportunity and social mobility based on merit; and a commitment to breaking up concentrations of wealth, particularly in land ownership.

I was eager to understand the country better than could be gleaned from newsworthy politicians, the rarefied world of the Treasury and my economist friends. It was necessary, first of all, to escape from the trap of spending one's time exclusively in the world of white Kenyans. There were, of course, some genuinely interesting and worthwhile white people. But the endless barbecues and dinner parties usually degenerated into a prolonged whinge about the unreliability of the servants, the decline in standards, and the last or next trip to the game parks. This refrain came typically from people who had until then led modest, unpretentious lives in cramped semis in Croydon and had been catapulted into a setting of space and beauty, waited upon by houseboys, cooks, ayahs for the children and gardeners. Most lived in the green suburbs with large gardens full of gorgeous tropical shrubs and drives flagged up by the owner's name – a style derived, I think, from the posher bits of Surrey.

When the novelty had worn off, boredom followed. Boredom was not much alleviated by Kenyan television or radio, whose idea of world news was a speech to a village meeting by the assistant minister for cooperatives. Drink and sex were popular distractions and many aspired to the kind of lifestyle captured in the film *White Mischief*: 'Are you married or do you live in Nairobi . . . ?' Few felt any real sense of belonging or involvement in the country, and many of the long-standing white residents made little secret of their wish to escape to the better-ordered, safer, more civilized environment of Rhodesia or South Africa. There was, however, a sufficient critical mass to sustain a film society, the occasional concert, and a national theatre in which I occupied a modest niche playing minor Shakespearian roles. An attempt to broaden out into a multicultural repertoire with *A Passage to India* was a dramatic and social failure. Apart from a small number of mixed families, university academics and culturally aware Goans, the different racial groups coexisted in different silos. All of this I found suffocating and I tried to escape.

Pamela Ogot had provided an entrée to the world of young,

educated Africans and to the university, where I additionally ran an evening class in economics. The university occupied an important but precarious place in the new Kenya. Its graduates would in due course become the professional elite and would fill jobs like mine. But it was in transition from a substantially Asian to an overwhelmingly African student intake, and from British syllabuses and degrees to a Kenyan identity. Rapid expansion and the dilution of quality led to resentment by many students who saw their efforts and degrees devalued. Poor African students from rural areas were thrown together with other races and tribes, causing considerable friction. Students who were the repository of all their families' hopes worked prodigiously hard but could not accept failure, however poor their performance.

There was also the intoxication of new ideas. Radical academics questioned the official view of politics and history. At a public lecture I heard, for the first time, a detailed historian's account of the Mau Mau which brought out the scale of the killing (of Africans), the abuses on both sides, and the state of virtual civil war between rebels and 'loyalists': subjects over which the government preferred to draw a discreet veil in the interests of 'unity'. The year 1968 also brought reports of student unrest throughout Europe and North Africa. For their part, the Kenyan authorities regarded the university as a potential threat and source of subversion. Many politicians (and soldiers) were uneducated and resented the privileged young men and women being subsidized to study. The inevitable happened: student demonstrations led to over-reaction. In 1969 the army was ordered on to the campus and many students were gunned down, raped or taken into detention. From then on, students kept their heads down.

I made other friends who introduced me to rural Kenya: Gilbert Ojwang, a Luo from South Nyanza, and John Ndero, a Kamba from eastern Kenya, both junior Treasury officials who, in return for a lift to their villages to see their families, were happy to offer me a few nights' accommodation. Theirs was a Kenya far from the main roads and the tourist routes. Their wives toiled the year round on small *shambas* growing maize and beans, keeping a few chickens and hauling water and wood for long distances. Their husbands' salaries paid for primary school fees and the odd luxury: toys or decent clothes. My modest Swahili and their modest English provided sufficient basic communication, but I missed many of the nuances. On one occasion I was offered a woman for company; whether this was a tradition or to accommodate the particular needs of Europeans wasn't clear. The expression of relief on the young woman's face when I insisted on declining her suggested that I did the right thing. On another occasion, one of Gilbert's less savoury relatives stole my (somewhat battered) coat and after an extensive search in the village the article was tracked down to his hut. My expression of indifference to the loss was misinterpreted as an act of great clemency and generosity, for had the thief been turned over to the police the magistrates would have certainly sentenced him to several strokes of the cane as well as imprisonment in Kenya's harsh, still colonial, penal system.

In a succession of visits I began to get a feel for the rhythms, and profound boredom, of rural life, far removed from electricity, public transport or markets. The journeys, across the rolling and fertile Kisii hills or the valleys around Machakos, revealed a largely unknown and beautiful Kenya but also an alarming one, since every inch of land to the tops of hills was already intensely cultivated by tiny plots; any additional population could only be accommodated by ruinously uneconomic subdivision or by migration to the cities.

Land hunger was the most explosive issue in Kenya, made worse by demographic pressures – Kenya had the world's highest birth rate (4 per cent) – compounded by grotesque inequalities. Kenya had lanced the political boil through a largely successful land transfer programme, taking a million acres from Europeans to allocate to small farmers, mainly Kikuyu. But there were other desperately overcrowded parts of the country, and some vast European estates – like those of Lord Delamere in the Rift Valley – that remain untouched to this day.

From other acquaintances – John Mwangale, a recently recruited Treasury graduate, an Abaluyha from Mount Elgon on the Ugandan border, and Mubia, who took me to his farm near Nyeri – I learned about a successful, commercially oriented dimension to African agriculture. Hundreds of thousands of small-scale African farmers were developing cash crops as well as maize: coffee; tea; pyrethrum (for insecticides); fruit and vege-tables for urban markets; horticulture for export; and dairy cat-tle producing milk for rural cooperatives. In some parts there was modest prosperity, and everywhere an eagerness to learn more about improved agricultural techniques such as the use of fertilizers, the optimum use of shading and terracing, scarecrows (hitherto largely unknown), and plant disease control.

I acquired abiding respect for the entrepreneurial skills of peasant farmers and a lifelong irritation with metropolitan, devel-opment theorists who opine that developing countries should stick to subsistence farming. I recall a particularly humbling long conversation with an illiterate farmer, a former Mau Mau detainee, who had a far clearer understanding of commodity futures markets and the impact of exchange-rate movements on agriculture than I had, and who expressed polite surprise that Cambridge economics graduates knew so little.

One of the few things about which white and black would normally be expected to agree was how appalling the Asians were. Indeed, it was a common conversational ploy by many racist whites, who did not wish to be overheard criticizing the new black rulers, to vent their spleen on the Asians. The Great White Hunters, the bores of the dinner-party circuit, with their endless anecdotes about tracking lions through the bush (from the safety of a jeep) were particularly contemptuous of this urban minority, which had no obvious interest in the great outdoors, in marked contrast to the idealized heroic African warrior, the Masai. Stories about the Man-eaters of Tsavo which, a century before, had caught and eaten large numbers of Indian workers when they were building the railway from Mombasa, caused particular mirth. For their part, populist African politicians were turning up the heat on the Asians for a variety of alleged misdeeds: overcharging or rudeness by Asian shopkeepers (or *dukawallahs*); lack of loyalty to the new Kenya (few had taken out citizenship apart from the Ismailis, who did so, en masse, on advice from their leader, the Aga Khan); lack of social mixing and intermarriage; Diwali fireworks; even the offensive smell of Hindu cremations. The simple truth was that the discriminatory practices of colonial times – when Asians were forbidden from owning land or entering the upper reaches of public service – had confined the Asians to trading, clerical and artisan activities, where they were now directly in the path of upwardly mobile Africans.

I felt particular discomfort at the anti-Asian mood building up in Kenya, which reached a climax with the exodus of

1968. Not only was there my relationship with Olympia, but some of my closest associates in the government, with whom I could have an easy conversation uninhibited by considerations of status or political sensitivity, were Asian: Nizar Jetha, an economist who asked the right awkward questions about tax policy; two very able statisticians, Parmeet Singh and Surjit Heyer; and the Treasury's sharpest financial mind, Ramesh Gheewala, who should have risen to the top on ability but had already reached his glass ceiling. Through them and others I was invited to numerous weddings and community events. I came to appreciate that the 'Asian community' was a largely meaningless racial construct, since it encompassed several religions and language groups with as much in common as 'European' Finns and Bosnians. Even within fairly homogeneous groups like the Hindu Gujaratis there were self-contained caste groups like the Patels, Shahs and Loharias. To the Kenyan Asians, however, I owed not just a happy marriage and family but probably my life. When I was stricken with a rapidly spreading infection of unknown origin, Olympia whisked me into the 'Asian' hospital, where I was, I think, the only European. After being put on the critical list for several days and pumped full of every antibiotic known to man, I stabilized and then recovered, mainly thanks to Dr Yusuf Eraj and his colleagues.

In other ways, too, I pieced together fragments of the complex society in which I lived. A Tanzanian friend, Nioni, who worked for the shortly to be defunct East African Railways, introduced me to the nightclub scene and the Congolese dance music which was, and I think still is, much preferred to the crude, plonking rhythms of most Western pop. I helped for a while as a producer of plays in a township called Jerusalem. Much of Nairobi's African working class disappeared at night to those mockeries of the Promised Land – another was called Jericho. They were mean, minimalist, crime-ridden, badly lit and distant from the city, the vision of some colonial town planner whose skills were transposed to or from Rhodesia or South Africa. The idea evidently was that Africans should be close enough to the city to be able to commute to work but far enough away not to cause trouble or overcrowd the commercial centre.

In Jerusalem, a group of youngsters had formed a theatre club performing African drama in English and, when a Peace Corps volunteer left, I was drafted in to help. My production skills were as rudimentary as their acting and the first night of our first big production was plunged into disaster when the leading man was picked up by the police an hour before the start. I let the cast down by resigning in the face of this and other obstacles. But I received a brief but vivid education in the lives of young people trying to educate themselves against formidable odds.

The same Peace Corps volunteer also encouraged me to continue his work with mentally ill children in Mathare. Mathare is now the site of one of the biggest shanty towns in Africa, but it was then in the early stages of growth and better known for the hospital. The stinking, caged, disturbed children, to whom I read and talked, survived, if little more: the underclass of an underclass. The wretchedness of their condition contrasted jarringly with the estate nearby: Muthaiga, home of the super-rich and the country's leading golf club.

These well-intentioned, if largely ineffective, gestures on my part contrasted with a more self-indulgent side to my lifestyle. Encouraged by Terry Libby, who had flown at university, I decided that I wanted to learn to fly. Nairobi's wonderful climate made it a perfect place to learn. Most of my savings went on flying lessons. I proved to be stunningly incompetent. I discovered that my rather disorganized and intuitive cleverness was a handicap, not a help, when it came to mastering the complex but essential routines necessary for pilot and passenger safety. I failed the pilot's licence exam three times and succeeded at only the fourth attempt, something of a record at the local flying club. The second failure was spectacular, when I did not take appropriate action to correct a spin and the plane narrowly avoided the control tower, followed by a simulated emergency landing in a field which I managed to make real. The examiner, a Rhodesian former Battle of Britain pilot, emerged from the experience shaking with fright. Eventually I scraped through and enjoyed solo flying in the breathtakingly beautiful landscape around Mounts Kenya and Kilimanjaro and over the Rift Valley. My carelessness almost proved my undoing, however, most notably after taking off from a landing strip on the slopes of Mount Kenya, when I forgot to adjust the choke and the engine started to die. As I drifted down into a forest some latent instinct for self-preservation saved me, feet from the trees. My nerve and my money ran out at about the same time and I gave up flying. I had, however, the malicious satisfaction of seeing my instructor, whose stories about my lessons entertained the club bar for months, barred from flying for crash-landing while drunk.

My personal debt to Kenya was immense. But, despite occasional visits with Olympia and our children to see their cousins in Nairobi, the country became a rapidly receding memory. When I returned again with Rachel, four decades later, I tried to recapture some of the past, and largely failed. Olympia's old home had disappeared under a property development; the house in the forest had gone, overgrown; Savosnik had stayed in Kenya but had died; Pamela I could not trace (but have done since); the once impressive finance ministry, designed to shock and awe more junior departments, was now dwarfed by skyscrapers. My brother-in-law was the only link with the past, with his family, and he had defied the pessimists, becoming one of the country's leading lawyers, a successful businessman and, now, a leading political figure too. I stopped searching and enjoyed the experience afresh, even marvelling at the animals in the game parks I had once affected to despise.

Chapter 6

Red Clydeside

To Glasgow I owe six good years: the beginning of family life with Olympia and two young children; some academic credentials; and a thorough education in the university of political life.

Why Glasgow? I faced a rich choice of economics faculty posts in Sussex, Cambridge and Glasgow. This was less a tribute to my abilities than a reflection of the fact that this was a golden age for university academics, with rapid expansion of job opportunities along with high prestige and relatively undemanding workloads. We decided on Glasgow on the basis of a warmly welcoming handwritten airmail to Kenya from the head of faculty, promising a lecturing post for me and an opportunity for Olympia to do postgraduate research.

The Glasgow to which we came had a grim reputation for poor housing, poverty, industrial decline, sectarian division and violent, alcohol-fuelled gangland crime. The reputation was a caricature of a much more complex reality which included much fine architecture, a rich cultural life, and a highly regarded university (in fact, two), the apex of an education system that, in many respects, produced better results than its English equivalent. But at that stage no one was seriously seeking to project the strengths and virtues of Glasgow, and most Glaswegians expressed their pride in the city through black humour and parody of the kind perfected by Billy Connolly.

My only previous acquaintance with the university had been the Debating Union, where a Cambridge colleague and I, as guest speakers, had been made to look slow-witted by the quick repartee of Glasgow student politicians, who had recently included the likes of John Smith, Donald Dewar and Menzies Campbell.

The university itself was not, like most others in England and Scotland, a mix of students from across the country but was overwhelmingly made up of local young people who had just completed their Highers (taken a year before English A levels) before embarking on a four-year degree. The students were, perhaps, as a consequence more conformist, less rebellious and more work-oriented than elsewhere, aware that they were on a conveyor belt to the Scottish professions.

The faculty in which I researched and taught had an ancient pedigree. Adam Smith was, arguably, the university's most famous son, together with his friend David Hume, and the continued relevance of his economic analysis after 250 years was reflected in the undergraduate courses. There were some birds of passage, like myself and Gus O'Donnell, later the UK's top civil servant. But the staff was mostly, somewhat uneasily, divided into two distinct groups. A group of Scots dominated the running of the faculty and the university, most of them formidably able but somewhat narrowly focused and conservative. Then there was a range of more exotic characters who brought variety and new ideas. Alec Nove was one of the world's leading authorities on the Soviet economy and he anticipated many of the issues that came to the surface under Gorbachev's perestroika. Ljubo Sirc, with whom I taught international economics, had come to Glasgow after a period in jail, under sentence of death, in Yugoslavia, where his views had clashed with those of communist fellow partisans. He analysed, and accurately predicted the failure of, the planned economies of eastern Europe – even the 'middle way' kind, as in Yugoslavia – and the eventual triumph of liberal economics. Radha Sinha did pioneering work on the comparative development of India, China and Japan. Our head of department, the Ulsterman Tom Wilson, had a gentle way of deflating the fashionable follies of government intervention. With a few exceptions, the department's leading figures reflected the underlying economic philosophy of Adam Smith, whose bicentenary was celebrated when I was in Glasgow.

The great strength of the Glasgow – indeed, of the wider Scottish – tradition of economics (called, quite properly, political economy) was that it firmly anchored economics in philosophical ideas. There was little encouragement for those, whose influence was growing elsewhere, who wished to turn the subject into a branch of mathematics or were slaves to reductive models. There was a genuine sense of outrage that Smith's ideas were being used out of context and for crude ideological positioning by people who failed to connect the market economics of the 'invisible hand' in *The Wealth of Nations* with his scepticism about the motives of businessmen, not least their endless quest to subvert the market. In his earlier book, *The Theory of Moral Sentiments*, Smith had extolled 'benevolence', 'sympathy' and 'compassion' as central moral principles.

In truth, I did not make a major contribution to the academic life of the university beyond my quota of teaching and finishing a PhD (on economic development and regional integration in Latin America), as did Olympia. And though Olympia and I had a tight circle of university friends and lived close to the university, we increasingly gravitated towards town rather than gown. In Olympia's case this was because she felt obliged, despite the conflicting claims of a baby and a thesis, to help contain our overdraft by teaching. She was recruited to teach history in a Catholic secondary, St Pius's, in Drumchapel, one of the three massive post-war council housing schemes built on the periphery of the city as homes for those displaced by slum clearance in the inner city. By the late 1960s the full awfulness of these schemes was beginning to become apparent: shoddy construction and damp; lack of decent public transport; lack of leisure activities, beyond the pubs; and the recreation of many of the social ills that were thought to have been banished by slum clearance.

Olympia's Catholic education and African teaching experience did not fully prepare her for the challenges of St Pius's. The Catholicism taught was uncompromising. Faith was instilled, not discussed. Olympia's attempts to introduce into the classroom a balanced historical assessment of Oliver Cromwell, let alone the atheists Robespierre and Lenin, produced an apoplectic reaction from the head. She also came to appreciate that in Glasgow religion is part of a strong tribal identity, and the pupils were clearly puzzled by their teacher's ignorance of some of the fundamentals, like the difference between Celtic and Rangers. Perhaps for this reason, or the head's wicked sense of humour, her duties were extended to include refereeing school football matches. I believe that the stories of this rather beautiful Indian lady running around a muddy pitch in a sari and high-heeled shoes entered into Drumchapel folklore. Olympia could cope with all of this. What she could not cope with was the resentful, and some-times aggressive, philistinism of the pupils. Unlike her African girls, who treated every second of teaching time as an opportun-ity and a privilege, many of the boys and girls of Drumchapel resented school and regarded it as irrelevant. She did her best to encourage the more academic pupils, but found that those she encouraged would be persecuted as a consequence. On one occa-sion she discovered that a particularly promising pupil was being regularly upended in a toilet bowl. Despite the insistence of our friends that comprehensive education was working well, and that Scotland had developed a superior variant of it, Olympia's experi-ence told her otherwise.

My own introduction to learning outside the groves of aca-deme was altogether more satisfying, starting with WEA evening classes and progressing to be one of the first generation of Open University tutors. The OU was an absolute joy, with brilliantly crafted, multidisciplinary coursework and eager, questioning adult pupils who had been given, and seized, a second chance and were determined not to lose it. I have been a strong supporter of adult education ever since and believe it is scandalous and foolish that so much priority is given to force-feeding reluctant teen-agers at school and university rather than adults who want to learn or relearn but, without help, lack the analytical tools.

Olympia and I also began to savour the, then, largely unsung treasures of the city. It was but a ten-minute drive to a concert hall to listen to Rubinstein, Menuhin, Claudio Arrau, Victoria de los Ángeles and others, or to hear Kiri Te Kanawa or Janet Baker sing at the increasingly acclaimed Scottish Opera, or to see plays at the innovative and lively Citizens Theatre. It didn't take me long to discover, too, that the big Glasgow football matches had an intensity and passion that I had never previously experienced at Elland Road in Leeds or Bootham Crescent in York. The first England vs Scotland international I attended at Hampden Park, with over 100,000 souls singing with one voice (I seemed to be the only Englishman there), was given added edge by the fact that England had recently won the World Cup but needed to be taken down a peg or two. Old Firm games had the intensity without the unity and as a neutral I struggled to comprehend quite how my tolerant, moderate Glasgow friends could mouth the sacrilegious banter and hymns of hate with such conviction. My enjoyment of these events came abruptly to an end at Ibrox on New Year's Day in 1971 when, in the excitement generated by two goals in the last few minutes, there was a sudden surge in the densely packed departing crowds. A few minutes later, a few yards from where I was standing, a hundred people were trampled or suffocated to death. The disaster deeply shocked the city. Olympia banned me from attending future matches.

It was in Glasgow that I seriously engaged in politics for the first time, in Woodside, a largely working-class ward wedged between the Great Western Road and Maryhill Road. When we first came to Glasgow, Olympia and I had rented a top-floor flat in a gloomy grey sandstone tenement in a rather elegant Victorian crescent, then somewhat dilapidated, though subsequently refurbished in the interests of conservation and enhanced property values. Our neighbour, John McFadden, was a Labour activist who enrolled me to help revive the local party and contribute the occasional day's campaigning in Argyll, where he was the parliamentary candidate. His wife Jean formerly apolitical, joined in as the first step on a long road to becoming Labour leader in Glasgow. He gave me a crash course in Glasgow politics, including the problems (and opportunities) presented by his Catholic religion.

The Labour rooms were gloomy, smelly and also small, which was just as well since even a well-attended constituency – let alone ward – meeting rarely reached double figures. Even these events depended on whether the party secretary, an elderly Irish lady, Mrs McCrory, was sober and remembered to appear with a key. The rooms had, however, been the scene, a few years before, of one of the more controversial parliamentary selection meetings of the period, chronicled in Paul Foot's *The Politics of Harold Wilson*, when the sitting MP, Neil Carmichael, was chosen.

The overall position of the Labour Party in Glasgow at that time was abject. Labour had dominated the city for half a century or more since the decline of the Liberals. In 1968, however, the council had been lost for the first time in decades to the Conservatives and their allies, the Progressives. A succession of Labour councillors appeared in court for fiddling expenses or taking backhanders. The Labour government of Harold Wilson was deeply unpopular in the wake of the 1967 currency crisis and subsequent austerity measures. There were factory closures and rising unemployment; and there was a Scottish dimension to the wider grievance about the North–South divide, with the SNP making deep inroads in working-class areas.

At this time the face of opposition to Labour was changing. Labour's traditional foes on the right were led by a group called the Progressives who depended on the wasting asset of politicial Protestantism. But in the late 1960s they were replaced by a new breed of Conservatives who managed to escape from their party's image, in Scotland, of plummy English accents and double-barrelled names, thanks to a group of smart young lawyers led by Len Turpie in Glasgow and Malcolm Rifkind in Edinburgh, and a formidable Glasgow Tory MP, Teddy Taylor. In later years, representing Southend, Teddy became a rather lonely and comic figure, but in Glasgow his populist instincts and sophisticated modern campaigning techniques frightened the Labour Party to death and he hung on, for an indecently long time, to a seat based on Europe's largest council estate. More important in the longer term were the SNP. They were then in the process of transforming their image from 'Tartan Tories' and eccentric men in kilts spouting Gaelic to a left-wing nationalist party appealing to the Clydeside working class. Some of their new cadres were seriously alarming and in England would have gravitated towards the National Front or the BNP. The SNP was beginning to establish a strong urban base which now, over three decades later, represents the main opposition to Labour.

All of these factors led the Glasgow Labour Party to look favourably on any new, positively motivated – even English – talent that could revive its battered fortunes. My energy and enthusiasm were seized upon and I was given responsibility for managing the next (1969) council election campaign in my ward (elections took place annually, by 'thirds'). My candidate was to be a tough shop steward from the Albion engineering works, Jimmy Gunn, for whom getting on to the council was to be the culmination of a career on the industrial wing of the Labour movement. He initially regarded me as some kind of strange extraterrestrial creature and I failed utterly to penetrate his particularly thick Glasgow accent. But we developed a rapport based on fatalistic humour as we lurched from one disaster to another.

Our election literature was made up of badly typed manuscripts which were reproduced on a hand-operated Gestetner machine and emerged hopelessly smudged, while I forgot the need for posters to have a legal imprint. My idea for injecting wit and novelty into the campaign was a slogan that captured the revolutionary spirit of the time: Ho! Che! Gunn! In the absence of a better medium we reproduced the slogan in chalk on Woodside's pavements and hoped that rain would hold off until election day. It did, but, in the gathering gloom on election eve, we hadn't realized that our most lavish display of electoral graffiti was located outside the front door of the Catholic church. After a call from an incandescent Father Murphy, Jimmy and I were set to work scrubbing the pavements the following morning while the bemused voters walked past to the polling station.

Election day 'knock-up' technology – which, these days, requires a Cray computer at least – relied exclusively on a loudhailer which was supposed to have the effect of driving the voters out of doors in order to save their ears from further punishment. We didn't win, but came surprisingly close on a bad night for the party in the city, and I acquired an unjustified reputation for electoral wizardry.

Shortly afterwards, the candidacy for the parliamentary seat of Hillhead became vacant. Hillhead became famous in the 1980s for Roy Jenkins's by-election victory, but was regarded in the run-up to the 1970 election as a safe Tory seat where Labour came a respectable second (and the SNP and Liberals aimed to save their deposits). The one glimmer of hope was the Tory MP, Tam Galbraith, who was rarely seen and had recently been identified in the press with a scandal. It involved an unusually intimate correspondence with the traitor John Vassall, which suggested at least the possibility of a homosexual relationship. Homosexuality had just been legalized and was still barely tolerated. Hillhead was a good place for an aspiring Labour politician to start, and the constituency party already had one in the form of a local schoolteacher. I turned up at the selection meeting more in hope than expectation and, to my considerable surprise, won. Unfortunately, I thereby made an enemy of the schoolteacher and his friends, who went on strike. More seriously for my long-term career prospects, I concluded, quite incorrectly, that the way to win a parliamentary nomination was to turn up on the night and wow the activists with a good speech.

The campaign was, however, enjoyable and rewarding. The constituency was small, densely populated and easy to cover on foot. It comprised three wards – Kelvinside, Partick West and Whiteinch – bordered by Byres Road to the east. I thought of it as representing a geological cross-section of Glasgow society. At the top of the hill, overlooking the Clyde, in Kelvinside – Glasgow's Morningside – was a stratum of grand red sandstone tenements of the respectable middle class, immaculately clean, with ornate stained-glass windows to brighten up the otherwise bleak stair-wells. I believe the area has now acquired some social leavening, but it then seemed to be inhabited almost exclusively by elderly ladies in mink coats who voted Conservative with unswerving loyalty regardless of political context or candidate – even the seemingly 'gay' Galbraith. As one moved down the hill through layers of social stratification, the tenements were less salubrious and the mink coats were gradually replaced by scruffy children and loud Glasgow grannies. At the bottom of the hill there were the worst and most squalid tenements, some already boarded up and waiting for clearance.

I suffered acutely from 'candidatitis', the candidate's disease of believing that victory is within reach, even when electoral arithmetic and political logic suggest otherwise. The illness was inflamed by an exceptionally committed team – led by another academic, Pat Shaw – and the national publicity I received for being the party's youngest candidate in Scotland. In the event, we managed not to go backwards on a bad night for Labour. And I received an unexpected boost as a result of putting my name on the ballot paper for one of the safe Conservative wards in the municipal election, which occurred simultaneously. By dint of knocking on large numbers of doors, or name recognition, or a fluke, this ward happened to achieve the biggest pro-Labour swing in the city. On the strength of it, I received a call from the Glasgow Labour leader, John Mains, a wily machine politician who had no interest in the parliamentary election whatever but cared passionately about winning back the council, where the real power lay. He told me that 1971 would be the Big Push and I was to be a key part of it.

He encouraged me to stand for a vacancy in the ward of Maryhill, potentially one of the safest in the city after Mains's own Gorbals seat. I duly appeared at a selection meeting at the Labour rooms, which were even bleaker than those in Woodside, and was invited to address a small huddle of mostly elderly people. The competition consisted of two sharp, assertive, snappily dressed young men, John McInespie and Gordon Kane. Both had a reputation for cutting corners and both, I believe, went to Barlinnie prison for expense irregularities some years later when they were councillors. I won the vote, but there was some soul-searching by the activists who couldn't quite reconcile me with their image of a Glasgow councillor. I was told later that the decisive factor was the vote of several Catholics who had been told that my wife taught at St Pius's and who assumed that my name, Vincent, identified me as one of them. This misunderstanding came back to haunt me years later.

I joined a team of two rather elderly but delightful and welcoming colleagues: Phil Stimson and Martha Johnson. The MP, Willie Hannan, was a peripheral figure, reflecting the peculiarly low status that MPs had in the city. They were mostly obscure figures, kicked upstairs to the Commons from the council or their trade union in reward for loyal, if undistinguished, service. Someone like Neil Carmichael, who had achieved the dizzy heights of parliamentary undersecretary for the Navy, was, in this company, a towering statesman.

I set about campaigning in Maryhill, though, in truth, the election was a formality in which I received over 60 per cent of the vote and a majority of more than four thousand over the SNP. But the significance of the 1971 election was that it was a landslide sweeping Labour back to power, helped by the fact that there was now a Conservative government in London.

The Class of '71 also included the former Speaker of the House of Commons, Michael Martin, and a clutch of new politicians who would come to dominate the city, including Jean McFadden and Sir Michael Kelly (as he became), a future chairman of Celtic Football Club, but then a Strathclyde economics lecturer. A similar electoral tsunami had occurred in Edinburgh, bringing in, among others, Robin Cook.

The new intake immediately came into conflict with the old guard. There had long been a strong whiff of Tammany Hall about Labour in Glasgow, with abuses of the considerable powers of patronage that shaded into outright graft. Councils were considerably more powerful then than they are today, with largely unfettered control over revenue from domestic and commercial rates, control over appointments – not just senior officials but individual schoolteachers, for example – and, in Glasgow, the opportunity to allocate a vast stock of around 150,000 council houses, increasing at four to five thousand a year. And until 1974 Glasgow was a unitary authority. In many respects, the early 1970s were the last big fling of municipal government, for good and ill. And the people who controlled the levers of power were substantial figures, much more important than MPs.

The issue of who should control the Glasgow Labour machine came to the fore immediately after the 1971 election when it became clear that the newcomers would not willingly defer to the established order. There were two overlapping groups in the old guard. One, led by the leader, John Mains, and the two Dans, Donnelly and Doherty, were of Irish Catholic stock and had seen the Labour Party as a route to respectability, influence and power. Another group, led by Sir William Gray, the formidable chairman of the Scottish Housing Association, and Tom Fulton, were not in any way sectarian but were interested in modernizing and rebuilding the city in a largely non-political, technocratic way. Bill Gray once told me that his greatest achievement was to have used slum clearance and council rehousing to break up the old Catholic and Protestant ghettos.

In addition to these, and strongly represented in the new intake, were two other, also partially overlapping, groups. One comprised the trade unionists, a large contingent that included Michael Martin; David Marshall, then a TGWU organizer and until recently a Glasgow MP; Jimmy Gunn, with whom I had campaigned in Woodside; and Albert Long, whose daughter I taught economics to and who much later, was Anne McGuire, was a minister in the New Labour government. The trade unionists had their base in the shipyards and engineering factories around the city and broadly reflected the left-wing perspective of the powerful national leaders of the time, like Jack Jones and Hugh Scanlon, and the communist-dominated Glasgow Trades Council (in which John Reid was active). The other group – mine – was made up of middle-class professionals, sometimes dubbed (by those who felt threatened by them) the 'pseudo-intellectuals': teachers, lecturers, lawyers and a Church of Scotland minister, Geoff Shaw, who would in due course rise to the top. The dominant personality in this group was Janey Buchan, a future MEP and the feisty wife of Norman Buchan, one of the leading Tribunite MPs. Her forthrightness and courage were allied to a sharp tongue and a remarkable capacity for making enemies. There was in Glasgow a socialist tradition dating back to the Independent Labour Party with such revered figures as Keir Hardie, Jimmy Maxton and John Wheatley, and many of our group identified with their uncompromising values.

Relations between the radical elements in the new intake and the old guard were already strained by an ugly argument that had broken out in the Labour Party shortly before it returned to power, centred on religion. There were two aspects to it. One was the Scottish dimension of hostility towards direct grant schools, which were seen to be a threat, as in England, to comprehensive education. There were several equivalent schools in Glasgow, but they happened to include a leading Catholic school, St Aloysius, to which leading members of the Labour group, in particular the prospective chairman of the education committee, sent their children and which they strongly supported. The other, broader issue was a challenge to faith-based education which split the city almost fifty–fifty between Catholic and non-denominational (in practice, Protestant) schools. The Irish 'troubles' were growing in seriousness in the wake of Bloody Sunday (in 1972), and there were genuine fears that the sectarian strife might spread from Londonderry and Belfast to Glasgow. For those worried about the febrile state of Glasgow society there were warning signs, including an invigorated Orange movement led by the local Ian Paisley figure, the Reverend Jack Glass. For a newcomer like me the marching bands of the August Orange parades merely provided entertainment for young children, but many Glaswegians – whether Catholic, Protestant or non-religious – regarded them with real fear. A group of Labour activists, including those in my own circle, started to agitate for school integration, and this led to a public rebuke from the cardinal and from our more conservative Catholic colleagues. I have since changed my views on the issue and now defend faith schools as an aspect of parental choice. But in that rather more polarized environment (and armed with anecdotes from Olympia at St Pius's) I became one of the 'troublemakers' seeking to upset the established order at a delicate time.

Once elected, I luxuriated for a while in my new status and delighted in the magnificent Victorian surroundings of the City Hall which were, alas, of rather greater dignity than most of the happenings within. Since I was simultaneously trying to be a councillor, an academic and a New Man, I often brought my three-year-old son, Paul, to council meetings, which was heartily disapproved of by some socially conservative colleagues but won me some firm friends among the women councillors. I tried from the outset to avoid the tribal breast-beating that passed for debate in the council and adopted a non-confrontational and constructive style, which I have tried to maintain to this day. It paid off immediately since my maiden speech, suggesting ways in which the council could facilitate economic regeneration in the city, received good reviews, including a big write-up in the *Scottish Daily Record* by a young journalist called James Cox who resurfaced many years later as the presenter of *The World at One* and as a neighbour in Twickenham.

A series of major issues then had the effect of heightening the tensions within the new Labour administration. There was a new Conservative government and an education minister, Margaret Thatcher, who was determined to stop the post-war system of providing free school milk. The decision caused particular outrage in Glasgow where levels of poverty were high and diets poor. There were living memories of rickets. Even those who were not exceptionally motivated by the issue of school milk saw the potential threat to local decision-making from a minister in London imposing her will on all councils, and on Scotland, regardless of local priorities. I took the lead in the Labour group, arguing for a strategy of passive resistance: refusing to implement the legislation. I was encouraged by John Mains, who saw this as an excellent issue on which to campaign and to rebuild party unity, which was coming under some strain. For a while, the resistance and the popular support we received had a unifying and, indeed, euphoric impact. But once senior officials started to spell out the implications of continued recalcitrance, including the threat of surcharges on individual councillors, resistance started to crumble. The revolt ended in the worst possible way, with a majority of us voting to continue the opposition and a minority, including most of the leadership, voting with the Conservatives and Progressives to end it.

This campaign established me, improbably, as a champion of the Glasgow left-wing and I milked the popularity it gave me. I rather foolishly confided to one of my colleagues that I found it incongruous to be promoting socialism in the council chamber and free-market economics in the university lecture rooms on the same day. I was reminded, unsympathetically, of a quote from Jimmy Maxton, that 'if you can't ride two horses at once you shouldn't be in the bloody circus'. I tried to assimilate the advice.

A growing polarization of the ruling Labour group on broadly left–right lines created the basis for the next big split, over council rents. We had hitherto been kept together by the political skills of John Mains, who had the knack of making most of us feel important and valued, and recognizing merit even where there were serious disagreements. He died at this particularly difficult juncture and Sir William Gray, who took over, though a brilliant administrator, lacked his political authority. The issue of rents was politically highly charged because the Conservative government proposed to tackle the whole system of cross-subsidy within local government, under which personal and commercial rates were used, at least in Glasgow, to keep rents low. There was certainly a case for reforming the financing of council housing and both Robin Cook in Edinburgh, where he chaired the housing committee, and myself in Glasgow produced papers offering a critique of the government's proposals, combined with alternatives. But, as with the school milk issue, even those who saw the need for reform were united in opposing centralist, Tory, solutions. There were, moreover, genuine difficulties in imposing large and rapid rent increases on low-income families, because even if they could gain access to the promised means-tested housing benefit they would face high marginal withdrawal rates and work disincentives.

Another rebellion was organized and history repeated itself with a predictable mixture of tragedy and farce. Glasgow was one of the last councils to comply with the new law – just soon enough to avoid the surcharges that were imposed on councillors in Clay Cross. The Labour group split along similar lines as before.

These confrontational issues did not arise in a political vacuum. There was, in the city at large, a political radicalization taking place in response to developments at UK level. The Heath government is now primarily remembered for the decision to enter the Common Market and for the miners' strike that effectively finished it off. But in its first two years the government was full of reforming energy and set a course later to be followed by Mrs Thatcher as prime minister. One of its most controversial decisions, made by DTI secretary Nicholas Ridley, was, in effect, to force the closure of Govan's Upper Clyde Shipbuilders (UCS), one of the city's main employers, rather than facilitate a rescue bid by a workers' cooperative until new investors could be found. Although Yarrow, further downstream, remained as a military shipbuilder, UCS was the last remaining outpost of an industry that embodied the city's manufacturing tradition and, directly and indirectly, employed thousands of skilled engineering craftsmen. There was remarkable cross-party support for the UCS workers, who were brilliantly marshalled by the communist shop stewards Jimmy Airlie and Jimmy Reid. Reid, in particular, was a magnetic speaker, powerful yet humorous, and his inaugural address as Rector of Glasgow University was one of the finest speeches I have ever heard. One of my friends, a university lecturer called Frank Herron, who came from a Govan shipbuilding family, subsequently made a compelling economic case that the costs to society of additional long-term unemployment exceeded any savings from the closure. But with hindsight, the closure was inevitable, later if not sooner, and although Ridley presented the government's case unsympathetically, as an English upper-class toff indifferent to the industrial heartland of Britain, he anticipated today's more critical approach to government intervention.

I was personally caught up in the UCS campaign and took considerable pride in marching along Sauchiehall Street with my son Paul on my shoulders, alongside Tony Benn, Jack Jones and other celebrities who came to Glasgow to join the massive protests. The UCS campaign also coincided with the rent rebellion and, indeed, part of the rationale for the latter was for the councillors to show solidarity with the workers in opposition to the Tory government in London. There was a mood of radicalism in the city which, while it was often couched in ideological terms, had a deeper cultural significance: an expression of the city's, and Scotland's, identity.

The climate of opinion also created conditions for a coup within the Labour group. A group of us who had been identified as radicals put forward the Reverend Geoff Shaw as group leader, and he won; while I was elected to one of the senior positions on the executive, in effect the Cabinet. I was very proud of this achievement since I had lived in the city for less than five years and was very conscious of my middle-class Englishness. I also liked to think that the coup was a turning point in the way the city was run. The group who seized control of the council, which included Jean McFadden, Bill Harley and Pat Lally, provided the city's future leadership. The takeover was portrayed, at the time, as a victory for the left. In one sense it was. And there was some overlap between the radical left of the Glasgow Labour group and the Communist Party, which was strong in the unions, if not electorally. There were also, at this time, the first stirrings of Militant. But, unlike in London and Merseyside, the Clydeside left had a strongly down-to-earth, pragmatic quality. Paradoxically, the main consequence of the change in the council was to open the way to new and more liberal ideas.

One change was a re-examination of entrenched attitudes towards housing. Housing dominated the city's political agenda like no other issue and accounted for 90 per cent of my casework as a councillor. The traditional approach was to clear the slums as rapidly as possible and decant the population into council housing: the three big perimeter schemes – Easterhouse, Castlemilk and Drumchapel – or multi-storey blocks near the city centre. Of the latter, the tower blocks of the Gorbals (Hutchesontown) won prizes and were initially regarded as a great success.

The only policy issue was how to speed up the rate of slum clearance and building. One of my earlier memories of group meetings was an earnest debate prompted by one of our colleagues who wanted to sell off the Kelvingrove Art Gallery, including Salvador Dalí's masterpiece *Christ of St John of the Cross*, to raise more money for council housing. Shortly afterwards, the fateful decision was taken to build the Red Road development, which later became notorious for its inhuman scale, insensitivity to the needs of families for space, and neglect of the practical problems of keeping stairwells clean and lifts functioning. There were some murmurings of unhappiness among councillors at the time, and we had access to a growing volume of literature warning of the problems created by multi-storey blocks of social housing. But an election commitment to step up the pace of council-house building proved decisive. We achieved close to five thousand in one year.

It was increasingly obvious to most of us, however, from our casework, that the strategy was flawed. As it happened, Maryhill had two of the better-designed and more popular schemes – Wyndford and Cadder – but it also had a 'problem corner' of low-grade, inter-war housing where the 'difficult' families were parked. The better local schemes could not, however, accommodate those displaced by slum clearance, and I saw large numbers of families desperate at the prospect of being exiled to the Gulag, as the big perimeter schemes were increasingly viewed. Other families hated the idea of their children being stuck twenty storeys up in high-rise flats. Initially, many councillors and housing officers refused to accept that there was a problem and developed a language for describing 'choosy' and 'difficult' people who lacked 'gratitude' for what the council had done.

But as dissatisfaction rose, there was a search for a coherent alternative. The Conservatives advocated more private housing for owner-occupation to leaven the lump of social uniformity of the inner-city multi-storeys and perimeter schemes. Although this was basically a sensible idea, and was adopted some years later by the Labour council, it was roundly dismissed at the time because it would reduce the space left for council housing. Moreover, it did not get to the root of the problem: that many of those who were being cleared and rehoused wanted to stay put in what the council regarded as 'slums'.

The problem came to a head in my ward when the council decided to demolish a series of blocks of old tenements. Far from being delighted at the prospect of being rehoused by the council, the residents – both owner-occupiers and private tenants – protested furiously and sought to reverse the decision. They were helped by a group of campaigners – dubbed 'anarchists' by the council – who had access to legal advice and pointed out that there were alternatives, including the refurbishment of the old buildings. I was initially caught between trying to help my constituents and defending the council, and unsuccessfully tried to persuade the council to change tack. A high-profile confrontation developed which attracted the press and television. When some of the residents were rehoused, their flats were boarded up, which then attracted squatters, and the remaining protestors – who would not accept offers of rehousing unless it was local – found themselves living in increasingly squalid conditions before they were forced out by the sanitary inspector. The rebellion petered out, but I was determined that it should not happen again.

Some months later, the council's planners turned their attention to another tenement block nearby, on the Maryhill Road. This time I surveyed the residents and found that most wanted to stay. Helped by the fact that I now held a more senior position after the internal coup, the council agreed to make Maryhill a pilot study for refurbishment. The idea was spreading and, helped by a unit at the university that had architectural and planning skills, more and more schemes of this kind were adopted across the city.

Another area in which new thinking was playing a part, and to which I made a contribution, was transport policy. In the early 1970s Glasgow's planners, like those in most big British cities, saw the future in terms of a network of urban motorways. The leading planning guru of the time, Colin Buchanan, argued for the separation of pedestrians and roads with a combination of car-free shopping centres and residential areas connected by fast car routes. Glasgow bought into this vision and Buchanan was, in fact, its main consultant. Leading councillors saw new motorways, like blocks of multi-storey council houses, as emblems of a modernized, dynamic city. The plan was already well developed when I arrived on the council and several motorways were under construction or planned, notably the main east–west route.

There was, however, already in the city a questioning of the new orthodoxy and I devoted myself to challenging it. I was galvanized in particular by a proposal to build a motorway through my ward designed to take commuters from the middle-class suburbs of Bearsden and Milngavie into the town centre a little faster. The fact that the motorway would be built on stilts through the middle of an attractive, low-density council-housing scheme, Cadder, and lead to the demolition of a large amount of perfectly sound tenement housing, appeared not to disturb the planners in the least. I mobilized the residents, who were unaware of the plans, to object. A still more controversial plan was for an inner ring-road which involved a stretch of overhead motorway very close to the medieval heart of Glasgow, and this enraged Glasgow's small but growing amenity and environmental movements. There was frustration, too, at the neglect of public transport: buses, which were crowded and increasingly expensive, and a ramshackle old underground system.

I was able to play a modest but useful role in changing the strategy by combining a local populist campaign, for public transport and against the motorways, with economic questioning of the technical assumptions behind the consultants' reports. I published an article in *New Society* that linked the controversies in Glasgow to the wider national debate. I had been appointed to the planning, highways and transport committees and spent much of my time on the council locked in battle with the planners and the highway engineers. After the coup had changed the balance of the Labour group, I was able, with allies, to kill off at least the excesses of the urban motorway programme. In particular, the Maryhill motorway and half of the inner ring-road were never built, and the council pressed ahead with the modernization of the 'Clockwork Orange', the underground railway.

The third change I was able to make was in understanding poverty and social deprivation. When I arrived on the council, poverty was seen in rather simple and mechanistic terms: basically, poor housing. The persistence of deprivation in the new housing schemes, and the seemingly insurmountable financial problems faced by many families, caused the emphasis to change. I launched a couple of initiatives that were then somewhat ahead of their time but did, I think, later take root. One was to establish a 'one-stop shop' advice centre in Maryhill. I obtained the funding for a Citizens' Advice Bureau, but was unable to recruit volunteers to staff it. Shelter later filled the gap. I also persuaded university colleagues to devise software for a system to help residents identify their benefit entitlements, then being made more complex by the new housing benefit and a means-tested family benefit, family income supplement, the forerunner of tax credits. IT systems were then a good deal more primitive than today, depending on punch cards to store data, and the project was considered challenging. Some of my more conservative colleagues were also appalled at the thought that raising awareness of benefits might encourage 'scroungers'. A pilot scheme was nonetheless approved and I believe that Glasgow maintained and improved the system subsequently.

One indirect consequence of this work on poverty was that I came to the notice of the Rector of Edinburgh University, a postgraduate student called Gordon Brown, who was putting together the *Red Papers for Scotland*, and he invited me to contribute. At that stage, Brown was known primarily in the world of student politics but talked of, like Robin Cook, as a coming man: very bright and with radical new ideas, part of an Edinburgh group developing independently of the Clydeside Labour heartland. The book had a wider significance in giving a voice to a new generation of Scottish Labour politicians, and while its socialist approach to policy has not stood the test of time, it has recently generated some good-natured repartee between the two of us, with speculation as to which of us has subsequently moved furthest to the right.

I recently revisited my own chapter, which is dense and rather dull but focused on the right issue: the extraordinarily entrenched, multidimensional poverty of inner-city Glasgow. Three decades on, the problems remain depressingly similar. When I was asked a few months ago to support a Lib Dem-led campaign against school closures in my old ward of Maryhill, I was struck by how little had changed for the better and by the still jarring contrast between the low living standards and low expectations of my former constituents and the thriving middle-class suburbs of Bearden and Milngavie a mile or two up the road.

Enjoying modest celebrity status as a high-profile Glasgow councillor took me into several bigger debates. One concerned devolution. There had long been a rift on the left between those of a nationalist bent, who emphasized Scottishness and Scotland's egalitarian and social democratic traditions, and the unionists, who dominated the Labour Party leadership. The unionists were led by Willie Ross, the secretary of state for Scotland in the first

Wilson government, who was a fine, principled and respected, but unbending, man. The rise of the SNP in the late 1960s in Labour's industrial heartland and a Tory government, apparently unsympathetic to Scotland, reopened this old divide. A key new factor was the discovery of North Sea oil and the nationalist slogan 'It's Scotland's Oil' had great resonance when Scotland was hit, no less than the rest of Britain, by an oil shock. A case began to be made for devolution, in intellectual terms, both in the Brown book and by Andrew Hargreaves, who happened to be an English correspondent in Scotland for the *Financial Times*. Some of the new generation of Labour politicians started to run with the issue of Scottish devolution. One was a rising star, John Smith. Another was John Mackintosh, a former professor who won a parliamentary seat in 1966 and was a brilliant, witty speaker who would surely have risen to great political heights had he not died young. Others included the MPs Jim Sillars and Dick Douglas, both of whom later joined the SNP. Although it took twenty-five years for the ideas to come to fruition, the Labour Party (and the Liberals, who were a growing force in the Highlands and a few urban outposts like Greenock) became firmly committed to devolved government.

I was then invited to join a group chaired by Bruce Millan, the most impressive of the Glasgow MPs, and a future European commissioner, which included Jim Sillars and a couple of able young activists, George Robertson and Helen Liddell, who were clearly destined for higher things. The group was charged with setting out an economic strategy specifically for Scotland when Labour returned to power. We were influenced by fashionable ideas of state capitalism that were then being refined by a group of economists around Tony Benn, notably Stuart Holland, but in Scotland there was more emphasis on practical ideas for regeneration, based on the model of the Highlands and Islands Development Board. Out of our report came the Scottish Development Agency, then Scottish Enterprise, which somehow survived Mrs Thatcher's bonfire of quangos and become a model for other regional development agencies. I have become less of an enthusiast for such bodies since then. But in the context of the 1970s and 80s a positive contribution was made by a body working pragmatically with the grain of the market, acting in support of business innovation, not as a tool of public ownership, and concentrating on infrastructure development.

The big issue of the early 1970s, however, was Europe, with Heath's decision after the Tories were re-elected in 1970 to negotiate UK entry into the Common Market. All of my friends and allies on the left of the Glasgow Labour group were viscerally opposed to the whole idea of Britain joining this capitalist club and they were seriously puzzled when I came out in favour alongside old enemies on the right of the party and the Tories. I was in a minority within the party – though supporters included George Foulkes, a young Highland MP, Bob Maclennan, and future European commissioners George Thomson and Bruce Millan, as well as Willie Hannan in Maryhill. I was drafted in by pro-European groups to make the case at public meetings across Scotland. These included debates with fierce critics of the European project like Robin Cook, who must have been grateful, when he later became a pro-European Foreign Secretary, that his earlier comments had not been recorded. Our proselytizing zeal was such that a group of us, under the leadership of George Thomson, were sent to Norway to support the pro-membership campaign there. There were bitter splits in the Norwegian Labour Party which our arrival did nothing to help heal. The Norwegian campaign was lost, permanently.

The other wider campaign in which I became involved was more personal. Olympia and I were one of the few racially mixed couples in the city, and the immigrant minority – mainly Asian shopkeepers and a small Pakistani community in the south of the city – was tiny. We encountered little prejudice in general, but there were periods of tension during the Kenyan Asian crisis and then later when Mr Enoch Powell made his 'rivers of blood' speech. At that time the atmosphere cooled noticeably and Olympia, when on her own or with me, attracted racial abuse on the streets. Teddy Taylor invited Enoch Powell to Glasgow and sought to make immigration an issue. We felt personally exposed and threatened and leaned heavily for emotional support on our friends, including Labour activists, who, whatever our other differences, were unfailingly supportive. I was drawn into the embryonic community relations group forming in the city, led by the city's first non-white councillor, Bashir Mann, and we were active in the anti-apartheid movement. In 1971 there was another upsurge of racist feeling caused by the exodus of Asians from Uganda. Fortunately, the Conservative government dealt with it decisively and honourably, making it clear that citizenship and immigration rights would be respected. Committees were organized around the country to welcome and absorb the refugees. I organized the Scottish committee and my councillor colleagues showed some courage in volunteering a number of council houses. In the event, few Ugandan Asians came to Scotland and, of those who did, many departed south after experiencing their first winter.

By the middle of 1973, Olympia and I had been in Glasgow for five years and had every reason to feel content. We were happy and settled with two young children in a comfortable, new, bought flat, with a warm circle of friends, enjoying the high quality of life the city had to offer and regular holidays in the Highlands. I had successfully completed my PhD, alongside my teaching, and Olympia was making good progress with hers. My political career seemed to be going from strength to strength, with a leading position on the council and a growing reputation more widely.

I was encouraged by the leading lights in the Scottish party to believe that, at thirty, I should be aiming to be one of the new wave of actual or prospective MPs – John Smith, Robin Cook, Gordon Brown, George Robertson – who could transform the party's fortunes on a wider stage. Then, a series of errors and misfortunes led to the collapse of the political dream and to my leaving Glasgow for good.

The first set of problems followed the announcement that Willie Hannan was stepping down as MP for Maryhill. I threw my hat in the ring. As the local councillor in one of the three wards making up the constituency, with by far the highest profile and a good reputation, I thought I stood an excellent chance. I had the support of several trade union branches and some solid friends among the activists. The competition did not seem, at first sight, all that strong: a trade union nominee, Jim Craigen, with good local connections but who had been away from the area for some years; and a councillor from another ward, Gerry McGrath, who had done little on the council and combined the positives and negatives of a stereotypical Glasgow Irish Catholic machine politician – expansive charm and wit, a great talent for networking, and a strong, clannish, preference for his kith and kin.

It soon became clear, however, that I was not going to win and that the next MP would be Craigen or McGrath. The first reason was incompetence on my part. I had not taken the trouble to work out the constitutional mechanics of how the Labour Party adopted candidates in seats that, unlike Hillhead, actually mattered. Having, as I did, a good following among the membership and supporters who were not members counted for nothing. Entitlement to vote came with being an accredited delegate to the general management committee from a ward or union branch or affiliated organization. While I had been cutting a dash on the council, and in the local community, Messrs McGrath and Craigen had been quietly ensuring that their friends were planted in dormant union or Co-op branches and formally approved as voting delegates. Just under fifty delegates were eventually authorized to vote, most of whom had never been to a party meeting before and would never do so again, while I could count on only half a dozen.

I had only myself to blame for this failure, but what happened next was worse. McGrath had a team of dedicated supporters, including Davie Hodge, a councillor who later achieved notoriety as Lord Provost for claiming as his own property a silver sword donated to the city by the Saudi royal family. They set about winning over the neutrals, and delegates committed to me, with an appeal to their Catholic religion. False rumours started to circulate about my (and my wife's) alleged support for sexual promiscuity, divorce, abortion, 'humanism' and 'atheism'. I had some form on the issue of faith schools, but was otherwise socially conservative. Nonetheless, I found myself answering lists of questions designed to isolate me from the devout. To their credit, a majority of the Catholic activists treated these approaches with the contempt they deserved, but some were undoubtedly influenced. My growing sense of paranoia was increased when, following a meeting at my home to discuss tactics, one young man, a Catholic teacher who had been effusively supportive in public, turned out to be a spy who passed the details of the discussion to the other side.

By the time of the selection meeting it was clear that I was there to make up the numbers and, after making a speech, I walked the streets of Maryhill with Donald Dewar, who had just spoken brilliantly but to no effect, and together we bemoaned the state of Glasgow Labour politics. In the event, Craigen beat McGrath by the narrowest of margins and there was a certain rough justice in the outcome. Craigen turned out to be a loyal, reliable and decent, but largely invisible, MP, which I think is what the local party really wanted. McGrath and his allies were badly tarnished by the reports of their sectarian activities and never made any further headway in local or national politics. Donald Dewar became MP for another Glasgow seat, Garscadden, based largely on the Drumchapel estate, and in due course reached the Cabinet and became Scotland's first minister.

I tried to rebuild relationships in Maryhill but serious damage had been done. Then, events occurred that put the situation beyond repair. On the eve of a planning meeting I was telephoned by an ex-councillor, John Dunne. He had won the pools, invested some of his fortune in local pubs, and given generously to church charities, which had given him a halo of virtue. One of his pubs, the Lord Darnley, now faced a difficult planning decision over expansion plans and the weight of council opinion was against his application. He accused me of being biased against him and tried to persuade me to vote for his application. His approach was seriously out of order, but when reporting it, somewhat emotionally, to the local party in Maryhill, I left the impression with some present that he was indulging in corrupt practices. My newly acquired enemies reported the meeting back to him in those terms. A libel letter followed. I secured the services of a good lawyer, Keith Bovey, who happened to be a leading light in the SNP and relished the prospect of a case exposing the sordid goings-on in the Glasgow Labour Party. The local party members were put through the ordeal of making formal statements about what they remembered having heard. I had sufficient support from Bovey to see off the libel action, but by this stage even my friends were beginning to worry that I was becoming a liability.

These events occurred against a background of uncertainty over the future of local government. Following a report on local government reorganization, Glasgow was to move, in 1975, from unitary to regional government (the future Strathclyde) with residual powers vested in a city-based district council. There was an almighty, undignified scramble for seats in the new structure, which added to the somewhat febrile atmosphere. I confronted the scenario of rebuilding from scratch a political career in a new system of local government that had less attraction, with the distinct possibility of never breaking through into parliamentary politics. I was in a comfortable but undemanding academic niche from which I was keen to progress. I decided to walk away.

Chapter 7

Latin Detours

One of the more bizarre twists in the long road to Parliament was my move from Clydeside politics to the non-political diplomatic service. A university colleague, Chris Mason, my predecessor as chair of the Cambridge University Liberals and a future leader of the Lib Dems in Strathclyde, had just enjoyed a two-year secondment to the Foreign Office and asked whether I might be interested in doing the same. Since I was looking for an exit strategy from Glasgow, the opportunity was too good to miss, even though I would have to withdraw from front-line politics and sit out the next general election in the neutral zone of Whitehall. The move would be a wrench for the family, which had by this time settled into the rhythms of Glasgow life. But Olympia understood, I think, the reasons for my restlessness and saw the possibilities, too, of wider horizons in London.

A potentially more serious obstacle was the Foreign Office security vetting. My friends included a fair sprinkling of Clydeside's revolutionary left, and my own loyalties were scarcely a secret. Moreover, there was at the time a preoccupation with left-wing traitors in government, following the Vassall affair, which had lurked in the background of my Hillhead election, and the earlier scandal of Philby, Burgess and Maclean. A Hong Kong policeman spent a week in Glasgow 'positively vetting' my application. he was either exceptionally astute or exceptionally dim because he was totally unfazed by, or uncomprehending of, either my political history or my alarming bank overdraft. His one serious line of inquiry was into homosexuality, a subject to which he returned in all our conversations. He was wholly unpersuaded that I could be quite as happily married as I appeared to be and trawled through my acquaintances for a secret male lover who might blackmail me. Whatever my failings, this was definitely not one of them, and I was told that I had passed my vetting with flying colours and could be entrusted with the nation's secrets. I expressed a wish to work on something interesting – the EU, the USSR or the Middle East – but the personnel department had already marked me down for Latin America.

The diplomatic service had a formidable reputation for putting square pegs into round holes but, not unreasonably, assumed that someone who had spent several years researching economic integration in Latin America and had passable, though halting, Spanish could contribute more in that department than those I had applied for. In between teaching, parental and political duties in Glasgow I had managed several visits to Central America. The countries of the region had been trying to bury their history of class and racial divisions, military oppression and petty nationalism in a modernizing project based on the European model, and I was there to observe, and encourage, this fragile experiment in cooperation. In the event, the project on which my somewhat geekish research was based failed abjectly while I was involved with it. Two of the countries – El Salvador and Honduras – went to war following riots at an international football match between them (the real *casus belli* being illegal cross-border migration), while three of them – Guatemala, El Salvador and Nicaragua – abandoned any pretence at democratic government and descended into vicious repression. My visits were superficial, but I saw and heard more than enough of the arrogant, reactionary, racist elite in Guatemala, and their frightened, brutalized Indian and *mestizo* (mixed race) subjects; the lavish lifestyles of the small clique of landowning families who controlled El Salvador; the thuggish goons who enforced the will of the Somoza dynasty in Nicaragua; and the banana republic of Honduras. Had I stayed and been more courageous, I would have been strongly tempted to support the embryonic guerrilla movements. But I remained an academic tourist-voyeur collecting material for a PhD and, as things turned out, setting myself up for a job behind a desk in Whitehall.

The grand Victorian splendour of the Foreign Office buildings on King Charles Street was designed for a global empire. The interior, now brightly refurbished, had in the 1970s seen better times, with the great rooms of state hiding a hinterland of dingy corridors and dilapidated offices. I took up my post as a first secretary. This was the grade at which the high-flyers were winnowed out from more stolid types who were destined for obscure embassies or the lower depths of consular, personnel and protocol work. In geopolitical terms, Latin America was somewhere in the middle of the departmental pecking order, boosted in importance recently by Venezuela's pivotal role in OPEC, the discovery of Mexican oil, and the political relevance of Chile after the Pinochet coup.

Cometh the hour, cometh the man. The department's newly appointed head was Hugh Carless, who was better known as the companion of Eric Newby in the latter's *A Short Walk in the Hindu Kush*. Hugh had elaborate good manners, a strong sense of status and protocol, and a slow upper-middle-class drawl which bordered on affectation and, I sensed, grated on Labour ministers and the bright grammar-school boys who had reached the top of the Foreign Office, like the permanent secretary, Tom Brimelow. Hugh was also restlessly ambitious and had a deep attachment to Latin America, a connection strengthened by his artistic Brazilian wife. His prejudices were somewhat reactionary and, to his credit, he made no attempt to conceal the fact. Despite some obvious differences, we got on very well and, I think, he saw my energy and ambition, and economic background, as a way of widening his own sphere of influence. In any event, he was generously indulgent of my numerous faux pas and careless staff work: failing to copy minutes to all the relevant departments; sending scruffy, smudged notes to ministers; and messing up the placements for diplomatic dinners at the Palace.

He did in due course rise quite high in the Foreign Office to become ambassador to Argentina, a posting that coincided with the Falklands War. Reading between the lines, I suspect that his soft spot for the Argentine military, and his eagerness, already apparent in the mid-1970s, to dispose of the Falklands as elegantly and quickly as possible, did not endear him much to Downing Street. In any event, he left the service without a knighthood and went to work for the Hinduja brothers, which was not the glittering end to a diplomatic career he could reasonably have hoped for.

My first staff meeting set the tone. It could have been an episode from *Yes, Minister*. Hugh announced that we were going to change our minister. Our departmental minister of state, Joan Lestor, was worryingly left-wing; almost as bad as the Marxist harridan at Overseas Development, Judith Hart. She was not the kind of minister who could be expected to hobnob with generals from Argentina and Brazil who held the key to lucrative deals with British companies, particularly for armaments. She also belonged to the cult of the Blessed Salvador Allende, which was becoming tiresome. Miss Lestor would be much happier looking after starving babies in Africa. A sounder man had been identified: David Ennals, an ally of the Foreign Secretary, James Callaghan. Minutes were addressed to him, not her. Latin American visitors were steered in his direction. A 'fact-finding trip' was arranged. Within a few weeks, the ministers were changed.

I should perhaps have protested at this masterly abuse of civil service impartiality, but I played along with it for reasons of cowardice, fascinated curiosity, and a preoccupation with settling my family in London. I also realized that Hugh was no fool; he had read very well the Foreign Secretary's mind and his distaste for the Labour Party's radical left. I knew that my relaxed approach to the left was not shared by many in the civil service establishment and intelligence services. This was, after all, the time when battier right-wing elements in the armed forces and intelligence services are reported to have seriously considered military intervention to oust the Wilson government. When inflation reached a post-war high in 1975 and the IMF was called in to help rescue the economy there was a palpable sense of national crisis which, for some, was attributable to the influence of reds under the bed, or in government.

In truth, my job – certainly in the early stages – was tedious and I struggled to fill the day productively. It led me to question the deployment of so many good brains – my colleagues were often Oxbridge firsts with impressive linguistic skills – in rather humdrum administrative work when, in their thirties, they should have been involved in serious decision-making. Even as a fairly elevated first secretary, my minutes had to pass through three tiers of bureaucracy before reaching ministers. An inordinate amount of time was spent pandering to the whims of visiting ministers and the social contacts of ambassadors. Underemployed diplomats in London would scuttle round, amid great drama, to deliver some pointless courtesy note from their foreign office to ours. I would spend much time reading and distributing political analyses from our overseas ambassadors and their staff which had already been covered, much more succinctly, in the British press. When Lord Rothschild's Downing Street think tank turned its reforming guns on the Foreign Office in 1975 there was a brief spasm of fear, but outraged ex-ambassadors were mobilized to launch a fierce counter-offensive in the Lords and *The Times* and the FCO survived the bombardment intact. My own, private, view was that Lord Rothschild had been far too indulgent.

There was, of course, a social life, which for some colleagues was a rich source of sustenance. The nearest Olympia and I came to it, however, was an invitation to a royal banquet. We dressed up as required, myself in a penguin suit and Olympia, absolutely stunning, in 'national dress' (a sari), but I forgot the problem of transport. At that stage we had a battered Mini estate used for camping, supermarket shopping, and carrying waste to the dump and the children to nursery school. The back doors were inelegantly held together by string. As we approached Buckingham Palace it became clear that we were somewhat out of place among the Rollses and Daimlers and we were interrogated for a long period at the entry gate before being reluctantly admitted. A Foreign Office colleague witnessed this episode and the story, suitably embellished, established me as an eccentric and fully paid-up member of the awkward squad. The event was given added spice by a diplomatic incident in the receiving line. Olympia offered the Queen a traditional Indian *namaste* instead of a handshake and, perhaps distracted by the boredom of innumerable greetings, the Queen appeared not to notice and continued to proffer her hand to be shaken. There was a prolonged stand-off as neither appeared willing to compromise until we were at last led away by clucking courtiers.

Since I was determined to make good use of my two years, and not just mark time, I set about making the job more interesting. I started with responsibility for Venezuela, Ecuador and Colombia, but discovered that I had a talent for office imperialism and, by the time I left, had taken over the Inca, Mayan and Aztec empires, also adding Fidel Castro's Cuba, despite some misgivings by security-conscious colleagues who were alarmed at the exposure it would give me to the intelligence services.

Hugh Carless was also smart enough to realize that, with the rise of OPEC, the big diplomatic growth areas were trade promotion in oil-rich countries and international economics. On the principle that in the kingdom of the blind the one-eyed man is king, I was put forward as a great authority on these economic matters, helping to create new areas of work for the Latin America department.

Hugh's biggest success was to outwit the DTI in taking the lead role in a big trade promotion push in Latin America. The Foreign Office rarely got the better of the Treasury in the endless territorial skirmishes; and the MoD guarded defence sales jealously, but the DTI was a softer target for predatory raids. Much to the fury of the DTI, I was made secretary to a CBI trade mission to Venezuela and Ecuador, and, on the back of it, spent six months involved in detailed trade diplomacy alongside leading UK companies.

The mission leader, Sir Peter Hope, was a remarkable character: an enormous, tall, bear of a man with an impressive intellect – he had achieved a maths first at Cambridge in two years – and a strong pedigree in business, the intelligence world and diplomacy. He had a withering contempt for the clubby amateurishness of the traditional British merchant banks and boardrooms where he worked and for the sheltered recesses of the diplomatic service. Caracas was one such recess, and when we arrived in the Venezuelan capital with our collection of British industrialists and bankers, the ambassador's aristocratic nostrils visibly quivered with disdain at this vulgar assemblage of tradesmen who were disrupting his attempts to build cultural bridges to the Venezuelan literati. Within hours, a list of dead wood, headed by the ambassador, had been drawn up and I was charged with ensuring on our return that it was duly chopped – or whatever more genteel form of demotion was permitted under Foreign Office personnel rules. It was the first time I had been exposed to this style of abrasive management after the cosy, protected environment of the civil service and academia. I found it exhilarating, despite the obvious harshness for some individuals who would now suffer a permanent black mark against their careers for having failed to jump to attention at the right moment. Sir Peter was surprised to discover that I shared his drive and enthusiasm, and we managed to energize the British contribution to what would otherwise have been a long ritual of courtesy calls and visits to steel plants and dams.

It was more difficult to energize our Venezuelan hosts. Venezuela was just discovering the vast riches that would flow from its oil, thanks to OPEC, whose founder and intellectual inspiration was a Venezuelan, Juan Pablo Pérez Alfonso. As in other oil-rich countries, oil money flowed into government; much was absorbed by senior ministers and officials and their business associates in the social elite, and a trickle emerged to be spent on the millions of poor people whose shanty towns clung to the sides of the steep valleys around Caracas. The country was nominally democratic, with the two parties (Acción Democrática, essentially social democratic, and COPEI, a Christian Democratic party) alternating in power. At the time of our visit, the presidency was held by Carlos Andrés Pérez, a clever, upwardly mobile politician with a populist touch who envisaged a transformation of the country through state industries (with a modest role for the local private sector). The extent of the venality of Pérez and his entourage only emerged later, but it was clear at the time that fabulous wealth was being created among a small number of well-connected people who hadn't worked or saved or taken risks to achieve it. Much of the wealth was on display, decorating the fabulously beautiful women with whom the country's leaders surrounded themselves. The greed, wastefulness and vulgar ostentation of the Venezuelan political elite help to explain why, two decades later, Colonel Hugo Chávez was able to overthrow it and install his own, populist, alternative.

Our hosts, then, took an obvious pleasure in having queues of gringos soliciting business from them and their arrogance was sharpened by a brittle nationalism, given historical shape by the exploits of Simón Bolívar in the war of independence from Spain. Our team managed to extract enormous and elaborate promises of future collaboration but precious few real orders. Such business as was actually secured from the Venezuelan government could mostly be traced back to a shadowy arms dealer and locally based Brit, Sir Arnold Smith, who drove around Caracas in a Rolls-Royce and entertained us at his remarkable mansion overlooking the city. My job was to ensure that the gap between aspiration and reality was closed in the aftermath of the mission.

On the visit I was also introduced to the hitherto hidden world of British intelligence. I had developed over the previous year a friendly relationship with Our Man in Caracas, a young man who was keen to make a splash in London with his reports from the front line. I had helped to put him on the map by hyping his rather insubstantial reports and copying them far and wide in Whitehall. Between us we succeeded in talking up Caracas as the new epicentre of the Cold War, and I managed to embellish several of his colourful accounts of Venezuelan ministers' love affairs and their tenuous links with Cuban officials to get the reports on to the Foreign Secretary's desk. This was more Graham Greene than Le Carré. But we helped each other to enliven our small corner of the geopolitical universe. In grateful appreciation of my help, he invited me to his favourite nightclub, became very drunk, and encouraged me to join MI6 (now better known as the SIS). The offer survived his hangover. I was invited to an assignation a few days later with the regional director of the service, who happened to be in town: a small, totally bald, portly man with dark shades who was introduced by my awestruck friend as the mastermind behind an anti-communist coup in Guyana some years earlier. We had several meetings over the next few days and it quickly became apparent to the MI6 man that my casual approach to security, poor linguistic skills and left-leaning politics made me utterly unsuited to this new career. I did not, therefore, follow in the footsteps of Lord Ashdown.

I remained, however, well suited to the role I had been given, orchestrating this initiative to promote Great Britain Ltd in Latin

America; organizing visits from Venezuelan ministers (and Pérez himself), and the less well-endowed Ecuadorians, to secure their elusive signatures on contracts; acting as a hub for some of the complex negotiations involving government guarantees; and passing the intelligence gleaned from intercepts or CIA contacts to our business friends to help them gain an advantage over their French and Italian competitors. In my more reflective moments the ghost of Adam Smith would appear to remind me that this corporatist world was the antithesis of everything I believed in. But the flattery of the captains of British industry and the envy of my departmental colleagues were more than adequate compensation.

There were, however, some firm defences in Whitehall against the potentially corrupting influence of excessive familiarity with the corporate world. On one occasion I tried to make a case for breaching the rules on export credit guarantees in order to favour a Clydeside shipbuilding company, whose representative had been on my delegation, and which was endeavouring to sell frigates to admirals in Ecuador. Ecuador's oil barely qualified it for OPEC membership and any big deals would have to be lubricated by what the French call 'credit mixte' – i.e. subsidy – outlawed under an international 'gentlemen's agreement'. I managed to mobilize the FCO, MoD and DTI in support of this bid, and my first-hand accounts of 'badly needed jobs on Clydeside' obviously touched the heart of the FCO minister who signed off my submission. It duly reached the Treasury and I was summoned to a meeting with the undersecretary responsible, a Miss Kelly, whose kindly manner disguised a formidable brain and ruthless effectiveness. She sat me down like a little boy at school and gently tore up my arguments one by one. Not only that, but she thanked me for serving up the most perfect example she had encountered of pandering to commercial vested interests, using fallacious, mercantilist arguments. She then treated me to an undergraduate lecture on the 'lump of labour fallacy' which I had infiltrated into my paper. The final humiliation came a few days later in the form of a letter from the Chancellor to the Foreign Secretary and I was required to explain why the Foreign Office had been so brutally routed by the Treasury. When my embarrassment had subsided, I acknowledged a greatly enhanced respect for the intellectual integrity and competence of the best of our senior civil servants, particularly in the Treasury.

My next escapade was to test the limits of the arms export control regime. I became increasingly concerned at the volume of lethal weapons that I was authorizing on a daily basis to go to fragile and unsavoury regimes. Expressions of disapproval would have confirmed suspicions that I was just a feeble-minded lefty, so I decided to challenge the system in other ways. One day a letter arrived on my desk from a manufacturer in West Bromwich who wanted approval to sell an armour-plated car – in effect, a mini-tank – to Fidel Castro for his personal protection. Since Castro had been on the receiving end of several assassination attempts it was clear why he wanted the car. The Midlands firm could supply it. My colleagues, and the DTI, were, however, nervous. Cuba was, after all, a communist country and the official guidelines said that export approval should not be given to arms sales to Cuba. I ignored nervous colleagues and approved the sale, arguing that this transaction could hardly be held to be an arms sale in the normal sense, and that it might help to facilitate our small but growing trade with Cuba and the blossoming of relations favoured by some ministers, like Mrs Hart. My superiors would neither approve nor reject my recommendation and passed the matter further up the chain of command with great alacrity. Eventually it reached the Foreign Secretary, Mr Callaghan who, no doubt recalling my role in the Ecuadorian frigates affair, saw trouble coming. He, in turn, referred the matter upwards, to Mr Henry Kissinger. A week or so later a reply was received from Washington to the effect that Mr Secretary Kissinger was surprised to be asked; he would never, otherwise, have known or cared about the matter, but, since he had been asked, the answer was 'no'. Castro survived without the armoured car. A few workers in West Bromwich lost their jobs. And the obsequious, one-sided nature of our 'special relationship' was starkly revealed.

My annexation of Cuba had occurred a little earlier when my room-mate, had asked me to cover for him during an absence. Nominally junior to myself, he operated independently and I gathered that he was being groomed for a role in the intelligence services, though he would always bat away my cheeky questions with diplomatic evasiveness. Unlike the gossips and misfits I had encountered previously, he seemed perfectly suited to the role of a spy, though, as with most of the spooks I encountered, his world view was deeply conservative. Nonetheless, he had resisted pressure from our ambassador in Managua to find a place at Sandhurst for the son of the appalling Somoza, until overruled by the head of the department. When he took time out to learn an East European language, I covered the Cuban brief competently and was allowed to keep it.

Anglo-Cuban relationships were minimal but for two factors. The first was a group of Labour MPs who retained a positive, perhaps nostalgic, view of Castro and the Cuban revolution and wanted a Labour government, at the very least, to balance its commercially driven ties with the juntas in Brazil and Argentina with friendly overtures to Cuba, and to distance Britain from the USA. Judith Hart was most clearly identified with this view. The second was the closeness of intelligence cooperation between Britain and the USA, which involved sharing data on communist states and, in particular, on the large Cuban embassy staff, most of whom seemed to have links with the Cuban equivalent of the KGB. My dealings with both our internal and external intelligence services left me with very mixed views. When dealing with specific issues and individuals they were totally professional, meticulous and immensely painstaking in piecing together detail without coming to premature conclusions. But whenever they let drop their prejudices on the wider political scene, these were invariably plucked from the *Daily Telegraph*, and occasionally reached out to the wider political fringes, as with the assertion I heard on several occasions that Harold Wilson, the prime minister, was an active Soviet agent.

Then, a large number of Cuban soldiers were reported as having joined the civil war that was unfolding in Angola. My own instinctive reaction was that the principal villains were the South Africans, who had launched cross-border raids into Angola. As the arguments raged among analysts internally and commentators externally, it became clear that there were two fundamentally different ways of looking at the world. On one hand, a lot of my diplomatic and intelligence colleagues saw it exclusively through a Cold War prism. Whatever our personal reservations about them, the South African apartheid regime, Ian Smith's rebel regime fighting Mugabe's ZANU (PF), and the residual anti-Marxist forces in Angola and Mozambique were 'on our side' against the communists, who were embodied by those Cuban troops. I represented the alternative view – shared (I hoped) by ministers – that the 'threat of communism' existed primarily because of those resisting majority rule. I saw at first hand, since I was part of the process, how briefings to the Joint Intelligence Committee and to ministers, and intelligence 'facts', could easily be coloured by one or other of these preconceived prejudices (foreshadowing Iraq many years later). Fortunately, even among the protagonists there was an underlying professionalism and I engaged in detailed, and basically good-natured, debates with Foreign Office research staff and the intelligence services about the precise sequence of events. On one important matter I was proved wrong: it transpired that Cuban troopships had set sail for Africa before the South Africans had invaded Angola from Namibia.

In another respect, however, I was vindicated. There was a mysterious department in the Foreign Office, the Information and Research Department, dealing with 'grey' propaganda: material that appeared non-attributably in newspapers and magazines around the world under the name of some academic or expert but was actually ghosted in the FCO. The head of the department, Ray Whitney, subsequently became a Tory MP. Much of its material was innocuous, even creditable. But from time to time articles appeared from the department that extolled the virtues of right-wing dictators who were allies in the Cold War, including General Pinochet. I felt I needed to act when it was clear that, in the context of the Angolan conflict with Cuba, material was appearing in support of apartheid in South Africa. I obtained the support of the acting head of the department, who had been up to this point studiously uncontroversial but on this occasion either shared my outrage or saw an opportunity to earn some brownie points with Labour ministers. The matter went to Anthony Crosland, the new

Foreign Secretary, who was incandescent to discover that civil servants had been churning out extreme right-wing propaganda under the noses of Labour ministers. The department was closed (I believe temporarily).

I was elated by the arrival of Anthony Crosland. He had long been a hero. His *Future of Socialism* was one of the most persuasive political tracts I had ever read and had played a significant part in moving me from Liberal to Labour while a student. He was not easily pigeonholed as 'right' or 'left', though clearly in the social democratic tradition. He was, or seemed, decidedly earthier than the other leading social democrat, Roy Jenkins. Crosland also contrasted sharply with Callaghan, who was very shrewd but deeply conservative and over-respectful of the flummery, fancy dress and protocol surrounding diplomacy. Crosland questioned everything, irreverently. He was particularly effective in gently deflating heads of department, like mine, who would argue that Latin America was the centre of the known universe. He firmly declined to spend his time massaging the egos of visiting foreign ministers or ambassadors. When he was eventually persuaded to pay a short visit to Latin America, it was on the strict understanding that he would return before Saturday evening's *Match of the Day*. Crosland sadly died at the end of my stay in the Foreign Office, to be replaced by his minister of state, David Owen. I did not get to see much of David Owen in his new role, but I know the FCO collectively groaned at the prospect of someone without Callaghan's gravitas and avuncular charm, and without Crosland's intellect and sense of fun, but with an ego to match both of them combined. To Owen's credit, however, he emerged from two years as Foreign Secretary with a considerably enhanced reputation and, unlike his predecessors, he made time to set out his approach to the job in a book on human rights. I encountered him again a decade later as my party leader.

Somewhat to my surprise, I completed my two years and a bit in the FCO on good terms with my colleagues, without having caused a diplomatic crisis, and with a big store of invaluable experience. I had no wish to stay on: Olympia and I would have dreaded the claustrophobia of embassy life, and my ambitions would not have been satisfied with a gong at the end of twenty-five years of service. My attempts to find a role in the private sector failed, however, and I went off to direct research on trade and development, especially in India.

Chapter 8

A Passage to India

The decade or so of my life as a professional politician is what, if anything, I am likely to be remembered for. But the decades of political exile that preceded it were enriching in a different way.

Satisfactory careers provide intellectual challenge and emotional satisfaction and integrate rather than separate professional and private life. I found those different elements in work on economic development and its links with international economics. One of the most fundamental economic questions is why some countries, and individuals, prosper and others live in poverty. That question leads to another: how can the world be better ordered to help countries and individuals escape from poverty? Years spent working in or on East Africa, then Latin America, then India, in academia, government, intergovernmental organizations and a multinational company, gave me a distinctive perspective both as an analyst and as an advocate. And through Olympia's extended family I was able to see the world not just through the windows of international hotels and taxis and the eyes of my professional contacts, but through a network of close and evolving personal relationships in India, Africa and the UK.

It is easy to feel a sense of despair and disgust about the abject poverty, rampant corruption and casual violence that disfigures so much of the developing world. But the big story of my lifetime has been the way in which the lives of billions of people, mainly in Asia, but also in southern Europe and parts of Latin America and even Africa, have been changed for the better; and the potential that an open international economy and liberal values have for doing much more. The current economic crisis may have the effect of changing the direction of economic travel, but it is unlikely to affect the growing relative importance of the big Asian countries. The economic and political transformation of India in the four decades over which I have visited it is both an example and a metaphor for this experience, although there is an understandable preoccupation with the part of the glass that is empty rather than the part that is full (or fuller).

My fascination with the process of development started with an overland student trek to India, via the USSR, Iran, Afghanistan and Pakistan, in a VW van. I shall always be indebted to Jim Potter, later a successful Cambridge-based businessman, and Geoff Heal, now a US-based economist of some renown, who invited me along for the ride. There were some abiding impressions, particularly once we had crossed the Soviet frontier. Visitors from the West were a rarity in the villages of the Ukraine and we aroused great curiosity, and also hostility and stone-throwing which we attributed to our German vehicle, this being barely twenty years years after millions had died in the Great Patriotic War. Soviet officialdom showed continuing interest in our papers and photographic equipment and where exactly we had spent each night, though the intrusiveness eased as we moved away from the main population centres. Nonetheless, I did manage to create a diplomatic incident when I struck up a brief friendship, conducted in pidgin German, with a pretty and flirtatious young woman on an open-air dance floor in a park in Kiev. I suspect that her gold teeth and my odour from weeks without a bath would have inhibited any deeper relationship in any event, but we got only as far as a vigorous rock and roll jive which was taken up enthusiastically by the rest of the dancers. Scandalized apparatchiks appeared and I was escorted away and given an angry lecture by one English-speaking guardian of public virtue on 'Western degeneracy'. I feared for the young woman, but I last saw her giggling helplessly with her friends.

These fierce standards did not seem to apply in the Soviet deep south and we discovered in Georgia decent food and wine for the first time, and managed to get hopelessly lost in Armenia along a road outside a missile base, to be offered some friendly map-reading from the guards. When we approached the Iranian frontier, it was politely explained that it wouldn't be a good idea to wander across the minefields and we were loaded on to a train with blackened windows and dropped at a frontier crossing point in the Iranian semi-desert.

Oil wealth, religious revolution and war have since reshaped Iran, but the Iran of the shah was orderly and moderately prosperous, with constant reminders of its great history in the well-laid-out cities and the magnificent blue-tiled mosques of Isfahan, Shiraz, Tabriz and Mashad (as foreigners we were not allowed to visit the holy city of Qum). Even in a short visit it was possible to pick up some of the tensions behind the placid exterior: in the sudden flashes of crowd anger we experienced in small incidents in the Tehran bazaar, where we stayed with a local family in proximity to the Shia shrines. (A week or so before we visited Mashad, a German tourist had been killed by a mob for showing disrespect.)

The Afghans across the border reacted to us quite differently. Instead of the Iranians' disconcerting mixture of obsequiousness and aggression, there was proud indifference. The cities of Herat, Kandahar and Kabul have since been largely destroyed by war but were then enjoying a long period of stability during which the country was courted by the USA and USSR with generous, competing, aid. In Herat, my friends fell ill from contaminated meat, which I had luckily avoided, and I spent the best part of a week 'discovering' the town. I found in the mosque a haven of cool tranquillity and spent many hours reading or daydreaming. Like the cathedrals of Christendom, the great mosques of Islam have the ability to inspire a sense of religious awe even in those who do not subscribe to their faith.

Nothing had fully prepared me for the culture shock of the Indian subcontinent: the heaving towns and cities of the Pakistani and Indian Punjab, bustling, squalid, noisy, smelly and garish. Every few yards held a surprise: some new variant of human or animal life. A narrow strip of tarmac across northern India – the Grand Trunk Road – served as an expressway, cricket pitch, public lavatory, shopping arcade, cow pasture, prayer mat, bedroom, garage forecourt, laundry and promenade. To navigate it was a feat of endurance and every stop produced a curious crowd.

The Punjab of the mid-1960s was not the prosperous economic powerhouse of later decades. It had barely recovered from the ravages of partition. The green revolution had not yet (quite) arrived. The year we passed through had seen a crop failure and there were hungry, destitute people everywhere; every temple or gurdawara or railway station was a Mecca for beggars.

The mood of the educated Indians we met oscillated between

on the one hand prickly pride and insistence that India's problems stemmed from British rule, and on the other a fatalistic despair. The shine had worn off the independence generation of Congress politicians – Gandhi, Nehru, Patel were dead – and corruption was reputedly rife. The armed forces had been routed by the Chinese three years earlier. A system of socialist planning had made little impact on poverty and India was stuck in what was called the 'Hindu rate of growth'. Even Pakistan seemed to be doing better. There were secessionist movements building up. A growing revolt by violent Naxalites among the rural poor was raising the possibility of a communist-style revolution; indeed, a genre of fashionable books like John Lewis's *Quiet Crisis in India* prophesied precisely such an outcome.

It was a relief to escape the chattering classes of Delhi, delightfully hospitable though they were. Our party split up and I headed off through Rajasthan to Bombay with Geoff Heal in the van. He became seriously ill, however, and we were rescued by a Methodist missionary in Baroda who undertook to send him back to Delhi on a train while I took over the vehicle. With all the impetuosity of youth I decided to explore the country on my own, heading directly east a thousand miles across the large waistline of India, aiming to meet the Calcutta–Delhi road somewhere in Bihar. My large-scale map suggested that India was traversed laterally by roads but, had I been more careful, I would have inquired what happened when the roads met India's rivers flowing north to south and feeding into the Ganges. When road signs, and sometimes the road, disappeared, I found my way with the help of endlessly friendly and curious villagers. After initial spasms of panic and fear, I came to trust India and developed a confidence that behind the alien masks of language and custom there was no malice and much goodness. I needed such confidence, because once I had passed the agricultural centres of Gujarat and cities like Indore, I was frequently lost and lonely.

I dealt with loneliness by picking up a stream of hitch-hikers. I learned a lot from a 'dry state' liquor inspector whose job was to identify contraband crossing state boundaries (which were, and are, in their tax and regulatory barriers to trade, a mockery of the idea that India is a single market). I gave lifts to several 'tribals', the Indian term for the original, or aboriginal, population, who occupy a position at the bottom of India's social hierarchy outside the caste system but alongside the 'scheduled caste' ('untouchables' or Harijans). I acquired a role as a makeshift ambulance driver, taking expectant women to the nearest midwife or, on one occasion, a bleeding body, more dead than alive, which had been on the receiving end of a wild animal. With ample spare tanks of petrol, a simple but adequate diet of chapattis, bananas and marsala tea (boiled with milk and spices), and using the van as a roadside hotel, I was able to cover substantial distances without mishap.

The rivers, swollen by monsoon rains, presented serious problems, however. There were no bridges or fords, only manually propelled ferries, like small rafts, designed for pedestrians and bicycles. The ever-inventive villagers realized that the rafts could just about carry a small van, which had to be loaded by driving along two narrow parallel planks. After great drama and the near disappearance of the van into a Ganges tributary, I managed to get it on to the first raft and off again; and then had to repeat the trick several times more. Eventually I reached an approximation to my destination; and headed back via Benares to Delhi, to a reunion with my friends.

There was a non-stop rush back for the beginning of term, but we had one more piece of drama. As we approached the Wagga crossing in Punjab, it was clear that there was something wrong. The traffic had thinned to non-existence and there were tanks and other military vehicles everywhere. We were reluctantly admitted into Pakistan but told that we were fortunate to be the last people allowed out of India before the frontier closed. War broke out the next day and the journey through Pakistan was punctuated by air raids and blackouts. In one small town we were detained for a couple of days as 'suspicious'. But the dash then continued and we arrived back, exhausted, ill and exhilarated in equal measure. I was left with abiding memories of India and a wish to return and to understand better what I had seen.

Two years in Kenya and several working on Latin America had increased my understanding of the complexity of development. Then, two events – one personal, one professional – drew me back to India. For several years after my marriage to Olympia both our fathers had ostracized us and declared that they would see us again over their respective dead bodies. Mr Rebelo was the first to show signs of flexibility and the reasons for the exclusion of Olympia from the family circle were being rapidly overtaken by events. By this time Mr and Mrs Rebelo had left Kenya to rebuild the family home in Goa and the suggestion was made that we might visit. The first opportunity was the wedding, in 1975, of their second son Celso, who alone of the seven children had resolved to marry a Goan girl from a good family and the right caste. Preparations were put in train for a family wedding at the village chapel in Verna, and our two young children were to have pride of place as page and bridesmaid.

Olympia had a deep emotional attachment to India but had never visited it, except as a child when she was sent to a Goan boarding school but was soon repatriated back to Nairobi, protesting bitterly about the heat and the food. Olympia's memories of heat boils and mine of tropical, post-monsoon conditions led us to assume that India was hot – period – and we dressed accordingly. We had, however, decided to start the visit in Delhi, which was experiencing an exceptionally cold winter. It was bitterly cold and our children suffered considerably from their parents' failure to appreciate the seasonal geography of north India.

There had also been a big political change in the decade since I had last visited. Mrs Gandhi, Nehru's daughter, had emerged as prime minister after a power struggle with the old guard of Congress and had won an election based on a populist programme of nationalization (of the banks) and spending promises. There was mounting unrest over a deteriorating economic situation and law and order seemed to be slipping out of control. She declared a state of emergency with dictatorial powers and we arrived in Delhi with the emergency in full swing. We saw a few glimpses of what that entailed. Olympia went to observe proceedings at a treason trial of a leading trade unionist, George Fernandes, who appeared in court in manacles. Opinion was divided among the people we met as to whether the emergency was an undemocratic outrage or a blessed relief. Those who took the latter view were particularly enthusiastic about the mass sterilization of many of India's poorer men, a campaign led by Mrs Gandhi's son Sanjay, which blurred the distinction between volunteering and compulsion.

For us tourists, the emergency meant the disappearance of beggars from the streets and taxis charging a standard fare.

Trains, Mussolini-style, ran on time, and we travelled around north India on the railway before heading off to Bombay to visit the bride's family. They lived in a middle-class suburb, Chembur, which, I later discovered, had recently been monitored as the most atmospherically polluted spot on earth on account of a petrochemical plant established nearby. The air was heavy with sulphurous smoke and most of the residents seemed to be dependent on asthma inhalers. But conditions there were heavenly compared with the settlement nearby which formed part of the largest slum in Asia, Dharawi, where the pungency of modern chemicals blended with the more ancient smells of tanneries and sewage. My hypersensitive Western nostrils and digestive system took some time to adjust to the overpowering stench and squalor, but I was reassured by my hosts that those Indians who had made it to a shack in this foetid rabbit warren of humanity were the lucky ones, having joined the conveyor belt of opportunity in a big city. Indeed, with each succeeding visit, the number of TV aerials and mopeds multiplied even faster than the size of the slum itself. There was also a prickly pride in the smells and smoke that symbolized industrial modernity, though a few years later Union Carbide would dispel such innocence. The film *Slumdog Millionaire* depicts life in this corner of Bombay (now Mumbai), then as now.

Olympia's brother Celso was one of the pioneers of this industrial revolution: a medical student, turned microbiologist, turned manager of one of India's newest breweries, in the township of Uran across Bombay harbour. To reach it we took a tiny, crowded ferry which ducked and weaved between the cargo ships and oil tankers before depositing us on a jetty nearby. In the monsoon season especially, such vessels had a bad habit of capsizing, but this one made it. The only forms of transport on land were an occasional trap pulled by a horse of such decrepitude that it seemed likely to collapse at any time, or a rickshaw pulled by a human being with even less flesh than the horse. We took the ethically dubious decision not to inflict the burden of carrying two adults, two children and several suitcases on the wretched man – probably thereby depriving his family of a meal. On subsequent visits a fleet of India's motorcycle rickshaws had arrived, but on this occasion the horse got us to the brewery.

The factory was remarkably well fortified, which, we discovered, was attributable to local labour relations. Like many of the islands on India's industrial archipelago, this one was populated by trade unions that claimed adherence to a particularly violent and uncompromising variant of Marxism–Leninism. My brother-in-law was a tough, uncompromising operator, whose skill in dealing with the unions had kept him and his colleagues from too much strike action or the dreaded *gherao*, when management would be locked in their offices without food, water or toilet facilities until they gave in to the latest demands. His job also required him to deal with the innumerable bureaucrats in Bombay or Delhi whose refusal to issue one of dozens of licences or permits could bring the factory to a halt, and these formalities were accomplished with the help of a suitcase full of rupee notes. We were exposed to the full force of India's angry managerial middle class, whose rage and frustration over bureaucracy, corruption and industrial unrest provided much of the dynamic behind Indira Gandhi's dictatorial emergency. Celso was a particular fan of Mrs G.

From Uran, there was a long and difficult journey by road to Goa, to the southern village of Verna, near Margao, where

Olympia's family lived. I was to visit Verna many times in subsequent years, yet the first impression remains etched in my memory: emerging over a bare, treeless plateau to see an implausibly emerald-green band of paddy fields and coconut palms stretching along the coast from the hills to the sea, with its ten-mile stretch of pristine sand, Colva Beach. And then, rising above the vegetation, numerous white churches, the legacy of Portuguese Catholicism. It would be dishonest to convey the impression, though, that this was an idyllic paradise designed solely to please the eye of a Western visitor; on a hill overlooking the sea stood one of the state's proudest monuments, a large fertilizer factory owned by the Birla group, which never appears on postcards but was, and is, an important part of the local economy.

In the densely populated coastal lowlands, along the main roads, there was a ribbon of old Portuguese haciendas, many then unoccupied and dilapidated, but later, when painted and restored, magnificent colonial buildings. They were owned by the leading land-owning families, among them Mr Rebelo. In a third of a century much has changed. At that time Goa had been 'liberated' by the Indian army barely a decade earlier (and although Olympia's immediate family subscribed strongly to this version of history, there were plenty of more distant relatives who lamented the passing of the Portuguese; indeed, some left for the 'mother country'). The Portuguese had left behind a moderately prosperous colony (by Indian standards), but one characterized by poor infrastructure, a sense of genteel decay, and an economy dependent on the bounties of nature rather than the intensive application of brain or brawn.

With my family I explored this corner of Goa. Opposite the

house was a small patch of jungle leading up to the plateau. On our first visit the woodland was alive with chattering monkeys and, as we emerged on the hill, there was a nest of cobras writhing in sexual ecstasy in the sun. Our initial horror turned to fascination as they indulged their pleasures unconcerned at our voyeurism. We were never to see them again, as development and increasingly busy roads pushed nature back. The plateau, however, retained its fascination, and on my last visit with Olympia, before she became too disabled to travel, we walked the country lanes up the hill behind the village cemetery, where the remains of her father were interred, to find an old Hindu temple in the arid rocky landscape which contrasted with the lush coastal lowlands a few hundred feet below. We found this spot to be a haven of peace, but when I last visited it, after Olympia had gone, developers were building blocks of flats across the plateau and a militant Hindu organization was rebuilding the temple as a statement of expansionary intent.

In the opposite direction, leading away from the back of the Rebelos' house, where the house-servant lived with her family and a couple of pigs were being fattened up for the next celebration, a maze of lanes and tracks led westwards to the ocean through the paddy fields. I never quite came to understand the Portuguese *comunidade* system of land tenure, which entailed a mixture of private ownership and collective rights and duties; but the Rebelo plot had been handed down in perpetuity. Mr Rebelo explained his plans for developing cash crops and, many years later, Celso and his family have indeed established a small coconut plantation interspersed with peppers and cardamoms. But coconut theft, meandering cattle and irregular water never seemed to make it a commercial proposition. I came to know very well the lanes to the sea, best enjoyed in the cool of the monsoon season when the rain has stopped and the paddies are full of water and young saplings. Over the years the lanes have progressed from sleepy walkways used by the occasional bicycle, cattle, barking dogs, hens, pigs, toddlers and budding young Indian Peles, to busy thoroughfares full of motorbikes taking farmers and their families off to the town and tourist vans ferrying foreigners to the beach hotels. And running parallel to the sea is a new railway, the Konkan, which connects Bombay to southern India.

When we first discovered Colva Beach, we shared it only with the fishermen, local courting couples and the occasional hippie. It has now become, if not quite the Indian Costa del Sol, a bustling resort with hundreds of Indian and European tourists from the nearby hotels, and local beach huts serving Goan fish delicacies and Celso's local beer (he having moved from Uran to Goa to establish a new brewery in partnership with a local politician).

The biggest changes have been in the quality of infrastructure and the rise in vehicle ownership. A generation ago our main means of communication were local buses, packed to overflowing but ridiculously cheap, running to the sleepy market town, Margao, now a bustling city with traffic jams to match. To get around Goa was an odyssey in itself, since the big rivers that run across Goa into the Indian Ocean had no bridges and there were erratic, sometimes hair-raising, ferry crossings. Now the road to Panjim, the state capital, is a major thoroughfare and, as if to make up for past neglect, there are two parallel bridges a few yards apart across the main river.

One unchanging delight is the city of Old Goa, once one of the world's greatest cities until cholera epidemics led to a drastic contraction in the seventeenth century, from which it never recovered. The magnificent baroque churches remain and their golden altars must have absorbed a sizeable share of the plunder from the New World. Goa was a Jesuit stronghold: St Ignatius Loyola is the most revered saint; and for those, like me, with a morbid curiosity, there are displays of the instruments of torture and execution that helped to ensure that Goa remained a particularly obedient and devout outpost of Christendom. I came to learn that piety was qualified by self-interest among the Goan land-owning classes. When the Portuguese arrived, the local elite was offered a deal: to keep their land they would have to adopt their conquerors' names and religion. The Rebelos, like other 'good families', are able to point to temple records that show them to be descended from the Kelkars, a Brahmin sub-caste. These historical details are not just a matter of curiosity but affect such everyday matters as marriage, landholdings, and status in the church and at village feasts. However educated and urbane, the 'good families' of Goa are as caste- and class-conscious as any others in India. And the genius of the Catholic Church was to have gathered and held to the faith this corner of India while respecting its idiosyncrasies, many of which predate Christianity.

My own acquaintance with Goa is framed by two marriages: Celso's which Olympia and I first came to celebrate, and, thirty-three years later, that of his daughter Vanita (now, like her Goan groom, an American citizen). To the latter I brought my second wife, Rachel; and other close relatives came from across India, the UK, the USA, Canada, Kenya and Zimbabwe. The family, like Goa itself, had become part of the global village while still retaining a sense of identity, attachment and home.

*

My interest in India was professional as well as personal. I was curious as to how such a sleepy backwater as Goa had developed so quickly and visibly and achieved living standards among the highest in India. Tourism is part of the story; and a lot of Indian government money went into making it a success. But there is more to it than that: multiple cropping and hybrid seeds on the farms; the transformation of industrial estates like that on the plateau above Verna from a sad collection of empty buildings into a collection of world-class Indian biotech and IT companies; and a generation of young people like my nephews and nieces who have acquired internationally recognized professional qualifications. Aesthetes and ecologists may question the meaning of 'development', but the transformation of living standards that I have seen within a generation is very real. More importantly, similar things were happening all over India, particularly in the south.

My exposure to Indian development might have been confined to the rather special case of Goa had it not been for a coincidental meeting shortly before I was to leave the Foreign Office. I had failed to find a role in the private sector, which I had been looking for, but happened to meet an old college friend, Sarwar Lateef, who was shortly leaving the Overseas Development Institute for the World Bank. He was looking for someone to carry through research work he had started on the European Union's trade policy as it affected emerging economies like India, and to take on a wider research management role in the ODI. I didn't need much persuading. He also passed on to me a consultancy commitment to write a substantial quarterly report on the Indian economy for the Economist Intelligence Unit, a task I carried out for the next twenty-five years.

The main inspiration behind the ODI project was K. B. Lall, the Indian ambassador to the EU and a former chairman of Hindustan Lever, who anticipated by a generation the opening up of India's autarchic, protectionist trade and investment regime. He wanted to ensure that the ingrained export pessimism of India's economic bureaucracy was not reinforced by trade barriers within Europe. My job was to make a convincing economic case to the European Commission to reform and liberalize the potentially prohibitive barriers for textiles and clothing, some footwear, and agriculture. In the course of this work, I came to understand a little about European trade policy-making processes, particularly as a result of sparring with the French-Vietnamese trade negotiator Tranh, a clever man who saw his job as maximizing access for developing countries' products while appearing to do the opposite. Some of my main adversaries in the policy debate, like the powerful textile industry group Comitextil, represented major employment interests, but other trade barriers were less strategic, like the tariff on one type of garlic designed to protect a small processing plant owned by a nephew of President Giscard d'Estaing. The protectionism that permeated European trade policy thinking, and corrupt practices such as this, had the effect of deflating the somewhat idealistic view I had held of the European project. I remained a supporter, on balance, but the support was tinged with a growing scepticism.

This work was worthy but was outside the mainstream of economics. I was able to remedy this omission with, I think, some genuinely pioneering work demonstrating that competing imports, of textiles and clothing, simply did not have the negative impact on jobs that was claimed by protectionists in Europe and the USA. The analysis made a contribution to the wider political debate, because there were strong protectionist under-currents within Europe, expressed through complaints about 'social dumping' from low-wage economies. I was drawn into a global network of economists, orchestrated by Béla Balassa, Ann Kreuger and Helen Hughes at the World Bank, who developed a coherent and liberal approach to trade and adjustment which has broadly prevailed (in spite of some considerable resistance) to this day.

On the back of this research, I produced my first serious book, *Protectionism and Industrial Decline*, which also drew on some detailed fieldwork in (disappearing) industrial Britain: the cutlery industry of Sheffield; the footwear industry of the East Midlands; and textiles and clothing more generally. Whatever sentimental value attached to traditional industries, workers and firms were adjusting to new technology and a globalized economy, and nothing positive would be achieved by trying to stop the process. I produced numerous papers and reports on the global textiles and clothing industry which helped to build the case for phasing out the system of protection, the Multifibre Arrangement, built around developed countries' industries: a process that was in due course agreed and is being implemented, without the disastrous consequences for textile-producing areas that had been predicted by the industry lobbies.

In parallel with this research and writing, I continued work on India, writing regularly, and made the acquaintance of a group of Indian economists who were questioning the conventional wisdom of inward-looking, planned industrialization. The most important of these was Manmohan Singh, who was then an economic adviser in the finance ministry but later, as finance minister and prime minister, launched and carried through the economic reforms that have taken India on to a much faster tempo of growth. Growth, in turn, is unlocking India's vast human potential and lifting tens, if not hundreds, of millions of people out of extreme poverty. Manmohan was a shy and rather uncommunicative man, whose personal humility and modesty – and incorruptibility – enabled him to survive and achieve considerable power in the piranha pool of Indian politics. Together with Deng Xiaoping in China, Manmohan could reasonably claim to have done more to improve the material human condition than any other political leader of the twentieth century.

I developed a close collaboration with another Indian economist, L. C. Jain, who had many of Manmohan's personal qualities but did not achieve the same pre-eminence, perhaps because he chose to operate through one of India's fractious opposition parties, Janata Dal, rather than Congress and the Gandhi family. The problem he was wrestling with – as someone who embraced Gandhian ideals and had a frugal lifestyle to match – was how to manage the necessary move to economic liberalization in such a way as to serve the interests of India's poor. Undoubtedly the policies that have been adopted have helped the poor, simply by virtue of economic growth stimulating demand for their services, but it has been a hit-and-miss process and the constant foot-dragging on reform by people claiming to be 'pro-poor' is one of the most serious factors holding India back.

Jain's view was that there were millions of artisans and craftsmen making fabrics and carpets, or jewellery, or wood and bronze artefacts, whose unique skills and livelihoods were gradually being lost in the face of mechanical technology and the Indian, middle-class consumer's preference for standardized, Westernized consumer goods – like clothes made from man-made fibres. But these artisans could have a future supplying high-value luxury goods in international markets where uniqueness would be valued, and paid for. It needed, however, supportive governments, at both ends, to lift barriers to trade. The book we produced, together with Ann Weston, we called *The Commerce of Culture*. In producing it we carried out a lot of fieldwork, trying to understand the progression in the value chain from Indian village to Western ship, the way craftsmen were organized (and often exploited), and how modest but well-judged intervention by Indian official agencies or NGOs could make a difference. Spending time studying and talking to the silk weavers of Kanchipuram, the gem cutters of Bombay and Surat, the bronze craftsmen of Moradabad and the carpet weavers of Kashmir, I had the predictably squeamish Western reaction to the sight of very poor people, sometimes school-age children, working long hours in poor conditions for low and unpredictable pay, while remaining dependent on marketing intermediaries who marked up the value of their produce by improbable percentages. But it was clear from the evidence we gathered that communities that were able to access world markets for their traditional artisan skills were conspicuously more prosperous than those that could not. Jain's political activism, backed by our analysis, concentrated on encouraging, not discouraging, trade and on helping the craftsmen to organize cooperatives in order to strengthen their bargaining power or to push up standards so as to ensure that the children in the carpet sheds received an education and had proper ventilation.

Some Western NGOs and pressure groups were, however, promoting the idea of 'self-reliance' as an alternative to the 'exploitation' involved in international trade, and urged consumer boycotts of hand-woven carpets from the subcontinent.

Since the practical alternative for most of the artisans and their families often involved destitution – for girls, domestic service or prostitution – I questioned not just the reasoning but the ethics of this approach. I also realized that, after several years working on trade policy issues, I was developing a somewhat bad-tempered intolerance towards people who questioned the merits of free trade.

Another growing obsession was my conviction that, from the early 1980s onwards, India had turned the corner in terms of both political stability and economic development. In the course of my quarter-century of reportage and commentary for the Economist Intelligence Unit, I produced around one and a half million words and built up a substantial bank of knowledge and understanding. How much of my relentless optimism, which strengthened on every visit, got through to the sceptical businessmen who were my target audience I cannot say. It is only very recently that mainstream opinion – in the City, leading multinationals and government – has shifted away from the established, lazy consensus that India was hopelessly mired in regulation, corruption, unstable coalition governments and slow growth.

While at the ODI, I had other responsibilities which helped broaden my understanding of development. One was to help place ODI fellows in the Caribbean. Nothing could have been further removed from the huge scale of India than the tiny statelets of St Vincent, St Lucia and Dominica (or even the more substantial Barbados and Belize). Each had its own fierce island pride and flourishing, competitive democracy, but all were struggling to establish any kind of meaningful economy beyond a precarious dependence on the global banana trade and on tourism. By Indian and sub-Saharan African standards, most of the English-speaking

Caribbean states were prosperous. But there was hidden poverty and frustration among underemployed young people, who found an outlet in emigration or crime. Small was beautiful, but also petty, parochial and dependent. The dependency remains. It has been profoundly depressing to discover, three decades after helping to place people to develop a strategy for diversification from bananas and sugar, that the banana states are still petitioning the European Union to continue indefinitely the special protection their products have long enjoyed.

In 1983 I was offered a senior post in the Commonwealth secretariat as special adviser to the secretary general. I had long harboured the prejudice that the Commonwealth represented the past rather than the – European – future. But its head, Sir Sonny Ramphal, was an energetic, charismatic figure who was succeeding in finding a positive, forward-looking role for the organization and I was attracted by the idea of working for him.

The secretariat was a difficult working environment. It contained some outstanding, highly motivated and hard-working people, notably Ramphal himself. But it also had the bureaucratic culture typical of other intergovernmental organizations, including the UN. The more senior appointments depended on political patronage rather than ability. Some governments offloaded deadbeats into key positions. Lazy but well-connected officials would wangle a few years in a cosy berth in London on diplomatic terms. The disparities in competence and application were compounded by cultural sensitivities. The deadbeats, in particular, would surround themselves with cronies and a protective coating of pomposity. It was not difficult to generate a perceived cultural or racial slight or to fall foul of status-conscious colleagues.

Somehow, Ramphal floated above all this and, during his tenure, the Commonwealth became a multilateral force to be reckoned with. The heads of government meetings, every two years, were atmospheric (if overlong and overloaded with pomp and formality). My first was in Delhi, and I was able to see the private sessions at first hand. Mrs Gandhi was at the height of her powers, having recovered from the loss of authority after the emergency. Mrs Thatcher was basking in the prestige of the Falklands War and a new electoral mandate. Bob Hawke was putting Australia on the world map. Lee Kuan Yew gave clarity and intellectual distinction to every exchange and Dr Mahathir spoke for the self-assured, emerging Asian 'tiger economies'. The heroes of African independence, Nyerere and Kaunda, had not yet been tarnished, at least abroad, by economic failure and Kaunda in particular was capable of gripping oratory (the impact was lessened when I discovered that his tearful outbursts, needing resort to a handkerchief, were an oft-repeated stock in trade). The hero of the hour, however, was Robert Gabriel Mugabe, fresh from his triumph over Ian Smith, articulate and charming, without a hint of the tyrant he was to become.

By the time of my fourth, and last, heads of government meeting the fascination of being a fly on the wall had palled and I became bored by the self-indulgence of many of the heads and the pointlessness of numerous interminable discussions on matters over which the participants had no influence. Except in relation to South Africa and apartheid, which became the only substantive issue on the agenda, and on which there was agreement to limited sanctions, there wasn't a great deal to show for having up to fifty heads of government spending the best part of a week together. Although I disagreed with her politics, I came to appreciate Mrs Thatcher's brisk and businesslike approach, designed to make progress on practical issues. My own role was a modest but interesting one, preparing and negotiating the communiqué which, in the economic field, involved triangulating the positions of the developed countries (usually led by the UK Treasury), the major developing countries such as India, and the large numbers of small states, particularly from the Caribbean and Pacific, for whom the Commonwealth was a more sympathetic and less overwhelming forum than the UN.

Ramphal's technique for keeping the Commonwealth at the centre of international diplomacy was to prompt a series of expert group reports on topical issues, to report back to the next heads' meeting. The Delhi meeting asked for a report on the international debt crisis which had overtaken Latin America but also some Commonwealth countries, notably Nigeria. I was asked to be secretary and scribe to a group that was to be headed by Lord Lever. Lever had had great influence as a Labour Cabinet minister and was credited with having negotiated the IMF rescue in 1976. He was an affable, highly intelligent man with strong, clear views and wished to use the group to promote his own ideas for solving the (mainly Latin American) commercial bank debt crisis through a big increase in financial flows guaranteed by the IMF. My tricky task was to produce a report that was not likely to be rejected out of hand by Mrs Thatcher and other developed country leaders, but would also address the concerns of the poorer countries with difficulties servicing official (government-to-government) debt. Lever himself became somewhat frustrated by these constraints and produced a book in parallel, written with a *Guardian* economic journalist, Chris Huhne, a future parliamentary colleague. Our report had, I think, some success in for the first time setting out an agenda for dealing with the debt problems of low-income developing countries; and the British Treasury – through successive Chancellors (Lawson, Major, Lamont and Brown) – made this issue central to UK international economic diplomacy, using Commonwealth meetings as a launch pad.

The debt report led to several years of work on private financial flows to developing countries. My colleague Vishnu Persaud, who oversaw the economic work and persuaded Ramphal to back it, saw that the economic nationalism that dominated the thinking of much of the developing world in the 1970s and early 1980s was gradually yielding to a more pragmatic approach to direct foreign investment by multinational companies, and to international capital markets. There was, furthermore, a niche in the marketplace of ideas. Developing country governments would resist lectures from Western governments on the subject, or the imposition of policy conditionality by the IMF and the World Bank. The main UN agencies, led by UNCTAD, and much of development academia were still immersed in the doctrines of 'dependency theory' and 'self-reliance'. We saw that there was a role for the secretariat, dominated as it was by developing country governments and staff, to promote a more economically liberal agenda which could be received sympathetically and with respect. After a series of seminars with finance ministry officials, Persaud and I published a report, and a book, on foreign investment and development which would now be seen as anodyne but was quite adventurous at the time. I went on to produce other reports on the role that international capital markets could play in generating different forms of external equity and loan finance for development.

Encouraged by the political response to this work, Persaud

decided to go one step further and set up a fund that would channel portfolio equity finance from City institutions into developing countries' embryonic stock markets. I was asked to carry the plan through. The idea was not entirely original. The International Finance Corporation had launched a fund of this kind and Templeton had established an emerging markets fund. But in the mid-1980s there was still widespread scepticism in City institutions about emerging markets and it was hard work attracting any kind of serious interest. Nonetheless, we prepared a proposal for the heads of government meeting in Malaysia, backed by a leading fund manager. Governments made a series of (modest) concessions that would open up their stock markets to portfolio investors. The fund was launched, and others followed with the Commonwealth brand. While the sums mobilized were modest, we acted as a useful catalyst and helped reduce the barriers of fear and suspicion between private investors and emerging markets.

Ramphal himself was not greatly interested in these rather technical matters but was preoccupied with the bigger picture: getting rich and poor, big and small, capitalist and communist, countries engaged in a 'dialogue' to produce consensus on the big international economic and strategic issues. He saw the UN as too cumbersome, procedurally hidebound and inhibited by the veto powers; the Bretton Woods institutions as too dominated by the West; the G7 as too exclusive. Two decades later, the G20 would emerge to fill this gap. But there was an appetite in the 1980s, among Europeans as well as developing country political and opinion leaders, to find some common ground outside the Reagan–Thatcher camp and that of the dinosaurs in the Kremlin (and whatever, mysteriously, was going on in China).

This was the climate that led to the Brandt Commission, and the Palme Commission, in which Ramphal was a key player. I played a modest role in these, but he asked me to play a big part in the third Global Commission, headed by Gro Harlem Brundtland, the Norwegian prime minister, which was to look at the environment and development.

Environmental issues, then, were a second-order issue in the Western world but were making an increasing impact, especially in Canada, Germany and Scandinavia. In the developing world there was a growing worry about the loss of tropical forests and dwindling water supplies, and thinkers like Dame Barbara Ward had started to sound warnings about widespread environmental damage. These various concerns had led to the UN Rio Conference in 1992 and the establishment of the United National Economic Programme (UNEP).

But there was still a vast gulf between the passionate warnings of environmentalists and the indifference of public opinion in most countries, and between the differing interpretations of environmental problems, especially as between rich and poor countries. The Brundtland Commission had the task of narrowing the gulf. The commission quickly got into difficulties when developed country environmentalists tried to steer it in their own direction: pessimistic about growth and resource use; romanticizing the simple, if primitive, world of the South American Indian tribes. An exceptionally bright Indian, Nitin Desai, was drafted in to head the team of scribes and to correct the balance and I was to work with him. The concept of 'sustainable development' emerged, and has become a mantra of the environmental movement. At its core was (and is) the belief that the alleviation of poverty is both an objective in itself and central to reducing environmental degradation. The disappearance of tropical forests was seen as owing more to the poverty of encroaching farmers than to the timber demands of rich countries (though, of course, overexploitation of forests for commercial use is a factor). Economic growth is to be welcomed, and is necessary in order to reduce poverty, but has to be modified in the direction of sustainability. These arguments may now seem contrived for political purposes, but were important then in securing a common approach among a very disparate group of countries.

In retrospect, one of the most important contributions of the Brundtland Commission was to pick up the early signals in the mid-1980s from a group of climate scientists who were warning about man-made climate change and global warming. I had helped draft the relevant sections and became fascinated by the issue. Then, the following year, at the 1987 heads of government meeting, the Maldives' president raised the issue of global warming and rising sea levels. He had read an article in a magazine on the subject: did it explain the partial inundation of his country of low-lying coral atolls, and could anything be done? A group was assembled under the British scientist Sir Martin Holdgate and I was made secretary. With the enthusiastic help of climate scientists at the University of East Anglia, a geographer, Martin Parry, at Birmingham, and an environmental lawyer, Philippe Sands, and through a series of case studies on the potential impact of sea-level rises in Bangladesh, the Maldives, Tuvalu and Guyana, we were able to pull together a report that was perfectly timed to address growing interest in the issue. The report, which appeared in 1989, was evidence-based and cautiously expressed; emphasized the potentially greater threats to poor people in developing countries, who would be more exposed to disaster and had less capacity and fewer resources to adapt; and argued for a combination of adaptation and prevention, the latter based on a cost-benefit approach. My attempts to explain these qualified conclusions to the press were not a success. The *Sun* ran an article describing global warming in terms of a Venus-like climate with streets running with molten lead. The report also provided Mrs Thatcher, who had been persuaded of the seriousness of the problem by Sir Crispin Tickell, with an opportunity to display her (now largely forgotten, but considerable) interest in global environmental issues. These took concrete form in the Montreal Protocol on measures to counter depletion of the ozone layer, which established a template for the much more ambitious Kyoto Protocol a decade later.

One personal spin-off from the expert-group report was that it attracted the interest of Shell's planning department, which had seen the enormous long-term implications of climate change and environmentalism for an oil multinational. This, in turn, led to an invitation to join them. Since my political interests had by this time receded into the background, I saw no reason to do other than accept and move on.

Chapter 9

Big Oil

Most politicians pontificate about markets and companies without ever having participated in any entrepreneurial venture more demanding than a school tuck shop or a fund-raising raffle. To a degree, this lack of experience doesn't matter. There are brilliant football managers who were hopeless footballers, and battle-winning generals who couldn't shoot straight. But when the government's Treasury bench is composed entirely – as it has been in recent years – of former lecturers, teachers, charity workers, criminal lawyers and professional politicians, it is difficult to believe that the quality of decision-making is not affected.

For many years my own understanding of the economic world was likewise largely confined to the public sector and to books. I had an acute sense of incomplete personal education. I looked, unsuccessfully, for a worthwhile role in the private sector. Somewhat late in life – now aged forty-five – I was invited to join Shell's group planning team and jumped at the chance. One of my attractions to them was that I was an economist who knew quite a lot about the developing world and about environmental issues and, in particular, about the new issue of climate change. Capitalist enterprises are often attacked for being short-term in their outlook, but this could not be said of Shell. It had made massive investments with a perspective of decades, and it was starting to worry seriously about the implications for an energy company of global environmental threats from greenhouse gas emissions long before governments or environmental campaigning groups had grasped the significance of the issue.

Shell's group planning is (or was) a unique institution in the corporate world. Many companies closed their corporate planning functions after the 1970s when there was a reaction against mechanistic forecasting and when headquarters staffing was stripped to its essentials in a leaner and meaner business environment. Shell's, however, survived and flourished, and those who led the planning team – Pierre Wack, Peter Schwarz and Ari de Geus – later became almost legendary figures in the rather specialized and lucrative world of business gurus.

Shell's team had earned its keep by developing a system of scenario planning which did not involve predicting the future but posed plausible if uncomfortable 'what if?' questions about the business environment. In a very large and successful company, largely invulnerable to takeover and inclined towards conservatism, senior managers saw value in this kind of regular internal challenge to their strategic assumptions. It had proved its worth in the late 1970s when it was almost universally assumed that high oil prices were here to stay. Shell planners warned that markets were working to reduce demand and increase supply and that oil prices could well crash for a prolonged period (as they did in the 1980s). This insight helped the company to survive and flourish in almost two decades of cheap (or low-priced) oil. When I joined, the company was trying to make sense of, and respond to, environmentalism, the cracks appearing in the Soviet Union, the growth of China, and the creation of monetary union in Europe. I was one of a handful of outsiders recruited to work on the scenario team addressing these issues and their attendant energy implications.

The company has changed in many ways in the last two decades, but the company I joined had enormous institutional self-confidence: a multinational which had grown and flourished for a century. It was, on the basis of market capitalization, one of the top three companies in the world, alongside Exxon and General Electric, and had an enviable balance sheet with little debt. It prided itself on its professional and engineering excellence, the loyalty of its staff and its ability to sail, like its oil tankers, serenely through rough waters that would sink most companies.

The unique corporate culture was the product of a marriage between Royal Dutch and (British) Shell Transport and Trading. The relationships were complex and have since been simplified and streamlined. But in essence the company was the same animal that had emerged before the First World War from the complementary interests of British and Dutch components. A British trader, Marcus Samuel, who started life selling shells on an East End market stall (hence the company name), developed an extensive business shipping Russian (or more precisely Azerbaijani) oil to Asia via the Suez Canal. In due course Shell teamed up with the Royal Dutch exploration company, which had been producing oil in the Dutch East Indies (Indonesia). The British arm contributed trading, transport, marketing and logistics; the Dutch, exploration and production technology. Roughly the same division of labour and corporate structure continues to this day despite the upheavals of war – the German occupation of Holland led, notoriously, to collaboration by the Dutch head of

Above: As a baby, held by paternal grandmother, Annie Cable, with my mother Edith (left) and a friend.

Above: Aged around 7 with my mother and the airgun shortly to be the centre of an incident with the neighbours.

Aged around 14 with my younger brother, Keith, on an annual week's holiday in Scarborough.

With adopted cousin John, who was later diagnosed with Huntington's Disease.

Above: (Kneeling.) Playing Macbeth, aged 17, with Marion as Lady Macbeth.

Right: Aged about 12, on a visit to London – including the House of Commons – with my father.

Father, Len Cable
(a lecturer in building
science at York Technical
College), testing concrete.

Above: As President of the
Union at Cambridge, Summer
Term, 1965. Amongst the group
is Norman Lamont (front row,
second from right).

Left: Speaking in the Cambridge
Union's 'No Confidence' motion,
1964.

Above: Olympia graduating from York University 1966, shortly before I met her.

Above: Olympia with her younger sister, Amata, on our wedding day at the Catholic Cathedral, Nairobi, July 1968.

After the wedding, with Amata; Olympia's brothers, Hugo (left) and Celso (right); and best man, Trevor Sweetman.

Above: Election photo as Labour candidate for Hillhead, Glasgow, 1970.

Above: With Shirley Williams, arriving at York Station for SDP election rally, 1983.

Celebrating election as MP for Twickenham in 1997 with Olympia at our home in Twickenham.

With daughter Aida on the day of her wedding to Stephen Kenny, 1999.

Above: With Dee Doocey – then election agent, now an MLA – and a model of the 2012 Olympic site.

The things which MPs do… abseiling for charity in Twickenham.

At Chelsea Flower Show, promoting beekeeping with the British Beekeepers Association, May 2009.

Party leaders at the Cenotaph, Remembrance Sunday, 2007.

With Nick Clegg.

Wedding of Paul to Agnesa Tothova, with Slovakian in-laws, younger son Hugo (left), mother (centre, seated), Olympia (third from right) and daughter Aida (right), 1998.

With Rachel, before the Blessing in the House of Commons Chapel, 2004.

With grandsons Ayrton (centre) and Charlie (centre, seated), Paul, Agi, Aida and Stephen, at home in Twickenham.

Shell, Henri Deterding – the switch from colonialism to decolonization, and then post-war nationalization (as in Venezuela and Indonesia).

It would be a caricature to say that the company reflected a creative tension between British accountants and Dutch engineers, but the distinction is recognizable. The Shell elite were trained at Delft, one of Holland's top educational institutions, a school of engineering and architecture. The exploration and production function of Shell, dominated by Dutch geologists and petroleum engineers, has always been based in The Hague and, particularly after recent corporate upheavals, is unambiguously the profit and power centre of the company.

The Dutch and British staff had rough parity at senior management level, with a slight Dutch majority reflecting the 60:40 shareholding. The marvellous bilingualism of the Dutch ensured that there was at all times excellent communication, in English, and the chemistry between the two nationalities worked extraordinarily well, as in other Anglo-Dutch groups like Unilever. Another eccentricity was the absence of a single 'boss'. Shell, as the wits often put it, was the last major institution in the world, apart from Yugoslavia, ruled by a committee, comprising (at that time) seven managing directors (four Dutch and three British). The executive chairman was *primus inter pares*, and when I joined Shell the post was held by Loew van Wachem, an austere, punctilious former mining engineer, regarded with some awe by the lesser mortals in the company. His particular obsession was trying to anticipate the iceberg that might sink his otherwise impregnable ship, frequently citing the experience of Exxon, which had almost capsized after the *Exxon Valdez* disaster. His instincts were to be proved right.

I had some difficulty, initially, adjusting to the rather rigid conventions and protocols that governed the daily life of senior managers and had evolved around lifetime employees who spent much of their lives as expatriates. In many respects it resembled the Foreign Office, with a civil service ethos, a strong sense of collective identity, and shared experiences in exotic parts. There was little sense of individual risks and rewards.

Nothing captured the spirit of the times better than the lunchtime mess for senior managers above a certain grade – almost all men and all white – near the top of the Shell Centre. Other ranks shared a cafeteria in the basement. Conversation in the mess was usually animated and always about the company. Managers talked about financial ratios and the beauties of the management matrix with a fervour that most men reserve for football. The former geologists, chemical engineers and accountants at the apex of the company generated excited, awestruck gossip as if they were pop stars. I was amazed, but also impressed, that the company could inspire such total devotion from its staff. A year after I joined, however, the mess was scrapped in a move to break down the rigid caste hierarchy, the first step towards converting 'old' Shell into 'new'.

The other key element in the corporate culture was the extraordinarily complex management structure and a system of interlocking regional and functional committees through which decisions were made. While this system provided checks and balances, it generated a top-heavy, expensive layer of middle management, later to be severely culled, and an aversion to rapid, risky, entrepreneurial decisions. The coexistence of tiers of management in both British and Dutch headquarters added to the complexity and the scope for office politicians rather than entrepreneurs to dominate.

The way in which the company maintained a business dynamic was by devolving a great deal of autonomy to the operating companies around the world. The head of Shell Australia or the Nigerian production operation was an immensely powerful figure, and while decentralization allowed business talent to emerge it also generated self-contained baronies whose mistakes were difficult to counter. Some subsidiaries, like Shell Oil in the USA, were almost entirely autonomous (which became a source of embarrassment when Shell Oil joined an Exxon-led coalition to dispute the science of global warming). The experiences of the company, and of other big multinationals, in relation to localism have considerable relevance to the (often simplistic) arguments about decentralization in UK politics. The exact balance between target-driven centralization and uncoordinated decentralization is, in practice, a very difficult one to strike, and Shell agonized over it throughout my time there.

I was lucky to be given a couple of assignments that introduced me to the top management. One was to prepare a presentation for the committee of managing directors on carbon taxes, working with the then chief economist, DeAnne Julius. Two things were striking about this project. The first was that a decade before British politicians started debating environmental taxes and global warming seriously, a company located a few hundred yards from the House of Commons was anticipating how to respond to that debate. The second was that – contrary to the popular, environmentalist, depiction of oil companies as dinosaurs resisting change – the response I received was that, properly designed, such taxes were a sensible and reasonable way to change behaviour and were compatible with the company's long-term aims, which included a switch from high-carbon coal and oil to gas and, eventually, to hydrogen.

The second task was advising the current Shell chairman, Jeroen van der Veeren, and his boss, Maarten van den Bergh (later chairman of Lloyds Bank), then both rising stars, about the future of Shell's businesses in Africa, many of them hanging on in strife-torn countries. These two individuals epitomized the best of Shell managers: extremely bright and hard-working, with an ability to think quickly and clearly both about practical, humdrum business issues and about the big picture. There were real dilemmas. The most chaotic and dangerous countries often provided the best business opportunities, since other companies were reluctant to take the risk of operating there. There was also a tension between the wish to stick with a country in bad times and to build a reputation for reliability and loyalty to local staff, and worries that the group's overall reputation would be tarnished by association with a brutal regime or a local partner with low environmental or ethical standards. These dilemmas were to be at the centre of work I later carried out in the group in relation to Nigeria after the execution of Ken Saro-Wiwa. My own instincts, reflected in my advice on Africa, were when in doubt to stay rather than run.

The main focus of my work in group planning was to help prepare a set of global scenarios: different stories about how the world might evolve over the next twenty years. For months our eclectic team of Shell insiders and multidisciplinary outsiders would argue and brainstorm not just about energy but about politics, economics, demographics, science and anything else that might shape the future. The freedom to think and explore ideas was remarkable: everything that universities and think tanks are supposed to be but usually aren't. Paradoxically, a private company had managed to create, better than in any public enterprise

I have encountered, a genuine collective in which a group of diverse and generally brainy people could work as a team, generating shared ideas, and in which the whole was substantially bigger and better than the parts.

For a very disparate group to gel and produce valuable conclusions appeared, superficially, miraculous, akin to assembling a troupe of monkeys and typewriters and discovering the works of Shakespeare. But there was actually method in the madness. The corporate world, and Shell in particular, has developed techniques of brainstorming that enable groups to transcend the egos of individuals and the passing ephemera of daily news. It is a pity that government and the world of politics are so resistant to the discipline of organized group thinking.

The basic structure of that particular global scenario exercise in the early 1990s – there have been several since – consisted of two archetypal stories about the future, neither predictions nor forecasts but plausible descriptions of the way the global business environment and energy markets might evolve: these to be used for the testing of business decisions. One of the scenarios, New Frontiers, described a post-Cold War world in which the forces of liberalization and globalization would be unleashed with unprecedented intensity. In this world, dominant new economic superpowers, China and India, would very rapidly (in historic terms) open up and become the economic centre of gravity of the world economy, balanced in part by those (mainly Anglo-Saxon) bits of the developed world that could adapt. The focus on the Asian giants now seems rather commonplace, but fifteen years ago it was counter-intuitive and rather alarming to executives with a rich-world or Eurocentric perspective. Equally uncomfortable, and also prescient, was the idea that brutal competition and global capital markets would expose all the cosy, protected, profitable businesses and relationships on which a multinational company like Shell depended for its profit.

The other story, Barricades, also described a world of globalization and liberalization, but one in which the forces of reaction would fight a strong rearguard action, bringing to the surface the politics of identity: resource nationalism in Russia and the Middle East, religious fundamentalism, and hostility towards immigrant workers and foreign investors. All of these elements are instantly recognizable today, though they were less obvious then, and they provided a basis for challenging the group's managers with the question: 'What would you do if . . . ?'

Since Shell is a (mainly) oil and gas company, the real interest of the work centred on what we had to say about energy. Here, what worried the company was the challenge of continued very low oil prices: a $10 per barrel world in which oil became like coffee, superabundant with new supplies constantly driving down the price. Such a picture, which loomed large in our storytelling, may seem bizarre after a year in which oil prices passed $140 per barrel and with venerable experts talking about 'peak oil' and growing worries about energy security. Nonetheless, there is a compelling logic to it which is worth resurrecting as an antidote to today's conventional wisdom.

Essentially, markets work in the energy sector as elsewhere. A period of high prices sets in train a market-driven response, in the form of more fuel-efficient vehicles and industrial processes, and a greater emphasis on conservation. At the same time, higher prices create incentives to explore further and produce in what were formerly uneconomic areas, like the North Pole and the deeper waters off the continental shelf. Shell's analysis showed that there were vast supplies of unconventional oils, in Canada and Venezula, which, when developed, would put a ceiling on the crude oil price in the long term. The concept of 'the world running out of oil', which was fashionable in the 1970s and has become so again now, was regarded as, in practical terms, bordering on the ridiculous. The only problem with the above argument is that the market processes take a long time to work through; it took a decade or so after the first oil shock in 1973/4 to reach a negative oil shock of falling prices. But it is a useful antidote to those who in current circumstances advocate energy policies on the assumption that prices will remain at high levels indefinitely. Indeed, in 2009 prices collapsed.

This immersion in the world of scenario planning took me to a variety of countries where Shell had actual or potential interests, to work with local management teams in applying this methodology to their businesses, in Brazil, Singapore, South Africa, Italy, Indonesia and, most interestingly and rewardingly, in the three big emerging economies of China, India and Russia. On the Chinese study, I was paired with a forceful Dutchman who was convinced (rightly as it turned out) that nothing could stop the juggernaut of Chinese economic expansion and that Shell should proceed at full steam to invest large sums in establishing a presence in the country. Although less informed, it was my role to be a critical foil, to point out the risks and difficulties of doing business in China. The Chinese did my work for me when they arrested a young female graduate from our Shanghai office, with whom I had been working quite closely, and charged her with espionage. After she had been in prison for several months, it was established that one of Shell's prospective business partners – a powerful state corporation – in a proposed chemical complex at Nanhai, near Guangzhou (Canton), had used its influence in Beijing to secure the arrest and was in effect using blackmail to achieve negotiating concessions. I never found out what price was paid and in what form, but the unfortunate employee was in due course released. Such was the natural caution of senior management that it took some years to clear the Nanhai project. I am told that the business in China is now growing strongly.

I was able to play a more important role in relation to India. On the strength of my research and contacts there, I was recognized as one of the few people in Shell with any background on India at all. The perception of India among the senior management in the early 1990s was very negative. They saw the country as chaotic, corrupt, unfriendly to business and generally hopeless. These perceptions had, of course, an element of truth, though conditions were, and are, improving rapidly. The general negativity had been heightened by a recent experience in Shell's one major venture in India, a chemicals joint venture (NOCIL) with the Mafatlal family. It was discovered that there was a large hole in the accounts, which appeared to be explained by payments to Indian politicians. Within twenty-four hours of the discovery Shell withdrew from the joint venture, reflecting the group's puritanical approach to business corruption.

Nonetheless, an energetic, young, recently appointed Indian general manager tried to revive interest, and I was asked to prepare India scenarios. I was sent on a reconnaissance visit with a managing director, the future chairman Mark Moody Stewart. Interest in things Indian revived, helped by a substantial oil discovery in speculative exploration drilling in Rajasthan. A variety of projects – refinery, natural gas terminal, gas pipelines – were seriously discussed. However, Indian national sensitivities around the oil industry combined with Shell's conservatism to prevent progress. But a substantial business is now being established in India. There has also been what must rank as one of the worst business decisions in modern times, when Shell sold off its Rajasthan oil well to a small Scottish exploration company, Cairn Energy. Cairn was subsequently able to realize two hundred times the value of the assets that Shell had accepted on disposal and has become a major oil company on the back of this single transaction. A mistake that would have sunk a small company went largely unnoticed in Shell.

The third exercise, on Russia, was the most challenging. Russia has vast reserves of gas and substantial reserves of oil, though much recent production has been wasted, feeding the energy-greedy heavy industry of the Soviet Union, and capacity has been badly degraded by communist management methods and lack of access to modern technology. The collapse of the Soviet Union and the prospect of a democratic Russia emerging under Yeltsin raised the possibility that Russia's gas and oil reserves might be opened up, an opportunity that whetted even the most jaded appetite among upstream oilmen. But the anarchic conditions in Russia were forbidding. I visited Moscow several times to meet Russian politicians and the new generation of liberal economists – Chubais, Illarionov, Yasin – who were trying to create a capitalist economy from scratch, and I consulted Western Kremlinologists, like my former head of department in Glasgow, Alec Nove, who had spent a lifetime analysing the weaknesses of the Soviet system. In trying to get a sense of the potential economic trajectory of the former Soviet Union, I looked at other catastrophic collapses like the fall of the Austro-Hungarian empire after 1918, and in the event this proved remarkably similar to what has happened in Russia. From such a tenuous basis and similar guesstimates of production, my colleagues and I were able to construct a picture of future Russian oil and, more particularly, gas exports, which has proved remarkably accurate, although it seemed implausible at the time. We constructed stories about the future of the former Soviet Union based on different assumptions about the relative strength of centripetal and centrifugal forces. Out of this work emerged a strategy, reasonably resilient to a range of uncertainties. Compared with BP, Chevron and others, Shell moved cautiously. The aim was to concentrate on peripheral regions like Sakhalin Island where the reach of central government was least likely to be felt. In the event, however, even this strategy offered no protection once Putin's increasingly self-confident and nationalistic government had started to flex its muscles.

The work, while interesting, was not all-absorbing and I was able fight the 1992 election in Twickenham without testing the patience of my Shell colleagues too badly. After four exhilarating years at Shell I had come to the end of my contract; and at Chatham House I was able in under two years to distil into print a large volume of work based on ideas developed at Shell and earlier: a book on globalization; another on China and India; a paper trying to capture the international dimensions of the rapidly evolving telecoms industry and the Internet; and numerous papers on trade policy and regional integration issues. Chatham House was not particularly well run and had the feel of an institution that had known better times. But it was a pleasant place to work: marvellously well connected, full of interesting people, and operating in the interesting terrain connecting academia and the world of policy. I became a minor celebrity in the field of international economic policy and, having accepted that I was unlikely ever to make it into Parliament, or to the top of any career ladder, I settled into an agreeable way of life, writing, reading, conferring and spending as much time as I could with Olympia.

I also made time to produce a pamphlet on the politics of identity for the new Demos think tank founded by Martin Jacques, the former editor of *Marxism Today*. Martin was a stimulating companion and encouraged me to write regularly for the *Independent*, of which he was deputy editor. He and Geoff Mulgan, the first director of Demos, were among the best and most creative political brains around at a time when an intellectual framework was being created for what all assumed to be a certain change of government. At Martin's house I met Tony Blair informally for the first and only time, his exuberant manner and easy charm making deep inroads into the assembled group, which I judged to be in varying stages of conversion from revolutionary socialism. A few days later I was invited to a meeting with Blair and the New Labour insiders and I had the Third Way explained to me, rather as if I was attending an Alpha course as a born-again social democrat. Unfortunately I was recognized as a Lib Dem, and when it was established that I was not there as a penitent convert, invitations ceased.

Out of the blue I received an invitation to go back to Shell as chief economist, and although Chatham House had been good to me, it took me only a few seconds to agree. Although the Shell job was not academically prestigious, it offered a unique opportunity to work on economic problems with the top management of one of the world's largest companies. I had developed a flair for communicating complex ideas simply and seeing the links between economics and the practical problems confronting business managers, and they would make good use of me.

I made an early impact with a monthly note I was required to prepare for the external board, executive managing directors and other senior staff, tackling the issue of the 'curse of oil'. There are some straightforward explanations for the fact that resource-rich countries so often fail economically. Their real exchange rates become overvalued, choking off other export and import activities. The economic 'rent' from resources is easily dissipated. With a few exceptions – Canada, Australia, Norway, Malaysia, Botswana – most resource-rich countries have wasted their wealth. What I thought to be rather obvious was shocking and alarming to colleagues whose lives were devoted to producing oil and gas. I think the ensuing debate helped persuade some of them to think more deeply about the policy environment of the countries in which they operated, and not to take refuge in protected physical and psychological enclaves. Nigeria was a test case.

A few days after I rejoined the company it found itself in the midst of turmoil consequent upon the hanging of the Nigerian campaigner Ken Saro-Wiwa by the military government. Shell had become the focus of a campaign by environmental NGOs alleging its complicity in the abuses of the dictatorship; its neglect of the environment of the Niger delta, where Shell (as part of a consortium) was the main private oil producer and operator; and, by implication, its responsibility for the death of Mr Saro-Wiwa. For the second time in several years a rather inward-looking company dominated by the concerns of professional engineers and managers suddenly found itself on the receiving end of highly effective and aggressive environmental campaigning. The Brent Spar affair had already left the company looking rather leaden-footed and environmentally insensitive, even though it had scrupulously followed scientific advice and government direction in proposing to dispose of a redundant oil platform at the bottom of the North Sea. Graphic filming of oil flares from Nigeria; emotional appeals from Saro-Wiwa's family and friends, including Anita Roddick of the Body Shop; allegations of leaking pipelines and neglect of local communities: all this formed a damaging charge sheet which the plonking responses of official Shell spokesmen did little to diminish. Shell undoubtedly suffered considerable reputational damage, and employees who had long boasted to friends and relatives about working for one of the world's best companies reported that they were being roundly attacked, even by their own children, for their involvement with such a wicked, exploitative operation.

The issue touched the soul of the company. The upstream business in Nigeria was the jewel in the crown of the exploration and production division, the company's elite corps. Many managing directors, past and present, had served time in the Niger delta; Nigeria accounted for one of Shell's largest sources of equity oil (oil owned by the company rather than managed on others' behalf), and a steady, if unspectacular, profit. And it offered enormous potential for expansion, in both gas and oil. While the critics may have exaggerated and distorted the position, there were some valid criticisms. Shell (and the other companies involved) had paid their taxes as required to the central government and had steered clear of Nigerian politics, but the truth was that the communities in the oil-producing delta were neglected and poverty-stricken and saw little or none of the oil money. While the many miles of exposed pipeline were frequently punctured by sabotage, too little had been done to clean up the local environment. And while the flaring of enormous amounts of associated gas was environmentally harmless locally (that is, apart from the carbon dioxide), and its waste owed much to the incompetence of Nigerian state enterprises, Shell had not been very proactive in using the gas.

One option being considered was to disengage from Nigeria. The reputational damage of the current exposure was huge. The Nigerian military government's stealing of resources had also reached the point where, not content with taking the tax revenue, it was no longer paying bills due to the company. And there was growing concern that corruption in Nigeria was so rampant that it was becoming difficult to insulate the company from it. There was another, opposing, view that Nigeria, despite its difficulties, had enormous long-term potential, much of it offshore and away from the angry communities and complicated delta tribal politics, but also in supplying the country's domestic market if the economy could be turned around.

Such a range of options lent itself to scenario thinking and I was asked to lead an exercise to help the Shell group and the Nigerian company decide their strategy. The general manager who oversaw the work was one of Shell's most impressive managers, with deep roots in Nigeria; he saw himself as a 'white Nigerian' and had spent his youth in the country, witnessing the massacres preceding the Biafran civil war. His top Nigerian staff were no less impressive: honest professionals with deep roots in the company and their communities – one, an Ibo, had kept an improvised oil refinery going in the bush, supplying the Biafran army with fuel until its final surrender. I came to appreciate, visiting Nigeria and listening to the staff, that Shell had a serious duty of care to these local employees and could not just leave the country in response to a political campaign back at base.

The scenario exercise was, I think, moderately helpful in clarifying the group's thinking about its future in Nigeria. It proved to be more valuable in another way. The company was looking for a way of communicating to the military top brass, and General Abacha in particular, that the gross corruption and human rights abuses could make it impossible for Shell to continue. But it wanted to do so in a way that did not come across as a threat or ultimatum, or as white men telling black men how to behave. The scenarios, which were essentially stories of the future, could be presented as parables or riddles, conveying a clear message but in a way that was not hectoring or offensive. So it was decided that I should present the scenarios to the president and his colleagues publicly at an 'economic summit' in Abuja.

The stakes were quite high. No one could predict how the president would react. He was a man who, reputedly, suffered from mental instability, including a fear of sleep, when he thought himself vulnerable to assassination. In order to prepare the ground, I was taken to meet him on two occasions, both at dead of night. I was prepared to meet an ogre. He was allegedly a man with a lot of blood on his hands, a private bank account of billions, and a public face on official photographs that gave prominence to his tribal facial scars and scornful leer. The reality was quite different. He was a small man, dwarfed in his northern robes, with an infectious belly laugh and a voice that swooped and soared in exaggerated cadences – like, I thought, Archbishop Tutu. After a few exchanges I was escorted away, leaving him to talk business with the general manager. I was then required to give a dry run of my presentation to Chief Shonakan, who had briefly ruled as head of state, and he advised me on the language to use to push back the frontiers of public debate on corruption and human rights abuses without bringing on a fit of presidential temper.

I wasn't sure whether to be flattered by the high-level attention or alarmed by what might happen if I enraged this African dictator. There was a large darkened hall and I could only see in front of me a line of bemedalled generals on a raised dais. My presentation of PowerPoint graphics – then something of a high-tech novelty – started with a fairly comfortable scenario story of the way Nigeria could develop if it followed through some modest reforms (which were nonetheless currently impossible to implement). The second I called the Road to Kinshasa, which was a description of Mobutu's failing state, with the unstated implication, that this was how Nigeria could become – and was becoming. The allusion to corruption and human rights abuses were, I think, clearly understood. There was polite applause led by the president and all was going well until the finance minister stood up to respond. Anthony Ani was a civilian in a military government and he was compromised by that, as well as by his corruption, in the eyes of most Nigerians. He sought to compensate by belligerent nationalism and saw this occasion as an opportunity to let rip. He launched into a tirade against 'this arrogant white man from London who has come to lecture us' and shrieked at the audience: 'There is no such thing as corruption in Nigeria.' There was a long pause for effect, but instead of the expected round of applause the president burst into peals of laughter. His colleagues and then the rest of the hall joined in. Crisis over.

I doubt that the presentation changed much, although I was told later that the 'Road to Kinshasa' and the 'Curse of Oil' had entered the vocabulary of the Nigerian chattering classes. The president did not survive much longer. He died mysteriously one night, his death variously attributed to his dicky heart, assassins or the excitement of a romp in bed with several prostitutes. The most hated ruler in the country's history, he died unloved and, having given military rule a deservedly bad name, has been succeeded by elected civilians. Shell's problems in the delta continue, however, with kidnappings and general mayhem depressing production. But no one now seriously argues that Shell should not be there.

The troubles that Shell encountered over Brent Spar and Nigeria were, however, part of a deepening set of problems. The self-confidence that I had first encountered in the van Wachem years was gradually ebbing away. Led by a senior planning colleague, Guy Gillings, there was a growing debate on the financial position, which appeared very comfortable but disguised poor returns on new investments. Shell seemed to be missing out on big acquisitions and big new country entries: Exxon had merged with Mobil; BP had absorbed Arco and, under John Browne, was making bold moves in Russia and the Caucasus. Shell's upstream division was no longer producing major finds. Brokers' circulars were no longer so flattering. Big reforms to simplify the management structure were launched, though the promised 'new Shell' was taking a long time to emerge from the bureaucratic 'old Shell'.

There was, however, strong leadership committed to change. Mark Moody Stuart was an impressive chairman who combined steely business discipline with a strong Quaker social conscience. He was succeeded by Phil Watts, who oversaw my work and whom I came to know quite well. Down to earth and direct, I liked him and admired the way he accepted past mistakes (as a former head of the Nigerian company) and tried to take on board elusive and unfamiliar new problems like reputation management. He was nonetheless a few years later at the centre of a major scandal when the company was found to have overstated the true position of its reserves. I know too little to comment on the detail, but I suspect that the company was caught midway in an awkward transition to becoming a 'normal', if very big, public company, having stripped away its checks and balances in the interests of efficiency, and having discovered that institutional shareholders now demanded and had real power over managers. Years before, the reserves problem would have been picked up by one of the cross-cutting committees; or, if it hadn't, the shareholders would have been none the wiser. Whatever the cause, the crisis forced a drastic streamlining of management, the establishment of a powerful chief executive accountable to an external board, and a recognition that the company is essentially Dutch and should be located in Holland. It is now unrecognizable as the company I joined except that, once again, it is looking down on BP.

When I returned to the world of politics I was forced to confront questions posed by so-called progressive politicians: do multinationals have too much power? Can they and should they act in a more socially and environmentally responsible way, even at the expense of their shareholders? Are the massive profits of oil companies 'excessive'? My answers to these questions no doubt reflect my indoctrination in the company. The power of multinationals, certainly in the oil industry, is now highly circumscribed by competition. Privately owned oil companies like Shell and BP are dwarfed by state-owned companies like Gazprom and Aramco. In the big markets they face fierce competition in retailing, refining, chemicals and upstream oil services. Except in the biggest, most technically sophisticated projects, the oil majors no longer have unique advantages. Also, my experience has been that the external pressures of customers and ethical shareholders, and the internal idealism and professionalism of many managers, make the modern oil company like Shell or BP very sensitive to the social responsibility agenda. And the massive profits have to be seen in relation to the capital employed. At high prices, oil companies can hardly avoid making money, but the expensive investments Shell is undertaking will lose money if prices continue to slump.

Two days after becoming an MP I was invited to join a *Newsnight* discussion on Shell's activities and to denounce the company I had worked for. I declined and said I was proud to have worked for Shell, which I think left Jeremy Paxman momentarily lost for words. But I meant it and I still do.

Chapter 10

The Long March

It was over a quarter of a century from my first contesting a parliamentary election to being elected to Parliament for Twickenham in 1997. I like to think that these years were not wasted. I was able to devote time to being a proper husband and father. I had a chance to learn from various working environments about the way government and business operate. Political failure and frustration also gave me the opportunity to reflect, from outside, on the political world that I wanted to join but could not. I have been constantly reminded that away from the rise and fall of personalities, the daily tittle-tattle of news, and the dramas being played out in the Westminster village, politics operates in long cycles and trends, making and breaking individual fortunes along the way. Along that road I have met a small army of prospective prime ministers and party leaders, many of enormous talent and potential, who have lapsed into obscurity or found their niche as commentators, consultants or academics, in local government or the media or NGOs.

It may seem odd for a liberal to find refuge in Maoist imagery. But the Long March conjures up for me both the trajectory of my own political journey and that of my party: endless skirmishes with small victories and defeats, long exile from the main theatres of political warfare and centres of power, all sustained by a determination to keep going and by hope of eventual victory.

For most of this period, politics occupied for me a status somewhere between a hobby and a part-time profession. It usually came third after family life and work. If I record the political events in more detail it is because of their wider interest. In reality, my life, like that of millions of other middle-class husbands and fathers, revolved around events that are now captured only in fading memories and selected highlights from the family photo albums: shared chores and shopping; children's tantrums and laughter, homework, exams, concerts, open days, Cub camps and Brownie badges, music and ballet lessons, train sets and Wendy houses; holidays, graduating from tents and caravanettes in Britain to luxury cottages in Italy; the endless dramas of the Rebelo family and the visits to see them in India, Kenya and Zimbabwe, alongside the slow disintegration of the Cables as my parents aged and died; birthdays and anniversaries, always celebrated in some style. We were, I think, more ambitious for one another than most families, perhaps more protective, certainly very secure and permanent. Even after cancer ate at her strength, Olympia was the dominant, regal centre of it, and I was content to be her consort. But from our first meeting in the staff room of the York mental hospital, she had always understood my passion for politics and helped me sustain it through the years in the wilderness.

The family upheaval involved in leaving Glasgow and setting up home in Twickenham mirrored an upheaval taking place inside the Labour Party. It was clear by the mid-1970s that the Labour Party was changing in a fundamental way. The traditional

tensions between 'left' and 'right', 'socialists' and 'social democrats', were often acrimonious and divisive, but were expressed
in a – broadly – common language by people who shared essentially the same values. A change then occurred that can be traced
back to a decision of the National Executive in 1973 to drop its
ban on 'proscribed organizations'. Most of us in the political
mainstream were only dimly aware of the existence of revolutionary Trotskyite groups like the International Socialists and
the International Marxist Group, which changed their names
with bewildering frequency and were differentiated from one
another by obscure but ferociously contested ideological debates
and incomprehensible personal quarrels. In the film *The Life of
Brian*, there is a dispute between the Judaean People's Front and
the People's Front of Judaea which captures this spirit. We didn't
see these groups as a serious threat. Trots like Paul Foot – who
before he joined the International Socialists had been active in
my local party in Glasgow shortly before my arrival – and Tariq
Ali were attractive and plausible figures who wrote and spoke
well and captured the mood of disillusionment on the left after
the Wilson government. The affable political activists who sold
Militant newspapers to the councillors in Glasgow City Hall
seemed harmless enough. So when a move was made to lift the
ban, there was little opposition. I recall questioning the proposal
in my local branch, but most of the activists didn't see a problem
and welcomed a move to integrate people who might irrigate the
shrivelling grass roots of the party with idealism and energy. The
full significance of this disastrous decision became apparent a
few years later, when I had moved to London.

When Olympia and I arrived in Twickenham in 1974 we joined
the local Labour Party, which was, on the surface, flourishing

politically and socially. Although the Conservatives had been running Richmond council and providing the MP forever, the Labour Party had a solid block of councillors from predominantly working-class wards, and in the second 1974 election the Labour candidate, Mavis Cunningham (wife of George), came second, defeated by Toby Jessel by 9507 votes. With a Labour government re-elected, morale was high and the political prospects looked good. The party provided Olympia and me with our first set of London friends, some of whom have remained close to this day. Reciprocal babysitting and fund-raising parties generated a warm comradeship which subsequent political strife never wholly eradicated.

The politics of race was very raw at that time and we threw ourselves into local anti-racism campaigns. The National Front had its headquarters in the constituency, in Teddington, and they were made to feel very unwelcome until they moved out. We were drawn into the anti-apartheid movement, in particular the demonstrations around the South African rugby tour in 1979/80, though these were more muted and the police more prepared than in the 1970 protests. They centred on Twickenham and were led by a young South African, Peter Hain. Some local party purists baulked at a campaign led by someone who had recently headed the Young Liberals. There were also dire warnings from some of the councillors that the Liberals were up to no good and were beginning to pose a threat in the borough. But, given my history, I welcomed the crossover of identities and, indeed, welcomed the Lab–Lib cooperation in government, which I had advocated a decade earlier from a Liberal perspective.

The growing threat from the Liberals locally was not, however, allowed to intrude on an internal conflict over the future direction of the party. The easy-going sense of camaraderie was gradually eroded by ideological and sectarian strife. Discussions at party meetings, which had hitherto centred on the future of the local swimming pool or the unhealthy dominance of office blocks in the town centre, turned to the growing potential for working-class revolution in the leafy suburbs of Twickenham. There were passionate debates about which particular subset of the Labour movement would be in the vanguard of the local revolutionary struggle when it came. We spent one evening debating whether messages should be sent to the leaders of the USSR and China, whose border dispute was threatening to divide the forces of world socialism.

Somehow, otherwise intelligent and idealistic people led or joined the descent into collective madness. Those who led the Gadarene charge to the cliff were, as individuals, often delightful and reasonable. One, Elmo Eustace, had long been venerated for having met Trotsky in his youth, but his utterances gradually metamorphosed from amusing comedy into vitriolic rants, which set the local party line. Another militant, Duncan MacPherson, I came to know and like subsequently when he became a Catholic priest and officiated at the wedding of my son Paul. They acted as catalysts for a growing sense of anger and betrayal against the Labour government among many of the activists.

The more moderate people in the party found themselves increasingly isolated. The councillors, who were fighting a (doomed) struggle against the encroaching Liberals and the adverse demography that was breaking up working-class communities, would find themselves harangued at party meetings for their reactionary tendencies. A particular target was the council group leader, Geoffrey Samuel, the headmaster of a comprehensive school in a neighbouring borough, who, in due course, left the party for the SDP en route to the Conservatives, who elevated him to be one of their leading local figures. Another was the hapless party chairman who, despite his protestations of being a leftist and Tribunite, was made to stand and confess to the crime of having sent one of his children (on a scholarship) to a fee-paying school.

I watched these events with a mixture of alarm and bemusement, and a certain semi-detachment since I was, after I had left the Foreign Office, involved politically mainly at a national level. However, I stood for the council and came a bad third, to the rising Liberals, a fact that my Liberal Democrat friends locally have not allowed me to forget.

I was active in the Fabian Society and produced a pamphlet arguing the case against import controls and the Bennite 'alternative economic strategy'. I also applied for the parliamentary nomination in a series of marginal seats, mainly in London, in the run-up to the 1979 election, and gradually began to appreciate the nature of the opposition. At Hampstead – then thought (wrongly) to be highly winnable – I got off to a flying start and at packed meetings of members won the nomination of four of the seven wards against competition that included Tessa Jowell, Ken Livingstone and Reg Race, the future MP for Wood Green. My supporters warned, however, that, while I might have the support of the grass-roots membership in the biggest wards, this meant very little. My four wards accounted for only a minority of votes on the general management committee, where support was piling up, from trade union branches and the main activists, for Ken Livingstone. His supporters identified me as the candidate of the right, which was an unfamiliar and uncomfortable position after

Glasgow. It was pointed out that I had failed all the tests set by the left: an unequivocal commitment to troops out of Northern Ireland; uncompromising support for Clause 4; nationalization and unilateral nuclear disarmament; opposition to 'wage controls', incomes policy and all trade union reform. Ken Livingstone, in comparison, had emerged as the champion of the left, competing with Reg Race for the backing of the more extreme Trotskyite groups. Ken beat me, albeit narrowly, and his supporters included several from wards where I had received overwhelming backing from the members. When we meet now there is some mutual admiration and a lot of common ground, but then there was an unbridgeable ideological gulf.Although I was angry at the time, I acknowledged that I had been naive and had failed to learn the lesson from Maryhill that the ability to make a good speech and attract the support of the broad, if passive, membership was quite irrelevant. It was the activists who mattered and, across London, the activists were now firmly on the hard left. I was better organized a few weeks later in the Hornsey constituency, but the outcome was the same; the nomination went to Ted Knight, leader of Lambeth Council and a standard bearer of Militant. I tried a few more London seats, but it became clear that unless I was willing to adopt the agenda of the left I was wasting my time. I don't claim any particular virtue in this respect. Like Tony Blair a few years later, I would probably have put on a CND badge if I had thought it would work. But my card had already been marked.

I started to disengage from the Labour Party, and since Olympia had become pregnant again, I effectively opted out of politics to spend more time with her and on my work at the Overseas Development Institute. Then, out of the blue, in 1978 I was approached by Tom Harris, the private secretary of John

Smith, the newly promoted secretary of state for trade. He had heard me speak on trade and development issues and seen my Fabian pamphlet and thought I would be a good special adviser. Checks were made and I was recommended by mutual acquaintances from Scotland, including Judith Hart. The ODI generously agreed to let me go and to hold my job open for some time, should I have to return after the pending general election.

I was invited to a meeting with John in his room at the Commons, and he tried to establish where I stood on the political schisms in the party. He was clearly deeply troubled by the advance of the hard left and was himself strongly pro-Europe and pro-NATO. Asked if I saw myself as a 'social democrat' or a 'socialist', I replied the former, which was the answer he wanted. He himself was close to Callaghan, the prime minister, and saw the major political battleground in the party as the trade union movement, where he had strong allies in the moderate unions like the electricians, shopworkers, postmen, textile workers and the GMB. I sensed a disdain both for the left – embodied in Michael Meacher, then a Bennite, who had been appointed his minister of state – and for the some of the more dilettante characters on the right wing of the party, particularly David Owen. He approached every issue with great political astuteness, which brought him into conflict with the permanent secretary, Leo Pliatzky, a former Treasury mandarin who wanted a minister more attuned to the apolitical concerns of the department. It was to be my job to act as a corrective to the technocratic advice of the mandarins, and Pliatzky made it clear that I was unwelcome and a threat to his position.

I took up my post in the run-up to the Winter of Discontent, and throughout the winter it became clear that the moral authority and political credibility of the Callaghan government were melting away. There was that awful, and terminal, moment when Sunny Jim appeared on TV suntanned and full of cheer after a visit to the Caribbean, sheltered from the reality of uncleared rubbish and bodies piling up at the mortuaries. Yet John's approach was positive and he clearly intended to make maximum use of his last few months in office to make an impact.

Among the more politically sensitive issues in the department were worker participation in industry, where John was keen to make progress following the publication of the Bullock Report; the design of sanctions against South Africa; and the conclusion to the Tokyo Round of world trade talks. On the last our views diverged substantially, since I was instinctively for liberalization. He was more worried about union reaction and the industry lobbies that were demanding a stop to tariff cuts, particularly for textiles and paper. Seeing the textile industry lobby in action – then led by the man-made fibre producer ICI – I recognized the seductive appeal to ministers of companies flying the flag and, standing alongside their workforce, demanding help to save jobs. A generation later, companies like BAe Systems have the same grip on government. In the event, Britain's concerns over these items did not prevent a multilateral agreement being reached through the EU, and John Smith was able to claim credit both for the successful negotiations and for putting up a fight for British industry.

In the last weeks of the government he made a serious effort, through his contacts in the union movement, to help me secure one of the parliamentary seats becoming available. But with Olympia seeking to manage a two-month-old baby and two other children, I was preoccupied and not able to follow up his offers of help. My political career in the Labour Party eventually ended in farce. After a lot of spadework had been done to help me secure a winning position at a selection meeting for a marginal Derbyshire seat, the family van gave up on the M1 ten miles from its destination and I eventually arrived too late to participate. After the crushing Labour defeat a few weeks later I parted from John Smith on good terms, but subsequently lost contact.

John Smith has, since his death, become a much-revered figure in Labour circles: the lost leader who would never have betrayed the soul of the party as Blair has done. Most of the compliments are, I think, merited. He was, indeed, very gifted politically and had a lawyer's talent for quickly assimilating a complex brief. He was also a conviction politician who represented the best aspects of the Labour Party's commitment to social justice. He was convivial and personally warm and approachable. What I have never understood, however, is his recent status as an icon of the left. In Labour Party terms he was firmly of the 'old right', patriotic (both in a Scottish and a British sense), respectful of law and tradition, and with a practical rather than ideological approach to policy. A misjudgement as shadow Chancellor in the 1992 election in not appreciating the unpopularity of higher direct taxes on middle-class voters is what he is now remembered for, by critics and admirers alike; but I sense that, given the chance to return to government, he would have been solidly centrist, albeit with less dependence on the slick, polished media-management skills of Blair's New Labour.

I saw the next three years of mounting strife in the Labour Party from a distance, being immersed in fatherhood and the controversies of overseas development. Links with some of the local

Labour activists were also strained by a personal decision over our children's schooling, which was a subject that aroused the righteous indignation of party activists like no other (and still does). Our eldest son Paul had been at the local primary school and we planned to send him to one of the two local comprehensive schools, while encouraging his considerable musical talent, as a violinist and pianist, through one of the London colleges of music. As the decision time approached, we were alarmed to discover that Paul, who has his mother's dark colouring, had been subjected to racial bullying by a gang that was heading for one of the two schools. Paul has an equable temperament and was not given to complaining, so when he did protest strongly we ruled out his going to that particular school. I attended the parents' open day for the other on the assumption that it had become our choice by default. The headteacher gave a speech on what a happy place he presided over, but was extremely coy about its academic achievements. I discovered that the previous year not a single child in the school had managed an O level in a science subject or a modern language. When I asked to speak to a head of department about this deficiency I was confronted by a character modelled on Dave Spart from *Private Eye* who harangued me on the subject of pushy middle-class parents obsessed by 'irrelevant' exam results. I am normally too polite and non-confrontational in such situations, but on this occasion I lost my cool, walked out, and resolved on the spot to look at other options outside the state sector.

Olympia regarded comprehensive schools without enthusiasm, having taught in them in surrounding boroughs as an occasional supply teacher and been appalled by the poor standards of discipline and low aspirations. As the product of a racially

segregated comprehensive in Kenya, she had no emotional investment in comprehensive schools. But she saw no way in which our
parlous finances would extend to private education. Nonetheless,
following my abrupt U-turn, our somewhat bewildered son was
asked at short notice to sit entrance exams for a couple of local
former direct-grant grammar schools, which had recently gone
private following Anthony Crosland's attempts to end selection.
He passed comfortably and at Hampton School he was offered a
music scholarship to cover half the fees. Any reservations I might
have had on the issue of principle were dissipated by meeting
the headmaster, a brilliant and inspirational educationalist called
Gavin Alexander, who was later to become a leading figure and
councillor for the SDP and then the Liberal Democrats. I took
on extra consultancy work to pay the balance of the fees and
we joined the middle-class exodus from the state system. Our
daughter Aida was equally bright and, encouraged by her mother,
was strongly feminist by the age of eleven and sought parity of
treatment with her brother. A year later she won a competitive
place at the Lady Eleanor Holles School, also in Hampton, whose
headteacher made no bones about her wish to see what was then
an obscure academic school eventually achieving parity with St
Paul's Girls, Roedean and Cheltenham Ladies' College (as it now
has).

Having become an unreconstructed class traitor in the eyes
of some of the comrades in the local Labour Party, I then compounded the treachery in the convulsions that overtook the party
in 1981. My initial reaction to the SDP breakaway was negative.
The SDP seemed to me unlikely to succeed and would further
weaken opposition to Mrs Thatcher's government, which was
becoming cordially hated in the wake of a recession. I felt more

comfortable with mainstream Labour figures like John Smith and Denis Healey, who had elected to stay, than with Roy Jenkins and David Owen. But the SDP acquired a momentum of its own as moderate elements in the Labour Party departed and the hard left seemed more than ever to be exercising a stranglehold, causing a further wave of defections. It is quite possible that had I stayed in Glasgow I would have remained in the Labour Party, but in the more polarized and febrile environment of London Labour parties few moderate people stayed behind. People I knew and respected drifted away or were pushed out. George Cunningham, for example, an independent-minded Labour MP who lived locally but represented an Islington seat, was forced out by a militant faction around Mrs Margaret Hodge. Local SDP defectors repeatedly called round to our house to appeal to me to join them and in the autumn I took the plunge, though not without some regret.

Civil wars divide friends and create strange new bedfellows. This one was no exception. The local SDP was a mixture of disillusioned Labour activists, a handful of ex-Tories, and a group of previously apolitical people who had been stirred out of apathy and indifference by the excitement of a serious new party being launched. The latter group in particular were very hard work, often having little clue about the basics of campaigning and a touching faith in the ability of new slogans and new faces to open up a short cut to national power.

An early task was to work with the local Liberals, who had made spectacular advances in the borough with their own brand of grass-roots community campaigning. Their leaders, David (now Sir David) Williams and Tim (now Lord) Razzall, were tough political professionals who were running rings round the stuffy, complacent local Tories and the beleaguered, retreating Labour Party. I think they saw the SDP as an irritating distraction but were smart enough to appreciate the Steel–Jenkins argument that the SDP was bringing in a new batch of recruits. They agreed a seat-sharing arrangement for the forthcoming 1982 council elections, which involved allocating SDP candidates predominantly to wards held by Conservatives, which would be won in a landslide but not otherwise. I was co-opted into the SDP team to stand in Hampton, then a Conservative seat but with an outside chance for the new Alliance. The only memorable feature of the campaign, which grouped me with two Liberals, Maureen Woodriffe and John Ison, was an unfortunately designed orange poster reading 'Cable Is on Woodriffe', which became a source of mirth in the Hampton hostelries.

The expected election landslide never happened, thanks to General Galtieri. A patriotic mood swept Hampton and the Conservative vote held up despite a deluge of leaflets, although the Alliance made gains overall and took over the council a year later after a by-election.

I was much more interested in the national scene and started to look for a seat to fight for the expected 1983 election, when the strength of the new Alliance would be tested for the first time. The candidates' circuit included future parliamentary colleagues, including Chris Huhne, but also some, like Polly Toynbee, Roger Liddle and Derek Scott, who later rejoined Blair's Labour Party. What really grabbed my attention was the candidacy for York. York was spoken of (without any evidence, as it turned out) as a place where the Alliance could be expected to 'come through the middle' from third place and was designated as a target seat. It was allocated to the SDP, though with bitter opposition from the local Liberals, as I later found to my cost.

My reasons for applying for the York seat were personal and sentimental as much as political. My father had died the previous year (in 1981) and I felt the need to visit my widowed mother more frequently, alone and lonely in the detached house in White House Gardens that had been the scene of my break from my parents over a decade earlier. In an emotional way, which I could never properly analyse, I felt drawn back to the city. I had a romantic notion of returning in triumph as its MP and believed that, for all our differences, my father would have been proud of me. Olympia would rather I had chosen somewhere closer, but indulged me, suspecting that my chances of being elected, and the consequent danger of prolonged family disruption, were not high.

One major reservation was that Alex Lyon, the sitting MP, was someone I knew and liked. He was a very decent man with a strong moral purpose and was, politically, closer to Methodism than to Marx; indeed, he was a lay preacher. I had worked hard in his winning 1966 campaign in York. By coincidence, his London home with his wife Hilda was a couple of hundred yards from ours in Twickenham, and I was frequently dispatched by the local branch to collect his subs and donations to local fund-raisers. As minister of state at the Home Office from 1974 to 1976 he had fallen out badly with Callaghan over immigration policy, not sharing the Labour leader's eagerness to placate the white working class, and over Northern Ireland, where he expressed sympathy for the nationalist movement. His rebellion coincided, and was linked in the public mind, with divorce from Hilda and remarriage to his former Home Office private secretary, Clare Short, who was later to become a major figure in her own right. His reputation in York took a battering and he was regarded as highly vulnerable in what was already a very marginal seat. I persuaded myself that I, not the Conservatives, would defeat him and maintain a progressive tradition in the city. My conceit was reinforced by assuming my superiority over the Conservative candidate, one Conal Gregory, a wine merchant who had no connection to the city at all, parroted party slogans like a speaking machine, and was regarded by friends and foes alike as dim – a judgement that was to prove seriously complacent.

Such was my level of self-belief and optimism that I wowed the York SDP – which had one of the largest memberships in the country – and they adopted me with an enthusiasm that reinforced my own. I acquired the most highly motivated and talented group of volunteers I have ever worked with, led by a York University academic, Ann Feinstein, wife of the economic historian, the late Charles Feinstein. She had a rare combination of brilliant organizing skills, political acumen and personal niceness that made our campaign professional, well funded and enjoyable.

As candidate, my first task was to understand and communicate our party message. The difficulty I had in doing so was the exact opposite of that facing the Liberal Democrats in recent years. It has been a genuine problem for the Liberal Democrats to say something distinctive and interesting when both leading parties are trampling all over the 'centre ground'. In 1983 neither Conservatives nor Labour had any interest in the centre ground. There was plenty of room for a moderate, centre party arguing for a mixed economy and a sensible blend of free enterprise and social justice. The difficulty was that, in a country with strong tribal politics, a third party was an unfamiliar idea, and we mangled the communication of it by presenting not one party but two, with different leaders and symbols and messy internal disputes on the ground.

There were, indeed, serious local problems, which even the most optimistic among my team found difficult to conceal. The liberal-inclined intellectuals centred on the university who flocked to the SDP represented a tiny fraction of York's population, which had a large, traditional working-class Labour vote in the big council estates and what was still in 1983 a strong manufacturing base of chocolate factories and railway carriage works. The Conservatives were also still deeply embedded in the city, thanks to years of campaigning by a highly motivated army of enthusiasts like my late father. The Thatcherite message that Britain's prolonged, humiliating national decline required shock therapy and radical measures had considerable resonance among frightened lower-middle-class voters; and the promised sale of council houses also drove a Tory wedge into the council estates. The university actually lay outside the (then) city boundaries, and the mobile, educated professional classes who were attracted to the SDP mostly lived in the rapidly growing suburbs in the constituencies of Harrogate and Ryedale.

More seriously, our fledgling Alliance was deeply and irreconcilably split. The Liberals had begun to win council seats in the city through community politics and refused to accept the allocation of York to the SDP. Their leader, Steve Galloway, was a hard-working and tenacious activist who had already become lord mayor of the city and had expected to fight the parliamentary seat. Even by the standards of a party with more than its share of bloody-minded individualists, he was (and, I understand, remains) in a league of his own. In my five years of campaigning in the city he refused to meet me, despite many overtures, withdrew all cooperation in Liberal-held wards, and made it clear to the local press that I and the SDP were unwelcome interlopers in his fiefdom. He attracted and repelled support in equal measure, and over twenty years later led the Lib Dems to victory in district council elections but then made mistakes that led to them being swept out again shortly afterwards.

Despite these handicaps, a local poll six months out, commissioned by the local press, showed York to be a three-way marginal, with Labour struggling under Michael Foot's leadership and, even after the Falklands victory, Mrs Thatcher far from universally loved. There seemed to be everything to play for and a real prospect of victory. The SDP should have won a by-election in Darlington in the run-up to the general election but failed to make a breakthrough and some of the sense of pre-election momentum was dissipated.

When the election came, however, there was real excitement and expectation around our campaign. The city had been used to two-party parliamentary campaigns for as long as anyone could remember and this was something different. SDP heavyweights came to town. Roy Jenkins spoke with me at a packed rally in the De Grey Rooms and was clearly excited and moved by the emotional intensity, the heckling and the enthusiasm. Shirley Williams attracted an enormous number to the market square but unfortunately caught the wrong train to York and eventually turned up after the longest hour and a half I have ever spent, trying to humour an increasingly restive crowd. Bill Rodgers came twice. I emerged the clear winner of a big public debate in the Guildhall, at which Alex Lyon was defensive and uncomfortable and the Conservative, Conal Gregory, provoked a constant stream of unintended laughter. I was helped by a wonderful picture of my photogenic eleven-year-old daughter surrounded by railwaymen at the carriage works, wearing SDP stickers and splashed across the front of the *Evening Press*.

On the doorsteps, I went from one emotional reunion to another: ex-school friends and teachers; my father's numerous admiring pupils; distant relatives I had last met in childhood; former girlfriends. On one unforgettable evening of door-knocking, I met and achieved a family reconciliation with my aunt Evie, the widow of my father's brother. She was suffering terribly, coping with the last violent and uncontrollable stages of my adopted cousin's Huntington's disease. This woman, whom I had been brought up to regard as the devil incarnate and as an overbearing, intolerable snob, was now totally broken with the burden of care and the humiliation of regular beatings from her once angelic son, trapped in his dying, uncontrollable body. Politics brought us together and made us laugh; she was a life-long socialist, which she had kept a secret from the Cable family, but on this occasion she would break the habit of a lifetime and vote for her nephew.

The cold political reality was that I was suffering from acute candidatitis, with a wildly inflated sense of what I could achieve personally. But it sustained my confidence and energy, and was one of the few parliamentary campaigns that I have actually enjoyed. Deep down I did not expect to win. But then in the last few days, the Labour vote started to collapse. Particularly in the working-class areas there was a big switch from Labour to the Alliance as people made up their minds in response to the national campaign. I also had one final stroke of luck. Canvassing on a council estate, accompanied by local journalists and a photographer, I encountered a boy with blood pouring from what looked like a severed artery in his arm, with a crowd looking on helplessly. With the application of simple first aid, I stemmed the flow of blood and was able to return the boy safely to his parents. This earned me press publicity candidates would normally die for, three days out from the election.

Of course, it wasn't enough. Despite doubling the third-party vote, I came third with 13,523 votes to Alex Lyon's 20,662 and the Conservatives' 24,309. In the cold light of day it was impossible to avoid the conclusion that embittered Labour activists had already drawn: that our – my – intervention had helped an unpleasant Tory defeat a basically decent Labour MP. But Labour's wounds were largely self-inflicted, added to the perverse consequences of a first-past-the-post voting system. And I believed that, if we could get so near with a third of the city effectively off-limits because of Liberal non-cooperation, a full-blooded united campaign would have come close to victory. With a mixture of pride and regret, achievement and disappointment, I returned to normal family life in London and to a new job as an international civil servant working for Sonny Ramphal and the Commonwealth secretariat. I sensed that the best opportunity I had had, and ever would have, to win a parliamentary seat had gone and that I should be realistic and settle for a different career.

I then made one of the worst misjudgements of my years in politics. After a year or more of procrastination, I allowed my name to go forward for the York seat again, this time in an open competitive selection against Steve Galloway. Some of my old SDP team flattered me into believing that I was an outstanding candidate and utterly indispensable. Nor did they wish to see Steve win the nomination after his petulant behaviour in 1983. I persuaded myself that it would be a useful way to keep in regular touch with my mother, now in sheltered accommodation. In reality, I had become an addict needing a regular fix of applause and publicity.

The easy bit was the selection meeting: a packed hall in the Quaker Meeting House. Although there were more Liberals than Social Democrats, Steve had plenty of enemies and I had speaking skills that he could not match. The rational part of me wanted to lose and acknowledge that it made far more sense to have a full-time candidate, however egotistical and wayward, than someone who would come for a few hours every few weeks. But I won.

It was downhill from then on. Steve, and most of the Liberals, again decided to boycott the campaign. My core team had either left, like Ann Feinstein, or lost their enthusiasm. Olympia needed support at home and my visits to York became more infrequent, resulting in minimal press publicity and further demoralization among the troops. The local press, and my opponents, realized that I was just going through the motions. One of the few things working for me was the personality of David Owen, who visited the city several times and who, despite a bored and disdainful manner, helped me to raise the profile of my flagging campaign.

When the election came in 1987, I struggled to find an agent until Walter Rich, one of the Quakers in our membership, agreed to act. We battled to get out literature. The month preceding the election day was bitterly cold and the volunteers shivered in an unheated campaign office. The national campaign went badly, with the two Davids sending out different signals and conveying to the public an image of disunity, which I knew all too well reflected the reality on the ground. Labour were altogether less shambolic than in 1983, with glossy literature, a softer, more moderate message and a plausible new candidate in York, Hugh Bayley. One of the ironic footnotes of the campaign was that in monocultural, monochromatic York, he and I both had multiracial families – his black, mine Asian – though I don't think our wives ever met.

Unlike 1983, the campaign provided no pleasure. I became ever more conscious that my personal links with the city were now very tenuous, as friends and relatives had died or moved away, factories closed and new, unrecognizable developments changed the landscape. I nonetheless felt a real sense of humility among people who were willing to back me wholeheartedly even through such a dismal and half-hearted campaign. Although my vote dropped back to under 10,000, it didn't fall far enough to help Labour recapture the city. After failing by a few hundred votes, Hugh Bayley had to wait another five years to take the seat, and the people of York were left with the dreadful Conal Gregory. I had nothing to show for five years of trying, albeit with diminishing zeal. I found it difficult to believe I would ever contest another election, or deserve to.

Far worse was to come. The family went on a week's break to the Lake District to help me overcome the disappointment and to plan together all the things we would do together to make up for the time I had spent shuttling to and from York. The weather and the setting of our holiday accommodation in the village of Hawkshead were perfect. We started to enjoy an idyllic holiday. Then Olympia became uneasily aware of a small lump in her breast. We reassured each other that it was almost certainly benign, but feared the worst. Our GP and the consultant to whom he referred Olympia at the Royal Marsden were optimistic, not least because she manifested none of the hereditary or environmental factors that underlie breast cancer. The biopsy, however, was positive; she would need urgent surgery and radiotherapy.

That evening, sitting together in a hospital ward absorbing the news, alternately crying and cuddling, is forever embedded in my memory. The previous twenty years of our married life had been buoyed up by the optimistic belief that we could handle any crisis, however difficult. There had been highs and lows, as in any relationship, and differences, but we had absorbed them, always looking onwards and upwards. The idea of mortality and physical decay was something new and shocking, and we struggled to come to terms with it. Whatever the advances in medical science, then and since, cancer was seen as a death sentence. My first task was to communicate all of this to the children waiting at home. In the event, they made things easy for me. They had already figured out what the problem was, and the prognosis, and were trying to reassure me, rather than me them.

Olympia's battle against cancer dominated the next fourteen years of our married life. The first round of treatment was not totally effective, so she needed a second. But after that she was pronounced to be in remission and equipped with a new drug, tamoxifen, which gave reasonable prospects of survival. Olympia's positive outlook on life reasserted itself and she resolved to live and enjoy each day as it came, in particular expanding her private practice as a piano teacher and supporting the progress of our children. Paul had by now won a place to read music at Cambridge; Aida was embarking on A levels; and Hugo, the youngest, then eight years old, was developing a prodigious talent in maths and a passionate interest in complex models and electronics. I drastically scaled back any travelling in order to be at home as much as possible. We immersed ourselves in new interests like ballroom and Latin dancing classes and even took exams.

Politics receded into the distance and I followed the traumas of the Liberal–SDP merger with detachment and incomprehension. After five years of trying to manage a divided campaign, it seemed blindingly obvious to me that the two-party Alliance model wasn't working and that a unified structure was required. The bitter disagreements I had encountered had precious little to do with ideology and everything to do with personal vanities and ambitions and the protection of turf. I had greatly admired David Owen's brilliant communication skills on television and his instinctively good judgements on big issues. But I had never much warmed to the man, and his self-indulgent conduct over the merger was, I thought, unforgivable. But beyond making a strong recommendation to the SDP members in York and Twickenham to vote for merger, I was not involved. I was baffled as much as angry that, with public opinion inflamed over Mrs Thatcher's poll tax and the Labour Party still far from providing a credible alternative (despite Neil Kinnock's impressive and courageous efforts), my own party should be tearing itself to bits instead of making political hay. This unholy mess contributed, as it had a decade earlier, to my becoming emotionally disengaged from politics, and I regarded myself as retired and redundant.

But, as happened in 1979 with the call from John Smith's office, another telephone call brought me out of retirement. An American friend from the local SDP, Malinda McLean, rang to tell me that there was now a vacancy in Twickenham for a candidate for the Liberal and Social Democrat Party (as we called ourselves). The sitting candidate, John Waller, had stood three times and, after bringing the Tory majority down to 4792 in 1983, had seen it go back up to 7127 in the 1987 election. He had become exhausted by the effort and his IT business was suffering. The sight of Lib Dem poll ratings in single figures, barely above the margin of statistical error, had, I think, persuaded him that further struggle was hopeless and a waste of time and money.

My initial assessment was similarly dismissive and I was loath to inflict more upheaval on my family. But Olympia persuaded me to think more positively. I had spent much of our married life dabbling in politics, in York at a distance, but here at last was an opportunity to work together in a campaign on our doorstep. She did not want to deal with her illness by sitting around feeling like an invalid but by living life to the full, and this was an opportunity to become seriously engaged along with me in local community issues.

Further reflection suggested that the position was not as hopeless as it seemed in the gloomy aftermath of the 1987 election. After all, Lib Dems were represented on the council in every ward in the constituency following a landslide victory in the 1986 local elections, though we knew it would be difficult to translate local into national votes. The Labour Party had been virtually wiped out and the Lib Dems would be the only plausible local alternative to the Tories once disillusionment with them seriously set in. The local Tory MP, Toby Jessel, was described, kindly, as a 'character' and had undoubted talents – but as a pianist, not a politician. His embarrassing gaffes were valuable ammunition for any half-competent campaign. Winning the seat was a long shot, but not impossible, and I decided to go for it.

I was not greatly loved by the Liberal establishment in the borough, who remembered me as a Labour opponent and were not impressed by my prolonged absences from borough politics. But in the event no local councillor thought it worth their while pursuing the parliamentary seat. I was the only local applicant and won the nomination quite comfortably.

The situation in Twickenham was in many respects the mirror image of that in York. In York my team and I had had inflated expectations, not justified by the political fundamentals. In Twickenham the problem was one of low expectations, despite it being a genuinely winnable seat. In the Borough of Richmond, Twickenham was the poor relation to Richmond both politically and socially: more marginal, with fewer of the leading local political lights, and less glamorous,

I was, however, fortunate in two respects. Shortly after I was selected, the party nationally, now under Paddy Ashdown, started to show signs of life. There was a morale-boosting by-election victory in Eastbourne. Mrs Thatcher's reign was coming acrimoniously to an end and there were growing numbers of disillusioned Conservatives looking for a home, provided it wasn't Labour. Paddy's military background and bearing were beginning to have an appeal to this group. And, locally, I began to assemble an enthusiastic group of helpers, led by my future agent, Dee Doocey, a local councillor with formidable organizing ability and a steely determination to succeed. She brought to bear a professionalism that contrasted painfully with the easy-going amateurism the party was used to and led to not a little friction. We had our differences, but our political partnership, more than any other single factor, took Twickenham from the category of also-rans to the front rank of Lib Dem seats. Malinda gave massive and unstinting support. Olympia organized two highly successful fund-raising events – a curry supper and a classical music concert – which helped to galvanize our activists and put her at the centre of a network of volunteers. Aida managed to get a youth branch organized. There was a palpable sense of optimism and purpose and the once remote possibility of winning now seemed less distant.

When the 1992 election came, the expected collapse in Conservative support failed to materialize, despite a sharp recession, growing home repossessions and negative equity. There was a mood to give John Major a chance and a lot of worry about Labour's high-tax alternative which swamped the impact of all our local work. We cut the Conservative majority from 7127 to 4901, which seemed scant reward for an upbeat and extremely well-marshalled campaign. The following day, however, the full significance sank in: we had advanced, while in Richmond and other target seats around London the party had gone backwards. It became clear that Twickenham was now the prime target seat in London and could expect maximum help. A boundary change would also assist us. When the Conservative tide finally went out, we were well placed to benefit.

After the years of toil and frustration, it now seemed, in the run-up to my fiftieth birthday, that there was finally a realistic prospect of a breakthrough and that I merely needed to plug away steadily over the next few years. Would that it had been so simple. Twickenham became a honeypot for other ambitious Lib Dem politicians and I had to fight to remain as candidate, while at the same time Olympia's health began to deteriorate in an alarming way. That long interlude before winning the 1997 election proved as difficult as any I had previously experienced.

After several years of tamoxifen, Olympia had been pronounced clear of breast cancer and she was advised to stop taking
further doses. I am not sure if this advice was inspired by medical science or by cost-consciousness in the NHS, but she felt she
should act on the advice. In any event, a couple of years later
the symptoms returned and after a further operation and radiotherapy, Olympia was told that the cancer had spread and had
reached her bones. Any hope that the illness was curable evaporated and we recognized that it was now only a matter of time.
The corridors and smells of the Royal Marsden became increasingly familiar. She had increased breathing difficulties and it was
eventually realized that a lung had collapsed. A further operation
reattached the lung to the chest wall, and for the rest of her life I
had to assist her twice a day to pump fluid from the lung with the
help of a device inserted in the side of her body.

She insisted on giving priority to our children, particularly
Hugo, who was now at St Paul's. She feared she would not survive
to see him beyond school. And she kept up her music as far as
possible, although the collapsed lung meant she could no longer
sing and her piano-playing was hampered by the damage done
by the excision of lymph glands. She needed practical and psychological support, which I tried to provide as best I could while
holding down a demanding job, now as chief economist, at Shell.

Politics took third place, to the mounting alarm of my friends
and allies in the local party. I realized too late that growing numbers of aspiring Liberal Democrat MPs were eyeing up the seat
and reports were circulating that the incumbent candidate was
not serious or no good. The presumed formality of confirming
my name on the list of approved candidates proved anything
but a formality and I spent a year fighting appeals in party

committees. At one point I was removed from the list of candidates, having supposedly failed a test on how to write a press release (it transpired that I had 'failed' for having forgotten to put a date on it). I developed a strong belief in conspiracy theories, but in my serious moments I realized that my job with Shell and my Labour background jarred badly with the grass-roots activists who controlled the process.

As an approved candidate my readoption by the local party should have been a formality; but a shoal of impressive competitors emerged, including Dick (now Lord) Newby, Sarah Ludford (now an MEP), Neil Sherlock, a rising star of the party and close to Paddy Ashdown, and Ed Davey, another rising star. The intense competition revealed personal hostilities and fault-lines in the local party which had lain dormant in the 1992 campaign. It became clear that I was in considerable danger of losing until a belated rescue operation was organized by Dee and Malinda. I won the selection by a handful of votes over Ed Davey and was saved from extinction by a battalion of elderly ladies brought in by a close ally and friend, Lisette Narain. Her remarkable personal history merits a book in itself. She had been a political and Christian refugee in Kemalist Turkey, where her father, a politician, had been murdered; then a nurse in the Gaza Strip; and latterly a local councillor; and, like us, she was part of a happy mixed marriage. It was deeply humbling to discover that friends and allies were willing to fight my corner for me, the more so as I was unable to explain the reason for my dependence on them.

One of the continuing awkwardnesses was that Olympia was determined not to disclose her illness. She was an immensely proud, as well as courageous, woman and could not accept being patronized or treated as sick. Not only the party activists but her own brothers and sisters were not to be told. I was obliged, therefore, to spin innumerable white lies to explain her prolonged disappearances and my own sudden absences and below-par performances. There were fearful rows with Dee and Malinda, who felt they were giving their all for a candidate who seemed less than fully committed and whose wife was only spasmodically involved. Whether they and others guessed the truth, I do not know, but the years leading up to the 1997 election weighed heavily on all of us. I came close to giving up on several occasions, but like a marathon runner approaching the finishing tape, I found it easier to stagger on than collapse.

When the election came, it was clear that nationally as well as locally a massive sea-change was under way. Dee's campaign was meticulously organized; Twickenham became the focal point for Lib Dem campaigns across London; and well before election day Toby Jessel was looking forlorn and defeated. The electoral avalanche swept away not just Toby Jessel but also the Conservatives in Richmond and Kingston, where Ed Davey won by fifty-six votes, and the two Sutton seats.

Olympia and I returned home in the early hours after the count, elated but exhausted. We were painfully conscious that I had finally achieved, at no little cost, both emotionally and financially, what I had set out to do over a quarter of a century earlier, but that her own life was now ebbing away.

Chapter 11

Political Triumph and Personal Tragedy

The first of May 1997 is remembered by everyone with even a passing interest in politics as the end of an era and the dawn of a new government laden with high expectations. Across the country there were minor excitements within the bigger drama, including the twenty or so Lib Dem gains: some beyond any reasonable expectation, in Kingston, Torbay and Carshalton; others, like the defeat of Norman Lamont in Harrogate, emblematic of the peaceful revolution of the night.

Set against these tumultuous events, the result in Twickenham was a little anticlimactic. Well before the end it was clear that we were going to win. There was a growing groundswell of support on the doorsteps and in the streets. The only rancour came from local Labour party activists, former comrades of fifteen years earlier, who had wanted to share in the New Labour triumph and bitterly resented a successful local application of the third-party squeeze which had long been inflicted on the Lib Dems in most parts of Britain. Tactical voting had been a key part of our campaign. I was the 'anybody but Conservative' candidate. When the results were in there was a convincing majority of over four thousand, which was a relief and a source of great pride to my team but it was dwarfed in significance by events elsewhere.

To have become an MP at the fifth attempt, twenty-seven years after my first attempt, was just a little too much to take in at first. I was convinced of the reality of it by the delight and pride of my family, which had shared the long years of frustration and disappointment. Becoming an MP by defeating an opponent is not, however, like taking on an ordinary job. There is no training, no handover, no infrastructure, no office, no staff; yet there are a thousand thank-you letters to write and a deluge of requests for help, advice, jobs or opinions. Exhaustion was made worse by abusive anonymous late-night phone calls from people who thought that I had committed an act worse than murder by removing their Tory MP.

Olympia and I tackled this new challenge as a joint project. She was by now considerably weakened. She realized that her time was limited and decided to use the last few years of her life assisting me and the three children. She helped me hire staff and premises, and organize surveys of local businesses and young people, as much as time would allow. But we also wanted time together and every day for a couple of years we tried to manage a walk in Twickenham by the river, or in Richmond or Bushy Park. This took precedence over other commitments, and my frequent disappearances from meetings and other parliamentary activities became a source of some disquiet to my staff and colleagues, who were not allowed to know the reason why.

Gradually some sort of order and system emerged, despite the handicap of working from an improvised office in Twickenham with a leaking roof and extremes of hot and cold. I came to appreciate that the key to being a good MP is good staff. After several false starts, I acquired superb staff for my Twickenham office, who have been with me ever since led by Joan Bennett, my PA and

Sandra Foyle, my case-worker. Together with Malinda McLean, my main party helper and supporter, and Dee Doocey, my agent, I had a rich, solid base, without which I believe no MP can function effectively.

The public perception of MPs and politicians in general was low, even before the recent expenses scandal rocked Parliament, though I have never found that the generality is applied to the particular. The problem is not so much one of hostility and disapproval as of ignorance and confusion. Even those who are well informed find it difficult to see the demarcation lines between local councillors and MPs (let alone MEPs and regional assembly members). As a Lib Dem MP in a borough with a Lib Dem council I have been widely assumed to be the Godfather who controls the parking wardens, approves house extensions, and ensures that the bins are emptied. MPs of all parties are assumed to be 'part of the government' and to have great 'power'. Because Parliament passes laws, MPs must have responsibility for the rulings of every judge or magistrate and have the ability to overturn court rulings. Our expenses to pay staff are assumed to inflate our salaries to fat-cat proportions. Elections are a particular mystery: I have spent hours in expensive houses, whose walls are lined with the world's great literature, trying without success to explain that general election votes do not go into a giant pot to choose the prime minister, but merely choose the local MP.

MPs are partly responsible for the fact that they are misunderstood. They rarely take the trouble to explain what they do; they claim credit for what others do; they blame others for things they are responsible for and compound the confusion by apologizing for things they are *not* responsible for. The categorization of MPs as 'good (or bad) constituency members' or 'good (or bad) parliamentarians' doesn't clarify anything very much. I would break the job down into a variety of distinct roles: representing and helping individual constituents through casework; being a 'local champion'; holding government to account through questioning in Parliament and select committees or by contributions to debate; legislating; issue-based campaigning; and being a party spokesman or member of the government. No MP can sensibly aim to do all of these, certainly not simultaneously, though some try. Some specialize completely. Some are lazy and do very little of anything beyond turning up to vote when required by the party whips. Those with small majorities, like mine initially, subsume all these various tasks under a constant preoccupation with being re-elected.

Within a week or so of becoming an MP I had my first queue at a constituency surgery. Most of my visitors really needed help or advice from a lawyer, the Citizens' Advice Bureau, a social worker, a local councillor or a police officer, but had been advised to see the local MP or else were curious to see the new man. My first customers (Mr and Mrs A) gave me a lengthy and indignant account of the insults, abuse and threats of their neighbours (Mr and Mrs B). I was sufficiently concerned to mobilize the police, the council and anyone else I could think of. A few weeks later Mr B came with a long and indignant account of the insults, abuse and threats inflicted on his family by Mr and Mrs A. I soon discovered that hundreds of hours of police, council officials' and MP's time had been absorbed by this dispute, which defied mediation and court injunctions and only ended years later when the B family finally gave up and left. A few weeks later I was drawn into another epic dispute between neighbours, this time with anti-Semitic overtones, between two families who claimed to be lifelong supporters of my party and were both incredulous that I should want to know the other side of the story. In quiet suburban streets there are often such murderous, all-absorbing, quarrels which have outlasted many wars. One that remains with me is a twenty-five-year-old dispute about an overhanging tree which pits one of my elderly party members against another equally elderly supporter. As an MP I am cast in the role of King Solomon.

My second client was an intense man who brought his files in a suitcase and told me ominously that my predecessor had failed to solve his problems over twenty years and he expected me to do better. After several months of correspondence concerning his unbelievably complicated claim for compensation from the MoD over a patent, I discovered that his patent was for 'an invisible battleship'. Following a lurid account of an MI5 plot to kill him, I realized, more slowly than I should have done, that he suffered from delusions.

The third in line was a Chinese man in exotic clothes and so camp and perfumed that his gender was in some doubt. He turned out to be the former gay lover of a local celebrity whose will was subject to a ferocious dispute with a local charity, which believed that the substantial inheritance was intended for a museum rather than for the Chinese lover. Responding to his requests for assistance I managed to alienate, in my first week as an MP, the whole cultural establishment of Twickenham. The relationship took a long time to rebuild.

Then there was a trader involved in a legal dispute with a leading bank which was pursuing him for an outstanding debt. It was clear to him, and to me, that the bank had made a mistake, and that a clerk had forged a signature to cover it up. He went from court to court, piling up unpayable legal costs. Bankruptcy and business failure loomed, but he insisted on fighting. Week after week he came, tears in his eyes, to plead with me to petition judges and legislate to change the law in his favour and rectify British injustice. Many such cases have come my way, and since my constituents can rarely afford legal fees I have perforce become an unqualified amateur lawyer, like most MPs.

There have been thousands of people over the years with genuine problems, many of them heartbreaking, some of whom I have been able to help. The biggest number are the immigration cases, mostly people whose papers have been stuck for years in a queue in the Home Office and who hope the MP can get an answer. There are undoubtedly some illegal immigrants cynically using every legal dodge and contact they can identify to regularize their status. But from my experience most are decent, honest people trapped somewhere in a Kafkaesque world between a country that they have long since abandoned or fled from and another that has lost their papers, or kept them in enforced idleness without permission to work, or passed them from one appeal or queue to another. And there are hundreds of long-standing Asian residents whose relatives back home are anxious to visit for a wedding or a funeral or to see their grandchildren, but who cannot complete the obstacle course created for them by British entry-clearance procedures.

The next biggest category are the young, mostly white, couples with young children in desperately overcrowded social housing, or else facing homelessness because their parents or friends can no longer cope with them sleeping on the settee, or because they are falling behind with their rent due to some muddle in housing benefit. There is often little that can be done to help because there is no housing available, they have insufficient 'points', or because of some procedural error they have made themselves 'intentionally homeless'. They will leave me angry and frustrated, and themselves blaming the council or 'the immigrants', as they head for family break-up or worse.

The constituency caseload is one of the core elements of MPs' work, and the best way to understand how central government legislation, local bureaucracy and markets impact on the public. I do not share the view that MPs should not be involved in 'social work', the inference being that this is a waste of time that should be spent on the benches in Parliament. I have become a firm convert to the view that electoral reform, when it happens, must retain this constituency link with individual voters.

The constituency link gives MPs their second role, as 'local champions'. Before becoming an MP I had little understanding of or involvement in local social activities. Life had revolved around family and work. Twickenham was where we lived: a commuter town and shopping centre, not a community. Olympia had once tried to become involved in the local arts world, but the conservative, middle-class women who dominated it had made it abundantly clear that they did not welcome a clever, argumentative Indian who upset their racial stereotypes by singing and playing Bach and Mozart rather well. We retreated into a laager of family and friends. Local party activists whose lives revolved around church, council, Scouts, charity fairs and school governorships found our lack of engagement troubling.

Everything changed the day I became an MP. Doors opened. Charities asked to me to be their patron. My wife, who had hitherto been treated as an alien from outer space, was greeted everywhere with bunches of flowers and beaming smiles. The diary quickly filled up with school visits, charity fairs, the inauguration of new vicars, concerts, Rotary dinners, annual general meetings of residents' associations, and allotment open days.

After exhausting the pleasures of flattery and of scattering gold dust in all directions, I began to appreciate that behind the endless whirl of activity and mutual back-slapping was something solid and serious; that the cluster of urban villages that I represented – Teddington, Whitton, Hampton, Hampton Hill, Hampton Wick, St Margaret's, Twickenham – had a dense and vibrant network of social activity. Mrs Thatcher's (probably misquoted) claim that 'there is no such thing as society' was palpably untrue; this corner of London suburbia was throbbing with enormous energy and spontaneous voluntary endeavour. Some would dismiss this activity as the preserve of the middle classes, often inspired by Nimbyism and scarcely concealed self-interest. But I took the opposite, view. I quickly appreciated, too, that there is an important role for an MP as a catalyst for all this endeavour, speaking up for community concerns with the benefit of a national platform. This has proved to be the most rewarding aspect of my work, personally and politically.

Looking back after twelve years it is possible to see where I was able to make a difference. Early on I met a local vicar in Whitton with a vision of providing respite in his church hall for local carers of elderly people. His spiritual and organizational qualities did not extend to breaching the defensive ramparts around the NHS and local government bureaucracy and the funds they controlled. I was able, with a few well-aimed cannon shots, to open them up, and the project has subsequently grown and flourished to meet an acute local need. Shortly afterwards I met a determined woman, Kate Turner, who had just embarked on a campaign to raise £6 million to build a children's hospice. Her conviction was absolute and she would have achieved her goal in any event, but having a friendly local MP promoting events, publicizing the issue of children's hospices and the lack of government support for them, probably helped.

A popular heated open-air swimming pool had been saved from closure by a community campaign in Hampton, but the campaign committee had tried unsuccessfully to elicit funds from the sports Lottery for restoration work, and I led delegations to see the sports minister, Kate Hoey, and the sports tsar, Trevor Brooking (getting his autograph while I was at it). The answer everywhere was a polite 'no', and I thought I had failed. But the enthusiasm generated by the campaign and a mass meeting had opened other doors and mobilized local fund-raising and the project succeeded, for which I received (perhaps excessive) credit. This particular experience developed in me a strong hostility to big national prestige projects – like the new Wembley and the Olympics – which, via the Lottery, suck money out of local community projects, many of which, unlike Hampton Pool, wither and die as a result.

As a result of such activities, I acquired formidable expertise in a wide, eclectic range of subjects. These included bees – campaigning for research into bee diseases; sewage – there is a particularly smelly plant nearby; military music – my constituency hosts the Royal Military School of Music at Knellar Hall; and scientific education – as MP for the government laboratories which lead the world in standard-setting for physics and chemistry.

The local champion role sometimes took me in the opposite direction from the approved party line. It was clear to me from my earliest contact with the Twickenham electorate that, despite my borough having the lowest crime rate in London, law and order was a massive local concern, mainly because of late-night violence and vandalism, connected with drink, and the explosion of graffiti in public places. The Conservatives had given me an open goal in the 1997 election when Michael Howard came to Twickenham and was quoted in the local press as saying that the area had too many police officers, when numbers had already fallen to their lowest level in many years. Having taken up the position that the Conservatives were too soft on crime, I stuck with the theme, despite the reservations of some nervous party activists. It also seemed to me the correct position to take. The wealthy could, and did, hide from crime (or imagined crime) in gated communities; the less well-off had to put up with vandalized, graffiti-scrawled estates. The police are a public service, then seriously underfunded and understaffed, no less than nurses and teachers. I combined local and national campaigning, established an all-party police group in Parliament, worked closely with the Police Federation, secured the first-ever (I think) parliamentary debate on graffiti, encouraged the build-up of police numbers locally, and organized a code of conduct for local publicans to challenge binge-drinking.

I am perhaps best known nationally for economic issues, but locally I focused on crime. This involved working with a pressure group, the Victims of Crime Trust, founded by two local police officers. One of them, Norman Brennan, was a brilliant publicist who claimed to speak (and probably did) for the gut prejudices of the Met's rank and file. They took up the cause of murder victims' families, some nationally known like Denise Bulger and Sara Payne, others more local and less famous. I discovered that in Twickenham's quiet streets there were victims of crime so appalling that a horror movie would not do justice to them. I began to understand some of the rage and frustration the victims' families felt as a result of official neglect and, in some cases, the leniency accorded to the killers. In due course, I established a parliamentary group to support victims of crime. The campaigns sometimes veered into vigilantism, but I took the view that it was better to be on the tiger's back than gazing into its mouth. And the campaigners are right to claim that victims deserve far more attention and sustained compassion than they normally receive.

Local and national campaigning for victims of crime was balanced by championing efforts to improve the local young offenders' institution, Feltham, which lies outside but very close to the constituency. A constituent on the staff urged me to visit, which I did several times before the extent of overcrowding, lack of exercise, self-harm, suicide and violence came to light. On one occasion I took Olympia, who noticed things that I overlooked: the lack of personal hygiene, showers that didn't work, inmates eating meals a foot or so from the cell toilet. My upbringing among the respectable skilled working class and lower middle class of York, and my later work in international roles, meant that I had probably had more exposure to village life in Africa and India than to Britain's criminal underclass. Some of those I met and talked to were hardened, uncompromising, violent young men, but others were confused children, often mentally ill, functionally illiterate and completely hopeless. Many were merely remand prisoners or minor offenders who had somehow been swept into Feltham, to be dominated and educated by established career criminals. I may have played a small part in exposing some of the inadequacies of the place, which is now somewhat improved.

The role of local champion has its dangers. Grass-roots community campaigning, on planning applications, for example, runs the risk of Nimbyism and the subordination of the wider public interest to protecting property values. On balance, I think the risk is worth taking. The bigger risk is that the wealthy and mobile vote with their feet and everyone else reacts with fatalistic apathy to changes decreed from above or generated by markets. By banding together and working collectively, neighbourhoods can exercise some control over their local environment. There will always be a mixture of motives – of low and high politics, of selfishness and idealism – but that is the nature of all political activity. The biggest meetings I have ever attended in Twickenham are those I have convened to mobilize protests against house building on public open space – recreation grounds and playing fields – and I would strongly defend the right of local communities to fight to preserve their environment against overdevelopment. Similarly, south-west London is much exercised by a campaign against the expansion of Heathrow, which is no doubt in part motivated by self-interest, but is also based on a wider and deeper concern for rebalancing environmental against narrow economic considerations and challenging the vested commercial interests of airlines and airport owners.

While local champions excel at catching fish in small ponds, sometimes bigger fish inadvertently stray in. When I first compared notes with a local Catholic priest about reports that had reached us of alleged neglect at a residential home for the elderly, Lynde House, we had little idea that we were dealing with one of the tentacles of a large business empire owned by the health entrepreneur and Labour donor Dr Chai Patel. Following a public meeting, I was able, working with a relatives' group and the press, to direct a spotlight through the murky waters of a poorly regulated sector to illuminate some of the abuses. These were subsequently confirmed in an official report, which I highlighted in a parliamentary debate. The affair, however, still rumbles on in the disciplinary hearings regarding the nurses involved. It is one of the more shameful features of British legal process that it can take not just years but decades, as Dickens would have recognized.

I have started, at some length, with the personal casework and local issues that dominate much of an MP's life and have only now reached the doors of Westminster. The emphasis is deliberate. The story of Parliament – certainly post-1997 – is of an august institution much diminished in status and influence, its powers having drained away to a mighty executive, to structures of international governance, notably the European Union, and to new bodies like the Scottish Parliament and the London Assembly. Successful MPs have had to reinvent themselves.

My own experience of Parliament went through a cycle familiar to many MPs: initially awestruck and intimidated by the tradition, the big occasions, the architecture and the reputation; then profoundly disillusioned by the pettiness, the tribalism, the time-wasting and arcane, archaic procedures; then gradually discovering that Parliament provides a unique platform for those who are patient and creative.

I remain to this day confused by parliamentary procedure and in awe of those who understand it. Legislation seemingly couched in the linguistic conventions of medieval scholars I have coped with, much as I cope with travelling on the Continent with my pidgin O-level French. In my first year or so in Parliament I was lost, relying on whips and friends to tell me how and when to vote and what to do. I had only one advantage over my peers: I was comfortable on my feet. I could speak spontaneously without notes, handle interventions without getting flustered, and ask ministers reasonably penetrating questions. I was surprised to discover how few MPs and ministers know how to speak in public without a script prepared by civil servants or a researcher. I realized how much I was indebted to the schoolteacher who had pushed me on to a stage at sixteen years old, and to my experience in the training ground for debaters at Cambridge.

But it didn't take long for a freshman MP in 1997 to realize that beyond the set-piece occasions, like Prime Minister's Questions and the Budget, there is little drama in the main chamber. With an enormous government majority, votes meant very little. We learned what was going on from Tony Blair's comments in the media and from press leaks, not from Parliament. With the Conservatives demoralized and inward-looking, buoyed up only by William Hague's wit, debates lacked urgency and energy, while the restrictions of parliamentary convention meant that my own party had few opportunities to shine.

Nonetheless, there are important rites of passage and one is the maiden speech. I spoke in the debate introducing legislation for the independence of the Bank of England, and spoke in support of a policy that my party had advocated for some years and was now being realized. Following Ruth Kelly, another new MP with an economics background, and after the traditional compliments to my predecessor, I was able within a few weeks of becoming an MP to have spoken, I think sensibly and positively, about a policy that, until the recent economic crisis, was the most successful and enduring of New Labour's years in office.

Opportunities in the chamber for a newcomer are limited, but

I was asked by my colleagues to introduce a debate on the euro, which invited interventions from John Redwood, Bill Cash and other sceptics. Another opening was provided by a ten-minute rule bill (which has no legislative force) on age discrimination, a subject I took up after being visited at my advice surgery by an ex-boxer, of remarkable physique, who had been refused a job in the Royal Mail because, approaching sixty, he was 'too old'. (The Royal Mail has since revised its policy.)

I discovered that one of the most useful parliamentary devices is the adjournment debate which can be obtained by winning a ballot of MPs and usually involves a thirty-minute exchange with a minister, without a vote being taken. In my first session I was able to gain confidence (and good publicity) with a succession of these: on MRSA (I think the first in Parliament), after a constituent with breast cancer had had her treatment seriously disrupted by this hospital infection; Equitable Life; security of tenure for residential-boat owners; airport expansion; compensation for a former POW who had been subjected to slave labour in Germany; and a questionable post office closure. These debates were a chore for ministers, most of whom read a prepared response without listening to my speech at all, but some of whom were helpful and compassionate (like Chris Pond, who ensured that the parents of a badly disabled son whose cause I had taken up were properly compensated for debts they had run up as a result of incompetence by his department).

But for the most part debates in the chamber had – and have – an empty, ritualistic quality, particularly after the opening speeches, and on an issue of major importance one can well be addressing an audience of a dozen, most of whom are waiting to speak and paying no attention. I plumbed the depths of disillusionment in a debate on the Stephen Lawrence inquiry. I had attended the inquiry hearings with my colleague Simon Hughes, had read the report carefully, had strong views, and had already acquired a reputation for contributing to discussions on London policing. I notified the Speaker that I wished to be called in the usual manner. I then sat for more than six hours waiting in vain, while an interminable succession of Tory and Labour MPs, mostly from outside London and who had never read the inquiry report, burbled on endlessly. Such experiences are common and help to explain why the chamber is usually empty. I vowed thereafter to use parliamentary time more productively.

One very productive use of time is the select committee. It was a rare privilege as a new MP to have ten minutes to interrogate the Chancellor or the Governor of the Bank of England, and the Treasury select committee did good work on economic policy issues, though necessarily constrained by the party make-up of the committee, with an in-built government majority. One issue that I persuaded the committee to investigate was the demutualization of building societies, having helped to lead a national Save Our Building Societies campaign. Even at the time it seemed obvious to me that good, solid institutions were in danger of being destroyed by the greed of their managers and 'carpetbagger' shareholders. I did not, however, fully anticipate at that stage the scale of the ensuing disaster or the key role that these converted building societies would play in destabilizing the financial system.

The large government majority also meant that the legislative function of the Commons was drained of content. This was (and remains) especially true of financial legislation – notably the Finance Bill, whose technical complexity is such that few MPs understand it. As a consequence, ministers read from a prepared script and opposition members from material supplied by lobby groups. For the most part, the immense and increasingly complex tax legislation is passed, scarcely touched by Parliament or understood by those who troop through the voting lobbies.

There are times when Parliament comes to legislative life: when the whips are off and MPs can exercise their judgement. The 1997 parliament had some serious and ethically difficult issues – stem-cell research was one – but by far the greatest passion was generated by fox-hunting. There was a genuine issue of principle at stake: the value to be accorded to animal welfare versus the freedom of hunting people to pursue a hobby of their choice. I came down on balance for abolition, but not without some liberal heart-searching, and consistently voted accordingly, though I have never fully understood the intensity of feeling generated by the issue on both sides.

For Liberal Democrat MPs the dominant issue of the 1997 parliament was our relationship with the Labour government. Paddy Ashdown's memoirs describe in detail his expectation of entering a coalition government and his attempts subsequently to play a role in the 'big tent' offered by Blair. Since all but three of our forty-six MPs had defeated Conservative opponents, it was clear who the main enemy was and who it would be at the next general election. But beyond a mutual interest with Labour in tactical voting at general elections, the attractions of continuing Paddy's close partnership with Blair in government were less obvious for those who were not sitting in joint cabinet committees. There was a steady stream of constitutional reform, particularly devolution, although these changes would probably have occurred in any event. There was a growing list of potentially damaging policies (like the abolition of dividend tax credits), follies (like the Millennium Dome) and cronyism (like the Ecclestone affair), where strong opposition was required. I was attached to the Treasury team, whose leader, Malcolm Bruce, was an uncompromising economic liberal and who pulled no punches in attacking Gordon Brown.

There was growing discomfort among the rank-and-file MPs with Lib Dem–Labour cooperation, sometimes vehemently expressed in parliamentary party meetings. I had never been particularly close to Paddy Ashdown and he had never shown any partiality to me. Nonetheless, I took the view that on balance he was right to try to maximize our party's influence in a context where the alternative was simply to watch from the sidelines a display of Labour triumphalism. Temperamentally, and after three decades in jobs that were far removed from tribal, political fisticuffs, I favoured constructive criticism and, where possible, a consensual approach, and always spoke in these terms in Parliament and among colleagues. I probably took this approach to extremes when David Blunkett as Education Secretary proposed student tuition fees. This seemed to me sensible since the universities were strapped for cash and students enjoyed a graduate premium in later life. I provoked a discussion in the parliamentary party, and after a long and heated debate it was clear that I was the sole dissenter from the view that we should mount outright opposition to fees. For my part, I acknowledged that good policy was bad politics and accepted my colleagues' overwhelming view.

The increasing disillusionment with 'the project' was in substantial part due to the failure to make any headway on electoral reform at Westminster. There were forty-six Lib Dem MPs, and had general election votes been reflected in the Commons we would have had over a hundred. The Jenkins Report produced an elegantly argued case for a PR system similar to that which now prevails in Scotland: a constituency-based vote system backed up by a list designed to achieve proportionality. The report was praised for its lucidity and prose style, but there was no way that the Labour government (let alone the Tories) would accept it. There was a simpler, less proportional version of electoral reform, the alternative vote, under which the constituency system would remain and voters would rank candidates in order of preference rather than with an X, and second-preference votes would be transferred from losing candidates. In this way, every winning candidate would have a majority of votes cast; tactical voting would be unnecessary and a vote for the third party in any constituency would no longer be wasted. Such a compromise was unattractive to PR fundamentalists but it could have been an improvement on the status quo. It would have been acceptable, too, to key figures in the Labour government, as I established in a series of meetings with ministers which I undertook largely on my own initiative but supported by the leadership (the subject has recently resurfaced as a possible, late, option for the Brown government to offer in a referendum).

In the event, this intrigue and private diplomacy came to naught because Paddy abruptly announced his resignation in 1999. Those of us who were not part of his inner circle were taken aback. The interpretation I put on his decision was that his dalliance with Blair had reached its limits and he wished to go out on a high, having judged that we could only go backwards at the next election, after a decade of advance under his leadership. He was wrong on the latter point, but from his personal point of view the decision to quit at the height of his career made sense.

To replace him, there was substantial support for Charles Kennedy, whom Paddy clearly disapproved of and had banished to the obscure outpost of rural affairs spokesman. I decided to support him, having been greatly impressed by his performances on television: articulate, witty and clever. Simon Hughes had strong support among activists who were enthused by his radical oratory and his record as a brilliant MP, holding on to Bermondsey in very difficult circumstances. In the event, three other candidates joined the field, including Malcolm Bruce, but Charles won with a respectable if not overwhelming vote. In the reshuffle that followed I was offered trade and industry; together with Phil Willis, Steve Webb and Evan Harris, I was one of the few newcomers to join our shadow cabinet.

The leadership contest roughly coincided with another serious deterioration in Olympia's health and thereafter, although I made, I think, a positive contribution in Parliament, I have little memory of it for my mind and heart were elsewhere. Olympia survived until a few days after the 2001 election, but for most of that time she was an invalid and reconciled to the inevitability of deteriorating health and a premature end to her life.

Shortly after I was elected, in the summer recess of 1997, news came from India that one of her brothers, Celso, had suffered a heart attack, and she resolved to go immediately to India to help out. Celso had defied his father to give Olympia away at her wedding and she had a soft spot for him, sharing the same highly strung and emotional temperament, including a fierce temper, but also gentleness and compassion. But her real motive for going to India was to say goodbye to her family, whom she did not expect to see again – while at the same time not disclosing to them the true nature of her own condition, for fear of causing distress. This mixture of love and deception was sustained with some difficulty, and her sister Amata, a consultant paediatrician in Bombay, could see that something was amiss and eventually coaxed the truth out of her.

This underlying tension apart, the visit was blissfully happy and Olympia and I had never been closer. We built each day around a long walk. Usually in the late afternoon, when the day was cooling, we walked along the road through the paddy fields the couple of miles to the sea. The monsoon rains had turned the landscape a bright green and the air was rich with the smell of damp earth and vegetation. Walking for pleasure is not an Indian habit and bemused villagers turned out to watch us pass until our eccentricity had become part of the daily routine. The sea was angry and dangerous and there were no tourists, so we could walk the vast, beautiful Goan beaches in solitude until sunset before returning to a family dinner.

Celso was recovering from the heart attack brought on by an unhealthy lifestyle and the stress of trying to run a brewery in India, with the endless hassle of government licensing and corruption, bloody-minded unions, and appalling transport and telecommunications infrastructure, not to mention ruthless competition. The heart attack was fortunately mild and the lifestyle adjustments had been successfully made; so there was some irony in Olympia, with irreversible cancer and a lung that barely functioned, acting as Florence Nightingale. But the visit brought brother and sister and the wider family closer together.

Throughout our thirty-five-year relationship Olympia was constantly struggling to balance the needs of the family and the expression of her own talents. She was too emancipated, talented and ambitious to accept the housewife role, like her mother and mine, but too emotionally entangled in the day-to-day distractions of family life to pursue a full-time career. The result, as for many women, was a messy and often frustrating combination of the two. But she achieved all the goals she set herself, even if not in a planned and orderly way.

She was a gifted teacher and wanted to teach. After the unqualified pleasure of teaching eager and appreciative African girls who understood the value of education, she was totally disillusioned by Scottish and London schools. The prospect of facing rows of bored adolescents yawning and burping their way through the school day filled her with dread. She switched between secondary and primary, full-time and supply teaching, without finding a role until embarking on private music teaching at home. This she did with flair and enthusiasm, and managed the business relationship with the parents as professionally as the teaching of scales and arpeggios. She took enormous pleasure in the achievements of her protégés, adults as well as children, and when she died many of them were genuinely distressed.

She also wanted to produce a major piece of academic research. Her PhD on the political history of the old republic of Brazil was a triumph over adversity: from a deeply hostile professor of Latin American studies in Glasgow, who did everything he could to discourage her, to the practical problems of writing amid the clamour of small children. I helped, baby-minding when she visited Brazil. But hers was the achievement. Unlike my own PhD, which was full of clever technical flourishes and equations designed to impress the external examiners but of no enduring interest, hers was a work of genuinely valuable scholarship. Hugo, our youngest son, has made it widely available on the Internet, where other scholars are hopefully making use of it.

Her greatest ambition was to be able to perform musically to a professional standard. When she returned to the UK she played the piano well and had a fine but untrained voice, but her understanding of music far outstripped her technical ability. She progressed from one teacher to another. But her ability to perform, even in exams, suffered from crippling attacks of nerves. Eventually she achieved contentment performing for her own pleasure, but at a very demanding level, and teaching, including our own three children. One of the decisions in my life of which I am most proud was overriding her objections and ignoring the parlous state of our finances to buy her a Blüthner grand piano.

Music became central to her existence. Rarely have Beethoven and Brahms been played with more genuine passion. But one of the consequences of breast cancer spreading into her lymph glands was that it gradually sapped the strength in her arms, and the collapse of a lung effectively terminated her singing. Her pleasures were increasingly vicarious and she was able to revel in her children's musical achievements. When she approached the end of her life, she was able to draw comfort from their recordings and from her favourite music. My regret is that we never recorded her.

As a mother who had always put her family before her career, Olympia wanted to use her last few years to ensure that our three children were as successfully and happily launched into adult life as it was possible for her to achieve. Paul, our eldest, had been the third person in our early married life: a placid, uncomplaining and lovable child. He had responded early on to his mother's enthusiasm for music rather than mine for conventional learning and sport. Too much time with books, he claimed, induced 'brain ache'. By his early teens he was accomplished on the keyboard and the violin and spent hours practising his instruments, while

Olympia and I, with the parental pride that accompanies gifted children, ferried him around endless music classes, rehearsals and concerts. This talent, and a flair for languages, earned him a place at Cambridge, where he also discovered his fine voice, singing in the St John's choir (then under George Guest and arguably the finest of the Oxbridge chapel choirs), and developed wide-ranging, sensitive musicianship which led him into conducting. By his mid-twenties he had a range of musical talents and accomplishments and a potential for singing and conducting at the highest level, but no obvious way into a notoriously cliquey as well as ferociously competitive profession. He had also acquired a beautiful wife, a Slovakian of Hungarian extraction, Agnesa Tothova, who was a talented singer in her own right, having been a finalist in the Lucia Popp competition at a young age. Like other eastern Europeans of her generation, she was making the transition from the constraints, but also the privileges, of the communist system, having been a star of the communist youth movement and an Olympic-standard swimmer as well as a talented musician.

Olympia could see the creative potential as well as the love in the relationship, but also the enormous practical obstacles to realizing their musical potential. Paul had landed a lead role in an experimental relaunch of Mozart's rather obscure unfinished opera, *Zaide*, at the Maggio Musicale in Florence, which gave Olympia and myself a pretext for a romantic break, staying in a nunnery on the hills overlooking the city. But the performance didn't lead anywhere. Olympia resolved to help and organized a concert at the Queen Elizabeth Hall on the South Bank for Paul and Agi to sing together. The orchestra of the Royal Opera House, Covent Garden, was hired for the occasion; our daughter Aida, now a commercial barrister, arranged corporate sponsorship; and

Olympia filled the hall by selling tickets to everyone she knew, including the outer fringes of her huge extended family. The occasion was a great musical and social success and gave some impetus to Paul's and Agi's singing careers. Some time later they recorded a CD with a top Czech orchestra, but it was released too late for Olympia to have the pleasure of hearing it.

Olympia also insisted that they were properly married in a church. She had little truck with cohabitation or a prosaic register office ceremony. The Catholic Church was again pressed into service, reflecting Agi's spiritual upbringing, and a wedding was organized in the fine chapel of St Mary's University College, a Catholic university campus in the heart of my constituency, with a reception in the adjacent splendours of Horace Walpole's remarkable Gothic house, Strawberry Hill. The guest list reflected our remarkably cosmopolitan family with the addition of a Slovakian branch. The fact that we hadn't a single word, let alone language, in common with Agi's parents, who spoke Hungarian, made little difference; body language and gestures got us through.

My politics only intruded once, when the very supportive priest, Father Devlin, had to withdraw at the last moment. His replacement turned out to be my nemesis from the Twickenham Labour Party, whose ideological journey from Trotsky to the Catholic priesthood had been even longer and more difficult than mine into Liberal Democrat politics. Olympia was exhausted but triumphant as impresario and organizer, having launched her eldest child into married life. Had she lived two years longer she would have seen her first grandchild.

Our daughter Aida was a very bright child, inheriting her father's stamina and capacity for sustained hard work and her mother's warmth, flair for organization and feisty temperament.

Trying, I think, to please both of us, she became a very accomplished pianist and was the only one of our children to develop a serious interest in politics. She followed her brother to Cambridge, where she got a first in law in her final year. She was far from being a reclusive academic and discovered the social side of undergraduate life more than I had done a generation earlier: rowing, long-distance running, and singing blues in a student band. Parental pride was amply satisfied when she performed with great flair Beethoven's First Piano Concerto in a public concert, and I still recall the moment when tears of pride and pleasure started to roll down Olympia's cheeks.

She subsequently sought to make her way as a barrister, but though she qualified, she found that while doors were beginning to open to clever, attractive women, there was still an assumption that they should stick to family and criminal law rather than the less familiar and more lucrative commercial bar. She eventually became a successful barrister-turned-solicitor in the City; but one by-product of her foray into the Inns of Court was that her pupil-master, Stephen Kenny, fell in love with her and she with him. Their marriage in Twickenham in the summer of 1999 was another great family occasion, the last before Olympia's health finally gave way. This time, despite a Catholic groom, we celebrated the wedding in Twickenham's parish church with a reception in the gardens of Marble Hill House nearby, a fine Georgian building overlooking the Thames, erected as a gift from George II to his mistress. While Paul's marriage had extended our family into a new part of Europe, this one took in the English establishment, including Stephen's uncle, the admirably independent law lord, Lord Lloyd. Olympia hadn't been strong enough to do a great deal more than participate but enjoyed the moment, much like

Vikram Seth's matriarch, Mrs Rupa Mehra, seeing her daughter happily married to an eminently *Suitable Boy*. We celebrated with a wonderfully romantic holiday, alone together, in the Italian Alps near Lake Como. Family holidays had been the highlight of the year for the last three decades. We were able savour this one, with Olympia feeling a sense of completeness.

Our youngest, Hugo, had carried with him since he was eight years old the knowledge that his mother had cancer and might well not outlive his childhood. He also laboured under the burden of high parental expectations, having shown exceptional potential at an early age, even in a bright family, along with considerable powers of concentration. As a result of prodigious hard work, and a lot of help at home, mainly from his mother, he won a scholarship to St Paul's and flourished academically, one of the strongest mathematicians and scientists in a school at the top of the academic tree. Attending school events, I was torn between my pride as a parent and a growing discomfort at the vast gulf that was opening up between the top independent schools like St Paul's and what became known as 'bog-standard' comprehensives. Every teacher at St Paul's was highly qualified, often with a PhD; discipline problems were virtually non-existent; there were magnificently equipped facilities; and every boy was encouraged to pursue breadth as well as depth, in Hugo's case music and running. I knew, as did Olympia from her occasional supply and music teaching at the local college, that even in educationally conscious and relatively affluent suburbs like Richmond, and even in the best-run and best-equipped of comprehensive schools, an altogether more modest set of expectations pertained. In our private world, Olympia had the satisfaction of seeing Hugo go to Trinity College, Cambridge, and collect a first in maths. She attended his degree ceremony in a wheelchair, unable to walk and in some pain. It was the last function outside home that she attended, apart from hospital visits, and was an event that encapsulated what she had lived for: putting her family before herself, and making a pilgrimage to the highest temple of this religion called education.

The final descent from illness to disability, from laboured mobility to frustrated immobility, had occurred the previous year on the last of our summer holidays together, when we had hoped to repeat the successful trip of the year before, this time staying at châteaux and hotels on the Loire. She began to experience spasms of extreme pain in her hip and an otherwise idyllic vacation acquired overtones of fear and foreboding. She refused, however, to accept that there was any link with her cancer and when we returned home insisted on physiotherapy for a 'pulled muscle'. A few weeks later she collapsed in agony and when eventually she consented to go to hospital it transpired that the bone had simply rotted away, breaking in several places. Such are the miracles of modern medicine that surgeons were able to pin the good bits of the broken bones together again. She was operated on over the millennium New Year, rotated between three Chelsea hospitals which respectively repaired the bone, restored a second collapsed lung, and tried intensive radio- and chemotherapy. Whatever may be said in criticism of the NHS, and I hear a great deal, the capacity of the system to deliver high-quality, sophisticated treatment to the acutely sick is miraculous to those who receive it.

I effectively lived with Olympia in those hospitals, largely empty over the holiday, talking and reading together. When she was asleep I answered the piles of constituency mail that had accumulated, bringing me the worries of Twickenham on which urgent and firm action was demanded from me and the government: noisy neighbours, children playing football against the wall, overhanging tree branches, the plague of *Cupressocyparis leylandii*, unwanted emails, dog turds, broken fences, uncut grass, fireworks, pavement cyclists, oversized house extensions, litter, parking fines, parking, parking, and more parking. Sometimes my heart rose a little when I was asked to intervene in more exotic causes: cruelty to bears in Chinese circuses, underage children employed in Arab camel-racing, or the loss of Ecuadorian rain forests. I did my best to be helpful to those who needed help and civil to those with less pressing needs. But my heart wasn't in it.

One night, hearing a lot of noise outside the largely deserted hospital, I went out to see the sky covered in exploding fireworks and wandered down to the source of the festivities on the Embankment. There I saw the vast crowds and it slowly dawned on me that this was the millennium. I felt totally detached from the celebrations, as if I was looking through the window of a house at someone else's party. On the way back through Chelsea amid the milling crowds, there was a church open, welcoming but empty. I sat inside, broke down in tears, and prayed for the first time in many years before returning to the now familiar smells and sounds of the hospital.

Thereafter, back home, Olympia was increasingly dependent, able to hobble about on crutches but little else. She was still determined to be positive and active. She tried to help me by telephoning and stuffing envelopes. She smoothed over quarrels among her family and among my activists, using the moral authority that comes from someone who was demonstrating every day more fortitude than some people manage in a lifetime.

She was also determined to stay at home, close to her family, and not to spend her last days in a hospital or hospice. Statistics show that the vast majority of the public wish to die at home among their loved ones in this way, but few manage it. I reverted to the role of carer and managed, just, to keep my own work as an MP going, with the help of a team of friends supplemented by periods of assistance from Olympia's sisters, her mother, and a much-loved aunt who came from Canada for a while. We kept going in this way for a further eighteen months, far longer than the doctors thought possible. I was not a perfect carer – often clumsy and forgetful – and I came to understand the emotional turmoil and exhaustion that afflicts many carers struggling with the frustration and inner rage of a partner or parent who is acutely aware of their failing physical powers and growing helplessness. We had a large stock of accumulated love and drew heavily on it.

Apart from friends and relatives we were indebted to the minister at the local Anglican church, Neil Evans. Despite being articulate and able to talk about almost anything, Olympia and I had never spoken to each other about spiritual questions and the meaning of life, and impending death. I had a broadly scientific outlook allied to a vaguely theistic set of beliefs, and a Christian sense of right and wrong, but nothing that could be seriously described as a living religious faith. Olympia's gradual divorce from the Catholic Church had been finally completed when she first visited the Royal Marsden some years earlier and a young Catholic priest, barely out of college, tried to give her the last rites, seemingly in order to stop any other denomination getting to her first. But something religious had remained, and whenever we visited a church she would light a candle and offer a silent prayer. Neil was an utterly unpretentious, undoctrinaire Christian, who could understand Olympia's condition and minister to her and he gave her considerable comfort.

After almost a year and a half of struggle, cancer had reached most of Olympia's body and, on a final visit to the Marsden, she said a final goodbye and thank-you to her consultant. Any hope that her last few weeks would be spent in uncomplicated tranquillity was blown by the imminence of a general election. Realizing my predicament, the party had a few months earlier sent me an organizer, Andrew Reeves, who worked around the clock to make sure that the local election machine was functioning effectively, even with a sitting MP who was something of a passenger. Blair's decision to postpone the election for a month because of foot-and-mouth disease gave him an extra month to prepare, but presented a new challenge for Olympia, who had willed herself to keep going until she knew the result. With the campaign properly launched, I tried to divide my time between Olympia and a few hours daily door-knocking. I did enough to realize that the election was drifting away from the Conservatives and that I was probably safe.

When I came back from the count in the early hours with a doubled majority, she was awake, waiting, and gave me a last smile. The following day she asked me to play Paul's recordings for the final time, we talked about the children's future and my hopes for the next parliament. After another night she stopped eating, her systems gradually closed down, and she died peacefully, her family around her as she had always wished.

We sought to make her funeral a celebration of her life, with humour and fine music, and Twickenham's parish church was full. The family that she had done so much to build tried to deal with its grief together and, as she would have done and would have wanted, immersed itself in work to ease its pain. She now lies in Twickenham cemetery, far from the countries of her origin and birth, but in a country she came to regard as home.

Chapter 12

New Millennium, New World

The new century started for me in the late autumn of 2001. I had spent the preceding few months in a daze, immersing myself in the details of funeral organization, the routines of parliamentary business, and finding solace in tearful family gatherings. Everyone who has been through bereavement, particularly of a partner after a long, loving relationship, will have imbibed the same cocktail of emotions as I did.

I decided to go to India in late summer to visit Olympia's mother, brother and sister, who had been unable to come to the funeral, and to take my younger son Hugo, who had no partner of his own to fall back on and who, I could see, was deeply affected by the loss of his mother. After his degree he had taken a year out to spend time at home with her, and her steady physical decline had taken its toll on him too. I treated the trip to India as part family duty, part pilgrimage, but also as an opportunity to renew old friendships. I had always found India immensely invigorating and energizing. This time, somewhere in the packed commuter trains of Bombay, the crumbling but thrilling streets of Calcutta, the bazaars and mosques of Lucknow, the gardens and boulevards of New Delhi, and my old haunts in Goa, I rediscovered my natural optimism and renewed determination to make the most of life.

In Goa, in my brother-in-law Celso's house, Hugo and I returned from a morning walk to find the television on and the in-laws gazing at pictures on CNN of smoke billowing from one of the Twin Towers in New York. A few moments later the second was hit and, along with hundreds of millions of others around the world, we watched, in real time, the two towers collapsing. What was clear, if nothing else, was that the political world I was returning to would be different, transformed utterly by terrorism and the Middle East.

A few weeks later my own life would be transformed too. I had made a resolution to revive the hobby of ballroom and Latin dancing which I had enjoyed with Olympia until she had become too weak, and also to make new friends, both men and women. I had an outstanding invitation – as the regional President of the United Nations Association – to talk to the New Forest branch. Near the front of the meeting was an attractive middle-aged woman whose elegant legs, enhanced by tight jeans, I kept noticing as I was speaking. At question time she rather forcefully objected to my economically liberal, free-trade approach to agriculture, arguing from the standpoint of a small farmer. We continued the conversation afterwards and I established that she had been a contemporary at Cambridge, Rachel Wenban-Smith, whom I remembered from a university party. She was now divorced, with a grown-up family, and working on affordable rural housing. The unresolved debate about trade and agriculture led to an agreement to return to the New Forest and visit her farm.

We spent the day walking on the beautiful moorland near the farm, which was an oasis of green pasture, home to her small herd of cattle and a few horses. We did not dwell too long on trade policy. That day we struck up a relationship that has provided both of us with love, fun, contentment, security and friendship ever since. My recollections of 2002, when the ominous build-up to war in the Middle East was taking place, are mainly of romance: weekend visits to the New Forest, long walks and log fires.

I soon came to realize, however, that the emotions aroused by bereavement and grief on my side, and desertion and divorce on hers, are not straightforward. I wasn't just a widower seeking and finding happiness in a new relationship, but the surviving head of a family whose dominant and unifying personality had died. My three children were, in different ways, puzzled and distressed to see their father disappearing so soon into a relationship with a new woman. I asked myself the question, which others were no doubt posing, whether the ability to move from a long, success-ful, loving marriage to another close relationship reflected some underlying shallowness or superficiality. I persuaded myself, and I think this is right, that good relationships have some common elements – emotional generosity, an ability to listen and will-ingness to communicate, patience and forbearance – which are transferable. My children gradually came to accept Rachel in the way I was accepted by hers, and we made visits in 2003 to Kenya to see Olympia's eldest brother Aurelio and to Goa to stay with Celso's family (where Olympia's silent mother brought Rachel posies of flowers each morning, as if to say, 'you are accepted'). We married in 2004, with a blessing in the House of Commons chapel, a joyful occasion for our families and friends as well as ourselves.

But I had been reminded, and continued to be, that even for a father the umbilical cord is very long, and that a much-loved mother is irreplaceable for a child of any age. I had warning of this a year after Olympia died when I received a distressed call from Hugo in Cambridge to Shetland, where we were staying with Rachel's friends; he was seriously stressed, suffering from acute back pain and had decided to pull out of an exam. Luckily, his earlier first proved enough to get him in to do a PhD at Imperial College, but he only started to enjoy life again when he went off to the USA three years later to embark on postdoctoral research.

Family acceptance mattered, but it did not overshadow the huge miracle of rediscovering romantic love in later life. We are bombarded with images of young love though, if most youthful romance is anything like mine, the reality is crippled by inexperience, shyness, embarrassment, overexcitement and fear – of pregnancy, inadequacy or rejection. We are rarely told that people in their fifties, sixties, seventies and even eighties fall in love. It is perhaps assumed that wrinkles and balding heads are an insuperable barrier to physical attraction, that sex stops at the menopause and its male equivalent, and that the simple shared pleasures of amorous affection diminish with age. I now know that those things are not true.

The years I have spent with Rachel have been brimful of emotions and memories: warm, comfortable and nourishing. Not that it was always easy. I had to adjust to someone not just of a different colour but a very different temperament. She had her own demons to conquer, reversing the loss of self-confidence that had come from her husband's desertion after more than thirty years of marriage. But age not only brings wisdom and understanding, but also the clarity of mind that comes from realizing that there are not enough years left to waste on self-indulgent quarrels.

It helped in adjusting to the emotions of loving a different woman that we met and built our relationship in, for me, a totally different world: centred on the idyllic setting of her farm in the New Forest. After a long and gruelling Friday constituency advice surgery, I would drive down late at night to the farm and find myself transported, as if on a magic carpet, to the depths of the countryside, which, as an urban or suburban man, I had often peered at but never absorbed. I would wake next morning to the sound of birds and the swishing of trees in the wind, before embarking on a few simple tasks, like feeding the chickens. And then the two of us would walk the dog around the farm perimeter, through groves of rhododendrons, across the parkland to the bluebell wood and on to the moors. As the song has it: 'if paradise was half as nice . . .'.

On these walks we planned the future. Rachel gradually introduced me to her family and friends and to her favourite haunts – Shetland in particular – and I did the same for her in Twickenham and York, where my mother still lived in self-reliant isolation. We prepared for our marriage. She retired from her job, which she loved, promoting affordable rural housing, to spend more time with me. She adjusted her lifestyle, in due course passing on most of her farm and selling the farmhouse to her elder son, and building a new home from scratch on the site of a former farmworker's cottage, alongside the pastures that feed her herd of Dexter cattle. I admit to not having made comparable sacrifices. My obsessive interest in my work as an MP received a fresh injection of pace as my domestic contentment energized my commitment and ambition. Fortunately, Rachel is also a political animal: she had once chaired the New Forest SDP, had stood for local elections, and had chaired Brockenhurst parish council for several years. Her politics do not have the passion and anger of Olympia's; but her views are held with conviction and are reflected in her 'green' lifestyle – and she is, like Olympia, unfailingly loyal and supportive of my work.

To make a long-term success of being an MP required a strategy. The first step was to buttress my majority, which was respectable – now 7250 – but not impregnable. To do this required continued assiduous attention to local issues, the local press and constituents' concerns. I had enjoyed this aspect of the work and it was no great burden to maintain a close interest and solid commitment. The second step was to make sensible use of Parliament. I was under no illusions. It was painfully apparent that Britain under New Labour had an elective dictatorship and our rulers had little time for Parliament, and even less for the views of MPs from a third party.

A sensible strategy seemed to be to exploit my one source of competitive advantage – to be able to talk seriously and sensibly about economic matters based on some practical experience of the world outside Parliament – so as to build up a reputation inside my party and in Parliament; and from that platform to influence the wider national debate in the media and the world of think tanks and policy formulation. The objective was modest but achievable.

I also wanted to make some contribution to the legislative process, which is, in theory, the main reason why MPs exist. I had an early stroke of luck in the first year of the 2001 parliament in winning a top-ten place in the ballot for private members' legislation. It was explained to me that I could take on a controversial piece of legislation, obtain some publicity and credit with the relevant lobby groups, and then lose, or else take a less controversial bill, which the government would support, and win. I wanted to do something worthwhile and opted for the latter. I was despatched to see a government whip, Tony McNulty, who set out the options with refreshing clarity: 'you play ball and I will make sure your bill gets through; you play games with us and you're dead', or words to that effect. Most of the apocryphal tales about the brutality of government whips have Tony McNulty at the centre of them. I warmed, however, to a man who didn't exude the faintest whiff of hypocrisy or false bonhomie, and delivered on his side of the bargain in a businesslike way.

I was offered a short list of private members' bills that the government would support but otherwise didn't have time for. I chose a bill designed to stiffen criminal penalties for pirates who breach copyright protection and steal intellectual property. Such piracy has become a major source of revenue for the criminal underworld and is seriously damaging to Britain's creative industries: the arts, particularly music and film, and computer software. Representing a constituency heavy with creative artists, scientists and inventors, like Trevor Baylis, there was also a strong local interest in intellectual property rights.I worked with a coalition of industries seeking to strengthen the law, did as I was asked, or told, and the legislation passed quickly, unamended, through both houses of Parliament. It was not exactly a triumph of debating skill and tactical brilliance – I was not the legislative driver but a chauffeur-driven passenger – but I have the minor satisfaction of having done something useful and seeing the key provisions of the Cable bill splashed across the screen every time I watch a film or DVD.

Being at last able to concentrate single-mindedly on the work of an MP paid dividends. I shadowed, successively, Peter Mandelson, Stephen Byers and Patricia Hewitt as each, especially

Mandelson, brought some direction and energy to the DTI. I made some impact as a result of promoting the policy of scrapping the DTI – which was designed to send the signal that good policy involved less, not more, government intervention and regulation. This earned me a page of compliments in the *Sun*, in a Richard Littlejohn column: 'the only Liberal Democrat policy I have ever agreed with'. I attacked the banks over their anticompetitive charges and abuse of their regulatory privileges several years before this was generally accepted as a problem; and opposed the bail-out of the private nuclear power company British Energy, heralding a tough and sceptical approach to new nuclear power. I built good personal links with Digby Jones at the CBI and John Monks at the TUC, but if I made a substantial contribution it was in introducing a more consistent strain of economic liberalism into our party's thinking, which had been hamstrung by conference resolutions calling for 1960s- and 70s-style industrial intervention.

Just over a year after the 2001 elections Charles Kennedy asked me to take over the economic brief, as our shadow Chancellor. This was a big move for me, to the heart of the party's policy-making, and promised a major role in the next general election campaign. It required some courage on Charles's part, since it involved moving Matthew Taylor, his close ally and campaign manager in the party leadership contest. I came to appreciate that, behind Charles's diffident manner and consensual style of leadership, there was a touch of steel. He also had a clear sense of political direction and saw an opening for us as a party that took us beyond the guerrilla warfare campaigning at which we had excelled, and beyond Paddy Ashdown's flirtation with New Labour.

There was a political space to be occupied appealing to people on both the traditional left and right: the former disillusioned with New Labour, and the latter, socially liberal Conservatives, unable to stomach Iain Duncan Smith's brand of Conservatism. For our party to exploit this new, eclectic mix required us to overcome widespread scepticism as to whether we were a serious party beyond the limits of local government and the occasional protest. A key step to establishing that belief was economic credibility. This I was required to develop by using my business background and establishing a more disciplined approach to money. We had been, somewhat unfairly, characterized by our opponents as spending more money on everything and being in favour of higher taxes as a matter of principle. With the help of David Laws, now an MP and part of my Treasury team, we were able to craft a more serious approach to spending priorities and budget discipline, and an emphasis on fairer, rather than higher, taxes.

While the continued but somewhat fading ascendancy of New Labour, and the hopelessness of the Tories, gave us grounds for optimism nationally, the position on the ground in my borough was quite different. The Lib Dems had controlled the council, led by David Williams, for almost eighteen years. The initial enthusiasm and idealism had become tempered by severe budget constraints and painful spending choices, and public resistance to one of the highest council taxes in Britain. Although the council had been led with considerable political skill, some unpopular decisions were taking their toll and in May 2002 the Lib Dems were swept out of power in a Conservative landslide. This change of fortune was a threat to the two local Lib Dem MPs, for we were now left very exposed; but it also provided an opportunity for me. Instead of being a tolerated and respected, but annoyingly independent, presence among party activists, I found myself in a leadership role, rallying the dispirited and defeated troops. I was helped considerably by the local Conservatives who, with a few honourable exceptions, embodied Teresa May's devastatingly self-critical description of them as the 'nasty party': mean-spirited and intolerant of diversity. More estimable qualities of administrative competence and a concern for educational standards somehow got lost in their atavistic tribalism, a problem the Conservative leadership continues to struggle with to this day. I became a successful community campaigner and helped to set my party back on the path to recapturing power in a reverse landslide four years later.

The early months of the 2001 parliament became dominated by an issue that future generations will puzzle over with some bewilderment: fox-hunting. But the tally-ho of the British hunters was soon drowned out by the bugles of the American cavalry arriving. In the months leading up to the Iraq War there was a growing amount of agonized questioning. In my own party the arguments ebbed and flowed in the shadow Cabinet and in the parliamentary party. We were, after all, the party of liberal internationalism whose leaders, from Palmerston to Paddy Ashdown, had supported intervention against tyrants. We had enthusiastically endorsed military intervention in Yugoslavia, Afghanistan and Liberia. Paddy, in particular, as one of the few modern politicians to have seen combat, had built his, and our, reputation on military activism. Most of our MPs (who, like me, had Conservative opponents) were nervous about being portrayed as 'failing to support our troops'. The 'evidence' about weapons of mass destruction, as presented in the government dossiers, was ambiguous; though by the time of the UK decision to join the war the more extreme claims in relation to nuclear weapons or long-range missiles were no longer being taken very seriously. The legal issues, too, were not clear-cut, though Tony Blair's pursuit of a second Security Council resolution provided a test we could all evaluate. The most persuasive argument for most of us was that intervention would be counterproductive: it would fuel Middle Eastern terrorism; would distract from the need to resolve the Arab–Israeli conflict; and would dissipate the political and military resolve to turn around Afghanistan.

Charles Kennedy chaired innumerable discussions and patiently winnowed out the strong from the weak arguments. Once it became clear that we would oppose the war, he sought to ensure that everyone was comfortable with the position and that we would be united. It was still far from clear at that stage whether he had made the right call, though the anti-war march and Charles's decision to address it ensured that we were speaking for a very large, angry constituency. The parliamentary debate on the decision to go to war was the biggest occasion of my years there. While there were some fine, independent-minded speeches from some Labour supporters of the war like Ann Clwyd, and opponents like John Denham, who had just resigned as a minister in protest – and from a handful of Conservative rebels like Ken Clarke and Ian Taylor – my abiding recollection was of the personal venom directed at our benches, mainly from the Conservative side. Charles struggled at times to keep going in the din, but the raucous taunts of 'Charlie Chamberlain' and 'traitor' gained him wider sympathy than Tony Blair's carefully reasoned arguments would otherwise have allowed.

Initially, with newspapers reporting that 'weapons of mass destruction' had been found and US 'shock and awe' producing a quick collapse of the Iraqi forces, it appeared that the military intervention had succeeded. We were endlessly taunted in Parliament by government über-loyalists like Jack Straw and Geoff Hoon who revelled in their apparent triumph. Jenny Tonge, my neighbouring MP, and I were confronted by ecstatic local Conservatives who demanded a military march past at the town hall to celebrate a victory comparable to Waterloo or El Alamein, at which the traitorous Lib Dem MPs could be exposed for their lack of patriotism. In the months and years that followed, however, our party, and Charles Kennedy personally, would be gradually vindicated.

I was, necessarily, a bit player in the party's campaigning on the war. I made a minor contribution, through my visiting fellowships at Nuffield and the LSE, in thinking through some of the possible economic consequences of the war, including the counter-intuitive idea that a war designed in part, at least, to open up Iraqi oil production might have the opposite effect of constricting supply and precipitating an oil shock. It happened, but only several years later.

My main task was to build up my party's credibility on the wider economic agenda, in particular by developing a critique of Gordon Brown's chancellorship that fitted our narrative but also resonated with the public. It had always seemed to me that the shrill sense of outrage that characterizes the speeches of most opposition spokespersons, on most subjects, is politically counterproductive and simply rather silly. This was especially so on economic policy, where the government had, at that time, a reasonably good story to tell. Michael Howard, who held the economic brief for the Conservatives, was clever and played the pantomime role well, but came across as insincere. His successor,

Oliver Letwin, by contrast, looked visibly uncomfortable in this world of parody and caricature and eager to get back to his job in the City or his books.

I decided not to try to compete, but simply to acknowledge Gordon Brown's successes objectively, before dealing with his failures, also objectively. Setting the right tone wasn't easy: too much praise would seem obsequious; too much criticism would seem carping and formulaic. I think I got the balance broadly right and have persisted with it: on the one hand, acknowledging the prolonged period of steady growth and rising employment, and the Chancellor's commitment to an open economy; on the other, criticizing the growing imbalance created by high personal debt and an inflated housing market; the overcomplicated, centralized system of micromanagement; and the catalogue of specific errors, ranging from occupational pensions and tax credits, through to the London Underground PPP and repeated U-turns on tax policy. Brown and I have maintained an amicable relationship, though I have been careful not to become too close and locked into his bear hug. I have seen enough of him to recognize not just his formidable intelligence, and even his considerable personal charm, but also a tendency to bully those misguided enough to hold a different point of view.

One of the key decisions made at this time – I think gradually rather than abruptly – was not to join the euro. I had often spoken in support of the project and of British membership on economic grounds, but once the decision had effectively been made by Gordon Brown not to join, there was little to be gained by continuing the argument. Once the ship had left the harbour it was pointless to swim after it, though for some years afterwards I sat on a parliamentary committee set up by the Chancellor, and continued, with his encouragement, preparing for the practicalities of e-day. I realized at the same time that I was myself also becoming somewhat more questioning about the European project as a whole.

Ever since the start of the debate over British entry to the Common Market forty years earlier, I had been a strong pro-European. I saw the European project as a form of practical internationalism, and its achievements in that respect have indeed been substantial: cementing peace between European enemies; opening up the borders of Europe to trade and, increasingly, movements of people; nurturing the emergence of first southern, then eastern, Europe to democracy and market economics. But I became increasingly frustrated and alarmed by the slowness of reform of the CAP; the frequently mercantilist approach to trade policy; the unnecessary intrusiveness of EU rules; the inefficiency and lack of control over EU budgets; and the unfailing ability of EU institutions to hoover up more powers and responsibilities, and to resist decentralization of matters, such as social policy and agriculture, that are best dealt with nationally. From being something akin to a Eurofanatic, I gradually acquired a degree of scepticism which reflected the public mood and that of many of my colleagues.

I had a major political break in the 2004 budget when Charles Kennedy, who as party leader was due to reply, didn't turn up. There was approximately an hour's notice and, to general surprise, I responded confidently and with spontaneity, earning some good reviews. In truth, it is a tradition of some absurdity that opposition leaders should respond to the Chancellor, and this was my subject. There was a lot of speculation among colleagues and the press as to the cause of Charles's absence, and the version that included alcohol featured on the charge sheet during the leadership crisis two years later. I was more than happy to accept the official explanation, a stomach bug, and felt indebted to him for the opportunity.

This minor episode did, however, crystallize growing worries that we were not capitalizing on the opportunities presented by an increasingly unpopular war and Labour leadership, and a Conservative opposition that was drifting badly. We were (and still are) in a transition from being a minor party which occasionally won spectacular by-elections and did well in local government, to a major party on a par with the other two. The seating and speaking arrangements in Parliament that give pride of place to the 'official' opposition in a bipolar house were reflected in much of the media coverage which, to our mounting exasperation, treated almost every issue (except the war) as an opportunity to pit Conservative spokesmen against government ministers. Our press officers battered endlessly at studio doors to get us a better hearing but succeeded only spasmodically. Any publicity was better than none. When the *Sun* took us sufficiently seriously to feature Charles Kennedy on their front page as a poisonous snake, and the *Daily Mail* took a prominent page to ridicule our policies, we were delighted. But our infamy was short-lived. When the Conservatives realized the full extent of the damage the Duncan Smith leadership was causing and summarily ditched him in favour of Michael Howard, there was a palpable sense in Parliament and in the press lobby that 'normal' two-party politics had resumed. Occasionally we broke the duopoly, as with the spectacular victory by Sarah Teather in the Brent East by-election, but that was soon discounted by commentators as a mere by-election exception, and the Labour Party got its act together to prevent a repetition in Hartlepool.

The mood in the run-up to the 2005 election was very mixed. We had much to be pleased about: there were more MPs and councillors than at any time in the party's living memory; our leader was popular and his credibility greatly enhanced by opposition to the war in Iraq; there was a serious professionalism in our campaigning and press operations, and in much of our policy-making; and we had a new generation of high-quality candidates who saw entry to Parliament through the Lib Dems as a serious career option. Yet there was also frustration as we failed to break through.

This session of parliament began with a death and ended with another: that of my mother. But the ties to my parents, latterly my mother, were much weaker than those to my wife, and my mother's death, though mourned, left few traces. For the last quarter of her life she had led a private, solitary life, avoiding company and shunning friendship and seemingly more content in her emotional self-reliance than in her earlier dependence on an overbearing husband, inattentive sons and interfering neighbours. The person she loved more than any other, her sister Irene in Australia, she had seen only once in the fifty years since Irene had emigrated. Early mental illness and numerous operations for bowel cancer in her middle age had taken their toll on her too. I stayed with her and maintained regular contact during the five years when I was fighting York, but with the onset of Olympia's illness my visits became less frequent; even then, she apologized so profusely for the inconvenience caused that a trip from London was made to seem like a journey to the North Pole. She moved into sheltered accommodation but shunned the communal area, imagining that the *Daily Telegraph* readers who occupied it would persecute her because of her factory-girl background and her infamous elder son's politics. But we did give her some real pleasures. The first was when she was persuaded to come to London to attend first Paul's and then Aida's wedding. After she had finished apologizing to station porters and taxi drivers for her Yorkshire accent, she enjoyed herself and revelled in the role of family matriarch. She coped happily with sharing a table at Aida's wedding with a real lord and lady. Had we warned her in advance, she would have stayed away.

A few years later, I took Rachel to meet her. At last, in her eighties, here was a daughter-in-law she heartily approved of: naturally kind, attentive and well-mannered, and with the added bonus of a public school voice. But, alas, about this time her memory started to go and she became increasingly confused. Daily routines became progressively more difficult and irritated phone calls to me from the warden more frequent. The management company running the sheltered housing made it painfully clear that helping dotty old ladies who had locked themselves out and were partially clothed was not part of a warden's job description, nor did it suit their corporate image. My brother and I were urged to move her (though she owned her own flat), and after a difficult spell in York District Hospital and numerous assessments, we moved her to an Abbeyfield home nearby in south-west London, specializing in senile dementia. Through the haze of confusion, she could dimly pick out the contours of an unfamiliar new world which had involved the loss of her home and home town, a long journey, and admission to an institution with locked doors and strange people. In one of her lucid moments, she told me of her horror that she appeared to have returned to a 'loony bin'. She had, I think, enough of a grasp of reality to hate the imprisonment, the dislocation of her routine, and the indignity of collective care. After a few weeks, she caught a new infection which she made little attempt to fight and died soon afterwards.

Her funeral was a sad little affair, with my brother Keith, his first wife, myself, my children and Rachel. She had outlived her sister and all her friends. Having spent all her long life in the city of York, she had been taken two hundred miles away to die. But the harsh truth was that the waves had closed over her life very quickly.

When the general election came, the party nationally started with just over 20 per cent of the vote and expected to pick up 3–4 per cent more during the campaign as we received more exposure. It was hoped that Charles's likeable and engaging personality (and a baby due imminently) would trump the clever but less likeable or engaging Michael Howard and a prime minister increasingly discredited by the war.

The campaign launch in particular was a very public disaster. Charles was not on form, which I assumed was due to new parental duties but his critics alleged was the result of a very bad hangover. He was widely blamed for stumbling over tax policy. But even if he had been on top form and memorized his lines, he would have struggled. The problem had been anticipated the previous evening and I had suggested sitting with him on the platform and intervening in the event that tricky questions came in, as they were likely to with Andrew Neil, Adam Boulton, Andrew Marr and Nick Robinson in the audience. Precedence, however, demanded that the chairman of the campaign committee, Lord Razzall, the chairman of the manifesto team, Matthew Taylor, the deputy leader, Sir Menzies Campbell, and a woman should occupy the available seats. My attempts to stage-whisper from the back of the room merely added to the journalists' hilarity.

Charles redeemed himself with a fine display in a set-piece interview on BBC with David Dimbleby, but the damage had already been done. The damage, in my view, was compounded by a conscious 'left of Labour' strategy, which reached its climax with our prize Labour defector, Brian Sedgemore. Brian was in any event stepping down as MP for Hackney and, while he had impeccably liberal views on social issues and had voted against the war, hostile newspapers gleefully pointed out that he was an unreconstructed Bennite who had once crafted Labour's alternative economic strategy. And while I did my best to communicate our tax policy, and while the idea of a 50p top rate and a local income tax were popular according to the polls, the insistence of our strategists on linking the 50p rate to spending commitments meant that, for very small sums of money, we could be portrayed as a high-tax, tax-raising party. This was not what many voters were looking for after Gordon Brown's big splurge of public spending and increased taxes. It would have been worse if the Tories had not put forward a highly implausible programme of tax cuts financed by improbable 'waste' savings; and if Howard Flight, their number-two economic spokesman, had not spoken out of turn, to be stripped on the spot of his job and his candidacy.

In the event, we advanced with a net gain of ten, compared with six in 2001. Objectively, this was a good result. But there was a sense of disappointment despite impressive advances in Labour-held seats. In politics as in economics it is expectations that matter as much as underlying reality. There had been no breakthrough. Charles's earlier talk of our 'overtaking the Conservatives' now sounded hollow. With some exceptions like my own seat, the

Conservatives had made advances against us in the south. Moreover, their campaigning techniques had improved greatly, making ours look rather antiquated. And immediately after the election Michael Howard had stood down with a view to promoting a new style of modern Conservatism under David Cameron. At this point strong leadership was required to recapture a sense of momentum, with new ideas in terms of policy and political activity.

For the first time, serious questions were raised by MPs about the leadership, going beyond routine Westminster grumbling and gossip. There was growing speculation about 'health problems' and about a likely leadership contest. But, not for the first time, a by-election came to the rescue. Patsy Calton, having just held the seat of Cheadle despite being in the final stages of cancer, died a few weeks after the general election, precipitating a particularly difficult battle. This had once been a Tory stronghold, a prosperous suburban Cheshire corner of the Manchester conurbation, and they were in full cry, fighting an energetic and highly aggressive campaign against our candidate, Mark Hunter, the Stockport council leader. As at Romsey and Brent East, Chris Rennard's team worked their magic; the MPs, led by Charles Kennedy, pitched in delivering leaflets and knocking on doors; and the election was won. A potential leadership crisis was postponed.

I spent the spare time I had that summer, including the hot afternoons during a walking and eating holiday among the *bastide* towns of Lot et Garonne in south-west France, writing a couple of booklets: one on public services reform, the other on the politics of identity, updating a paper I had written for Demos a decade earlier. Lurking at the back of my mind was the thought that, if there were a leadership contest, it could be helpful to be known as someone who had something interesting to say.

The recess was followed by one of the most politically damaging party conferences in recent years, dominated by leadership speculation. Just over three months later Charles Kennedy would be gone, amid considerable bitterness. The full story has been told with admirable clarity and objectivity by Greg Hurst in his biography of Charles. I don't have a great deal to add beyond some detail that was important to me. I would become one of the central figures in the coup to change the leadership, but, as Greg acknowledges, I became involved only very reluctantly.

When serious agitation started for a change of leadership, my initial view was that I didn't want to know. I was happy with the leader we had. He was still popular and had a fund of credit from the Iraq War. He had been personally helpful to me, though we were not close. I discounted many of the stories I heard as the product of personal grudges or frustrated ambition. Even when I was persuaded by people who had no axe to grind and who knew him well that there was a problem, I took the view that there might be a heavy cost to ousting a popular leader and that the main alternatives being canvassed were unlikely to be an improvement.

I remained of that view while most of my shadow Cabinet colleagues had already been persuaded of the need for a change. I was finally convinced in a one-to-one meeting that we had sought with Charles to clarify the situation. I went in expecting him to say 'yes, there is a problem, but I am dealing with it and I hope I can count on your support'. I would then have pledged support and tried to help defuse the rebellion. To my surprise, he categorically denied any knowledge of specific incidents that even his loyal staff had acknowledged. I have since been told that a state of denial is a characteristic symptom, but I didn't understand that at the time and merely felt let down.

With hindsight and, perhaps, more cunning, I should have seized control of the rebellion at that point and turned it to personal advantage. But I was persuaded to play a more modest role, communicating to Charles the collective lack of confidence of his shadow Cabinet colleagues and the need for an elder statesman figure, Sir Menzies Campbell, to take over and stabilize the party. My concern at this point was that the process should be as respectful of Charles as was possible, and hopefully give him more time, though there was a counter-view that speed was of the essence. I left at Christmas 2005 for a visit to Sri Lanka – to open a village built in the wake of the South Asian tsunami of the year before by the efforts of some of my Hampton constituents – and to the wedding of one of my Indian nieces in Goa. I left behind in my constituency office safe the sole copy of a letter seeking Charles's resignation, signed by eleven of my shadow Cabinet colleagues, and hoped against hope that the situation would resolve itself in my absence. Far from it: someone in the shadow Cabinet leaked the contents, and I arrived back home to a media barrage on my doorstep. I played my role as deliverer of the letter; someone had destroyed Charles's last defences by leaking his medical records; and he was gone. There was immense ill-feeling in the parliamentary and wider party among those who did not know the facts and some who did. The whole episode was the worst I had experienced as an MP and left me, and several others involved, feeling soiled and diminished.

If the end of Charles's leadership was messy, the opening moves in the succession were equally so. There had been a tacit understanding that in order to minimize conflict, we should rally behind Ming Campbell. There were plausible alternatives to provide competition, but no one foresaw that Mark Oaten's and Simon Hughes's private lives would emerge into the public domain, crippling both their leadership campaigns.

Then Ming, as acting leader, stumbled very badly in early outings in Parliament, his elegantly authoritative, gentlemanly demeanour crumbling in the bear-pit atmosphere of the Commons. His leadership bid was seriously weakened and the door was ajar to a new challenger. I felt too committed to move. Chris Huhne saw the opportunity and moved quickly to exploit it. As an ex-journalist, he was highly effective in seizing media opportunities. The majority of MPs and peers rallied round Ming and he won, though serious doubts had been created by the campaign, which were never fully dissipated subsequently. I was left wondering what might have been had I not stood back, though I had the consolation of being chosen by our MPs, on a tight vote, as deputy leader.

Chapter 13

A Taste of Leadership

An obsession with leadership is not unique to the Lib Dems. For a decade and a half the Conservative Party was dominated by the consequences of the overthrow of Mrs Thatcher and the failure of Messrs Major, Hague, Duncan Smith and Howard, in turn, to revive their fortunes. Labour had a similar problem in the 1980s and clearly does so again. An American-style presidential system has quietly evolved, in which the personality of the leader matters more than the strength of the supporting team. Parties have become like Premier League football teams, whose managers no longer just pick the team and decide tactics – the Attlee model of leadership – but are the repository of all the hopes and fears of supporters. They get the credit if their team play well and the blame if they play badly, as if the players themselves have little competence or inspiration beyond the magic communicated by a Special One. The pre-match wind-ups or post-match recriminations between Fergie and Arsène, like prime minister's questions, have acquired a significance way beyond their limited content. The most dangerous positions are either to have responsibility for a political Chelsea, which is expected to win and which has the backing of the super-rich but then disappoints – the Conservative problem until very recently

– or to manage a top team, which has fans with high expectations, a great tradition, big potential and some excellent players,
but which hasn't the resources to break through to the very top,
like the Lib Dems. Or at least, until now.

For reasons described in the previous chapter, the end of
Charles Kennedy was inevitable but painful and damaging to
all of us involved. Ming Campbell's brief reign was unhappy in a
different way, and while his downfall was equally inevitable the
manner of it reflected badly on the political class as a whole, and
its commentators, as well as on us as a party. To watch a decent
man being kicked to death is not an edifying spectacle. To see
cartoonists in otherwise liberal newspapers depicting a sixty-five-
year-old as a geriatric has-been with a Zimmer frame went way
beyond political wit.

On one level, the Ming dynasty, as it came to be called, had
some successes. Indeed, the underlying strengths of the party
in adversity had been made apparent in a by-election in Ealing
Southall in June. The Conservatives were widely assumed to
be the main challengers to Labour; they chose a good-looking,
well-connected, local candidate – an Asian Cameron – and
received strong endorsement from the local press and defect-
ing Labour councillors. We fought a traditional campaign, with
MPs and party leaders working alongside volunteers from all
over Britain stuffing envelopes and delivering leaflets. Although
Labour won comfortably, the Conservatives were relegated to
third place.

Leadership questions remained, however and centred on two
aspects of Ming's performance. One was his negative portrayal by
political commentators. After twenty years of being listened to
with deference and respect he was not psychologically equipped

to deal with the noisy hostility and mockery of the Commons. By the time he was launching well-prepared, sharp questions, that battle had already been lost and he had been written off by the press gallery.

Secondly, a naturally conservative, cautious, risk-averse approach to issues is valuable in a team, but was not what was required when the Lib Dems were in danger of sinking out of sight. Ming was courteous to a fault, anxious not to upstage or embarrass colleagues, but also, particularly in the field of foreign affairs, in which he had considerable expertise, concerned not to stray too far from the responsible, nuanced position he would have taken as a minister.

Whether for these or deeper reasons, our poll ratings sank and his personal rating remained poor. Nonetheless, there was a spirit of unity at the 2007 Brighton conference and much good-will towards the leadership, based partly on the assumption that there would be a general election immediately or by the spring, and that Ming would then either lead the tricky negotiations necessitated by a 'hung' parliament or would graciously step aside with the thanks of the party and make way for Chris Huhne or Nick Clegg, whose embryonic leadership campaigns were much in evidence.

Gordon Brown's decision not to proceed with an early election was disastrous for his own credibility and authority. But it also blew this comfortable scenario apart. I think that Ming, as a sensitive man, was painfully aware that the traits that made him personally respected and liked were not those now required for political survival or to lift a struggling party. The new political situation exposed Ming to speculation as to how he could survive up to two and a half more years of this parliament; but most of us in senior positions in the party had no appetite for another leadership battle.

On the weekend of 10/11 October there was dreadful press coverage and I believe Ming decided to go then. I never discovered the precise sequence of events that precipitated the resignation, but during the afternoon of the Monday I was sought out by Ming's chief of staff, Archy Kirkwood, and told that Ming had resigned and that I, as deputy, was now the leader until a leadership election could be held. The party president and chief executive mapped out a timetable; we agreed a public statement; and I was whisked off to meet the leader's staff whom I had inherited.

Once the shock had worn off and the frenzied round of interviews had subsided, most of them alleging plots that did not exist, I was able to reflect on the challenge ahead. Party morale was low; membership and income were falling; MPs were torn between a sense of relief and foreboding that the downward spiral could continue. I could not claim that my reign was overburdened by expectations: the reaction of colleagues was closer to pity and sympathy than envy, and the summit of their ambitions for me was not to make a bad situation worse. They also made it clear from the outset that I should not think of being anything other than a caretaker leader. The point was made, with varying degrees of subtlety, that since Ming had been judged 'too old' at sixty-six, the party and the public were unlikely to turn to a sixty-four-year-old. Now, they said, was the time for a 'new generation'. I resented the advice at the time and the lazily ageist assumptions behind it, but without the backing of a critical mass of MPs there was no way forward. I ended my second day in a state of deep gloom, mixed with a growing sense of panic, for next day was my first prime minister's questions. I didn't sleep, trying to dream up a question and working out how to handle the inevitable wall of noise, aggression and ridicule that I could expect.

Prime minister's questions is an event like no other in Parliament: a packed, noisy, irreverent Punch and Judy show, far removed from the decorous but flat and soporific atmosphere that surrounds most parliamentary business. But parliamentary reputations are made and lost there, regardless of any wider or more useful political talent. Liberal Democrat leaders have had a particularly hard time, subject to taunts and shouting from both the two larger parties. Paddy Ashdown never lacked self-confidence, but his memoirs recall his frustration and rage at never being taken seriously in this context. Charles Kennedy did lack self-confidence – unlike TV, this was not his medium – but was treated more sympathetically in general. Ming's difficulties I have already described. Our leaders also lack the practical and psychological support of the Dispatch Box and are therefore forced either to look down at notes, which attracts screams of derision and looks bad on television, or to speak from memory or inspiration, which risks disaster. The opposition leader is allowed six questions, which allows for a serious argument to be developed. The Lib Dem leader is allowed two, which have to be kept brief in order to head off barracking. Dennis Skinner and his friends sit a few feet in front and Tory wags to the right. In the ten years I had been in Parliament, my three predecessors, and our party troops behind them, had regarded this part of the week as an ordeal to be endured rather than a political opportunity. They also faced Tony Blair, who had developed a mastery of this par-ticular medium and specialized in the good-natured but brutally dismissive put-down. I had the advantage of facing Gordon Brown instead, and having shadowed him at Treasury questions for several years I knew that he was in many respects cleverer than Blair, but lacked Blair's finesse and performance skills.

My strategy from the outset was to be meticulously prepared. The material was my own, but I had a skilled team to bounce ideas off several hours before the event, and help with a range of carefully crafted options for the two-stage exchange, taking into account Cameron's possible questions, and every conceivable reply by Brown – all, then, to be memorized as far as possible. The difficult bit is to hold all this together in the face of a cacophony of noise, trying to judge when to wait and when to plough on so as not to lose the timing and the punchlines. I was deeply indebted to the drama teacher who, half a century earlier, had made me overcome my fear of live audiences by fixing a member of the audience in the eye and talking, one to one, shutting out the terrifying mass of faces.

The first two outings went well and attracted favourable comment, which gave me the confidence to attempt more aggressive questions, and finally jokes, including 'Stalin to Mr Bean'. From Brown's responses, then, and in a succession of prime ministerial statements and the debate on the Queen's Speech, it was clear that he had no capacity for repartee beyond clumsy, predictable, flailing blows which were easily countered by changing the angle of attack. I was naturally flattered and encouraged by my favourable reviews, but valued most the revival of morale among my own troops. I was amazed that at the heart of government there was no one who could help Gordon Brown improve his technique.

I also discovered in those few weeks a character trait of my own that I hadn't previously identified and didn't much like, but which proved invaluable. I rather enjoyed putting in the knife. Years of trying hard to be fair and reasonable were cast aside. It wasn't that I had any personal animosity towards Gordon Brown; quite the reverse. I think that at the core of it was a suppressed rage: the feeling that I could be doing his job, and doing it much better.

Apart from making a success of PMQs and other set-piece parliamentary performances, I had one overriding objective, which was to keep the Liberal Democrats in the front of the news by responding rapidly to new issues with an approach that was distinctive, challenging and – hopefully – reflected our underlying values. My party has never been short of ideas, thoughtful policies, talented politicians and strong convictions, but has had difficulty getting into the mainstream of national debate. There is a tendency in the media to portray every issue in simple, dialectical, two-party terms, and to regard our party as a minor nuisance, to be reluctantly given a walk-on part in any serious drama. It is, however, simply unprofessional to blame the 'meeja'. If we have suffered badly from neglect over the years, we have perhaps acquiesced too easily in the role assigned to us, maybe through lack of energy and abrasiveness.

The lesson of Charles Kennedy's political success on the Iraq War was the need to muscle in on the story; to take risks; to challenge; to avoid being sucked into any cosy establishment consensus; and to tap into popular idealism, anger and frustration – the politics of protest. Although we were distinctive on civil liberties and environmental issues, despite rather half-hearted attempts by David Cameron to move into that particular space, there was no early successor to Iraq as a defining issue, and the result was growing invisibility. We had to raise our game.

All of this is not a criticism of my predecessors, since I had been at the heart of efforts, at least in relation to economic policy, to forswear easy, populist campaigning stunts in favour of policies that gave us credibility. There is a tension in any opposition party between the need to milk public applause and seek the approval of well-read newspapers on one hand, and to appear credible as a party of government – competent, responsible and economically literate – on the other. As leader, however, I decided to take risks and sail closer to the wind, helped by an excellent media team and a press officer, Puja Darbari, who understood exactly what I was trying to achieve and was brilliant in securing the necessary publicity.

The first issue that surfaced, within days of my becoming leader, was the imminent visit of the king of Saudi Arabia, and an invitation to Buckingham Palace to attend a banquet in the king's honour. I decided to stay away, partly to protest at the kingdom's appalling human rights record, but also to draw attention to the cynical way in which our own government, and its Conservative predecessor, had been corrupted by the massive Al Yamamah arms contract. Most recently, the Serious Fraud Office had been stopped by ministers from pursuing a bribery investigation into BAe Systems' dealings with Saudi Arabia. The issue had become an important one for the party, and I had introduced three debates in Parliament on the subject. The king's visit was a golden opportunity to raise awareness of it. My media team were 100 per cent behind my proposal to boycott the Saudi visit, but some colleagues were very nervous: the Palace and the Foreign Office would be deeply offended; my gesture might be seen as anti-Arab and/or anti-Islamic; BAe Systems jobs were at stake; precedents would be set for future leaders and future state visits. I decided to ignore the objections while making it clear that I was not advocating a general boycott of Saudi Arabia, but did oppose the accolade of a state visit and the obsequiousness with which our government was treating the House of Saud. My main worry was that no one would notice or care what the acting leader of a third party thought. But they did. There was an enormous groundswell of support outside the Westminster village and what I said clearly touched a raw nerve.

Another opportunity was presented by the growing crisis in the banking sector, centring on the Northern Rock bank. I had already created a stir at the time of the earlier run on the bank in September by attacking the government's decision to bail out the bank with loans (as opposed to protecting the depositors without taking it into public ownership). I also publicly blamed the senior management of the bank for recklessness and personal greed, a view that clashed badly with the official view that they had simply been the victim of bad luck, a US-generated credit crunch. It soon became clear that the government had taken on a vast, open-ended commitment to lending enormous sums – up to £30 billion – with only partial security; that the senior management had indeed behaved very badly; and that the government's preferred option of being marriage-broker for a private sale of the bank was unlikely to work or, if it did, would reward private speculators at the expense of the taxpayer. With help from my Treasury team colleague Matthew Oakeshott, a City expert who shared my instinct for an aggressive approach to the issue – unlike the Conservatives who kept their heads well down – I challenged the government's handling of the matter. We advocated temporary public ownership as the best way of protecting the state's enormous stake in the bank and ensuring that any upside from a subsequent sale would accrue to the taxpayer, not to someone like Richard Branson.

Such credibility as I and my colleagues won over this issue was due in part to long-standing warnings about the problems that would arise from rapid expansion of bank lending to households, much of it secured against a bubble in the housing market and resulting in high levels of household debt. The immediate trigger for the Northern Rock crisis lay in international capital markets rather than our domestic property market. But Northern Rock's wild lending spree pumped up our housing bubble. And the coincidence of falling property prices and a pronounced economic slowdown, which I had warned of for several years, was beginning to become a reality, though at that stage only just beginning.

Gordon Brown's other embarrassments came thick and fast: bitter and personalized criticisms from service chiefs; the loss of personal data on twenty-five million people due to extreme carelessness by HM Revenue and Customs; allegedly illegal and certainly very questionable handling of party donations. Any opposition leader would be seriously remiss not to turn this succession of disasters to advantage. My challenge was to ensure that the Conservatives did not monopolize the airwaves and to find the right blend of serious criticism, righteous indignation and humour to capture the tragi-comedy of Gordon Brown's decline.

The political commentators were complimentary, sometimes gushingly so. I worried that I was being talked up so that my predecessor and successor could be talked down. I also marvelled at the low threshold at which political criticism switches to adulation. A few weeks earlier David Cameron was being treated as a cross between Churchill and Abraham Lincoln for the rather modest achievement of having memorized a speech; now I was acquiring cult status on the back of a few well-directed one-liners, after a decade's worth of serious speeches and articles, and even jokes, had previously sunk without trace. Still, I decided not to worry too much about the problems of success, but to enjoy it.

The delicious icing on the cake came when my press officer and the production team of Andrew Neil's late-night show, *This Week*, used my long-standing interest in ballroom and Latin dancing to pair me with Alesha Dixon, the talented and beautiful winner of *Strictly Come Dancing*. Becoming the envy of every man in Britain, with an invitation to write about dancing, rather than politics, for the *Mail on Sunday*, would have been beyond my wildest imaginings three months earlier.

Chapter 14

Fame, Fortune
and Notoriety

We are all entitled, as Andy Warhol reminded us, to fifteen minutes of fame. I have been fortunate to enjoy some for two years, beyond the more parochial recognition in my constituency and party. I am conscious that fame is transitory. For most of us, and for opposition politicians more than most, there is also the serious limitation that it is disconnected from power and decision-making. But I am grateful for the opportunity, as long as it lasts, to communicate political ideas and ideals to a wider audience, to promote my party, and to realize some personal ambitions that have been incubated in obscurity for decades.

This has occurred unusually late in life. Older politicians, like older people in general, are expected to fade away quietly to make way for those who are younger, fresher, more ambitious and energetic. A gentler, less demanding, more dignified role awaits in the Lords or on the boards of companies or charities. I can certainly see the disadvantages of gerontocracy and would not want us to emulate Mao's Chinese politburo where eighty was middle-aged. But our opposite stereotype is no better. I have discovered, by accident rather than design, that age is not inversely correlated with energy and commitment.

I am, nonetheless, very conscious of mortality. I had never seen anyone die until the person closest to me died in 2001. I have, ever since, lived with that experience, and one of its legacies was a determination to live life to the full, to squeeze as much as possible out of every day, conscious always that time is slipping away. Having the additional blessing of a very contented second marriage has made it easier to be focused and single-minded. As a consequence, I work harder than I have ever done, and more effectively. Age greatly increases productivity. Articles that would have taken days to grind out now take an hour or so. My wonderfully efficient PA, Joan Bennett, ensures that every minute is sensibly utilized. I have developed some skill in improvising speeches and presentations, and this economizes on time and effort and actually helps to build a rapport with live audiences. So I do many more. Occasionally, what my wife Rachel calls the T-word – tiredness – creeps in subversively, but then older people need less sleep, and a little R & R goes a long way.

I am often asked why I am not the party leader and whether I still want to be. The unexciting truth is that I am perfectly happy as I am, playing the role of number two to Nick Clegg. As I noted earlier, there were a few days after the resignation of Ming Campbell when I sounded out colleagues about a leadership bid, but it was clear that there was a collective wish to move on to the new generation that Nick Clegg and Chris Huhne represented. I settled into the role of acting leader for a couple of months and was reconciled to handing over responsibility after our enormously protracted leadership process.

In those weeks I satisfied myself, and surprised others, that I could handle competently or better the role our leader has to play in Parliament and the media, as well as motivating our troops in the party and the country. My reaction at the end was: been there, done that. I have, moreover, many faults, but vanity is not one of them. I have always moved effortlessly from the spotlight to the shadows and there is a particular pleasure to be had from enjoying prominence and (in my case, modest) power without feeling the need for them.

I am not the only politician in Westminster to have discovered that there are more satisfying roles than being a party leader. Iain Duncan Smith and William Hague have both reinvented themselves. They, like me, now have the best of all worlds: an enviable degree of respect and affection, and considerable influence, without the intrigue that surrounds those who control access to the greasy pole of preferment, and the need to explain every minor gaffe or justify every disappointing opinion poll.

I can now look at the party's future, and my own, with more detachment than if I carried all the burdens of leadership: the endless ridicule and abuse from opponents and commentators; the importuning for jobs, peerages and influence; the resentment of sacked colleagues and lack of gratitude from promoted protégés; the untimely press leaks and prolonged publicity droughts; opinionated, unelected supporters demanding that their views be accepted; councillors, backbenchers and MEPs pressing for greater recognition; superannuated peers fighting old battles; and the likelihood that none of this will lead to any more long-term recognition than a painting on the wall in Portcullis House, probably tucked away in an unvisited corner.

Being leader of the Liberal Democrats has been described as one of the toughest jobs in British politics, and with good reason. There is a high level of responsibility – for leading sixty-three

MPs; three thousand councillors (more, now, than the Labour Party); a bevy of lords and MEPs, MSPs and Assembly Members – and it includes maintaining, and building upon, the 20 per cent or so of popular support we can reasonably expect. There is the hope rather than the expectation of imminent national power, so the loyalty of supporters has to be based on trust and team spirit rather than the prospect of spoils which keeps Conservative and Labour politicians motivated. We are regarded by our two main opponents as a nuisance, an added, unwanted complication and a worrying uncertainty, and they try to deal with us by ignoring us or resorting to ridicule. The media, especially that which is unsympathetic to our cause, reflects these tactical ploys and even editors or journalists who want to be fair-minded find triangular debate difficult to accommodate. As a consequence, our leaders find it difficult to be heard. There is a daily battle to get a slot in the main news for the leader or a leading spokesman. Leading the Liberal Democrats is like leading a biblical tribe of nomadic pastoralists across a semi-arid landscape, constantly looking for the water of favourable publicity. There are frequent droughts, for which the leader is held responsible. What sustains us is a sense that there is a promised land.

Nick Clegg is well equipped for this difficult task. Apart from the obvious qualities of intelligence and articulacy, he has a strong character and equable temperament, which will emerge in the heat of a general election battle; a clear sense of strategic direction; and sufficient resilience to cope with the endless pinpricks, disappointments and unflattering reviews that are the lot of leadership. My impression is that he is big enough to welcome a high-profile deputy, and we have formed a good partnership.

*

One of the more gratifying experiences of the recent past is having (among various awards) been chosen as Parliamentarian of the Year. This award is the result of a poll of MPs of all parties and is all the more appreciated for reflecting non-tribal support. The experience has led me to reflect on what being a parliamentarian actually means.

It is easy to make the case that Parliament today is a decayed and marginalized – indeed, corrupt – institution. I described earlier the way in which power has seeped away to the executive, as well as to Europe and regional assemblies and the Scottish Parliament. Large parliamentary majorities and the discipline of the whips mean that votes are rarely close or significant. Good oratory is very rare. Abysmal, obsequious speeches on the government side can be a passport to the front bench, where the toadies can enjoy a long ministerial career, reading speeches written by officials and fortified by party propaganda inserted by a special adviser. Oral questions are often based on hand-outs from the party spokespersons and those that are remotely taxing are not answered or invite a partisan response. Serious debates are usually very badly attended once the lead speakers have departed, and often before. And MPs can expect to read in the press, especially after the expenses scandal, that they are greedy freeloaders with their snouts in the trough, enjoying a lavish lifestyle at the taxpayers' expense. Even those of us who emerged unscathed and without criticism from the scandal have been diminished by the popular view that parliament is a thoroughly discredited institution.

But a strong case can also be made that Parliament can rise to the big occasions and, at its best, is still a significant democratic force for good. The ritual of Prime Minister's Questions, for example, can sometimes be little more than a noisy, childish bun-fight. But it also exposes more vividly than any other medium the ability (or not) of prime ministers and potential prime ministers to think quickly on their feet and to communicate their messages simply, clearly and under pressure from three to four hundred noisy MPs. My perhaps overrated, and certainly over-repeated, quip at PMQs about Gordon Brown's transformation from Stalin to Mr Bean would not have had the impact it did in any other context. William Hague's wit and Michael Howard's forensic cross-questioning did not, in the event, translate into wider politi-cal success, but Gordon Brown's failure to master the medium has done much to undermine his credibility and self-confidence; Iain Duncan Smith was seen to be 'not up to it'; and Ming Campbell's leadership never recovered from early stumbles in the face of sustained barracking.

Parliament also stages some fine debates amid the dross. A good minister will stand his or her ground and take repeated interventions, turning them to advantage in building a case. I have been appalled, as many others have, by the recent torrent of Home Office legislation, which my colleagues estimate has pro-duced over three thousand new criminal offences; but I could not help but admire the way Charles Clarke and David Blunkett, in particular, argued their brief. Tony Blair's defence of the Iraq War may have gone against the grain, but was undeniably impressive. The best debates tend to be on controversial issues that cut across party lines, like the recent legislation on human fertilization and embryology, though they are often spoilt by wickedly unhelpful timetabling.

The British parliamentary tradition of legislative trial by debate can reach impressive heights, but has been corrupted by the ruthless guillotining of controversial new laws. The moments of high drama are, moreover, diluted greatly in their impact by interminable discussion of the detailed clauses, with a handful of MPs struggling to swim through a treacle of incomprehensible verbiage produced by parliamentary draftsmen.

Behind the confrontational aspects of Parliament, my experience has been that, off-camera, relations between MPs from different parties are generally amicable and businesslike. A lot of work is done through all-party groups. I established two – for the police and victims of crime – working with professional and pressure groups, and was able to help raise the profile of important issues. One of the most effective cross-party campaigning groups I participate in brings together opponents of Heathrow expansion. The de facto leader is John McDonnell, an independent-minded Labour left-winger, whose constituency includes the proposed new runway, and he sets the tone in blunting whatever ideological axes we try to grind.

I do not wish to exaggerate the extent of cross-party and non-party working. As an opposition spokesman, I take good care to keep my distance from government ministers, while remaining on affable, first-name terms. Despite shadowing Gordon Brown for five years, and an acquaintance going back thirty years to when we collaborated on the *Red Papers for Scotland*, I have had little contact with him beyond friendly banter centred on his affected or real surprise that we were on opposite sides in spite of a good deal of 'progressive' common ground.

There was a short time in October 2008, at the height of the financial crisis, with our leading banks close to collapse, when Alistair Darling tried to generate a cross-party approach. The spirit of national unity lasted several days, until the Conservatives judged that it would help a Labour government and work to their disadvantage. I realized a few months later quite how incendiary such talk can be in our tribal political culture, when I referred in passing in my Mail on Sunday column to the public perhaps wanting to see a government of national unity in an emergency. It was seized upon as evidence that I was agitating for a place in the Brown government: wrong, but a damaging accusation in a system predicated on inter-party rivalry and conflict.

There is an underlying problem with our model of strong government and weak Parliament. Governments find it easy to guarantee the passage of almost all legislation unless it grievously offends their own party. Even then, many government MPs can be bought off by being given jobs (the 'payroll vote'), plum positions on select committees, perks like foreign travel for those who are flattered by such offerings, and promises to help resolve constituency issues. There remain a handful of irreconcilably independent-minded MPs in any parliament who are described as the 'usual suspects'. Parliament has been blessed on the Labour side by characters such as Jeremy Corbin, Frank Field, Kate Hoey, John McDonnell, Dennis Skinner, Bob Marshall-Andrews and Mark Fisher and, before they severed their links, Clare Short and George Galloway – the latter the best natural orator in the House. Among the Tories, there are Bill Cash, Sir Peter Tapsell, Douglas Hogg and Richard Shepherd. But only very rarely do the usual suspects attract a sufficient number of other rebels to put the government's majority at risk.

If Parliament is to flower and to challenge the power of the elective dictatorship of government, more is needed than an occasional, accidental, hung parliament. There are several essential changes. One is to end the winner-takes-all system whereby one disciplined party, with a minority of support among those who actually bother to vote, can wield almost untrammelled power on the basis of an artificially large majority. The Scottish parliamentary model has shown in a UK context how it is possible to combine a constituency-based system – which has undoubted merits, as well as attractions to existing MPs – with greater proportionality. A second is, through reform of the House of Lords, to ensure that there is an effective revising chamber which can give new legislation a more satisfactory cross-examination than the usually derisory, token review given by the Commons. There is now a broad consensus that such a chamber would have to be predominantly elected in order to enjoy democratic legitimacy. Third, in the present poisonous atmosphere of public cynicism, there is little appetite for more politicians, so any reform would have to be accompanied by a substantial scaling-back of the number of MPs and lords, with a more austere and disciplined approach to pay and expenses.

Political celebrity status is not achieved by parliamentary performance alone. There are some very able parliamentarians – fine speakers, conscientious attenders, knowledgeable authorities on procedure, incisive questioners of ministers, cunning tacticians – whose names are largely unknown outside their own constituencies (or perhaps even there). They can be forgiven for feeling frustrated at the national media publicity that some high-profile colleagues, including me, succeed in attracting. I share some of the bemusement. Only a couple of years ago my idea of a good week in the media would have been a splash in one of the two weekly newspapers serving my Twickenham constituency, an interview on the BBC News channel, and an occasional outing on an agenda-setting programme like *Today* or *Question Time*.

Politicians have a symbiotic relationship with news and political journalists. They need and nourish each other like the tick birds that feed off the parasites on the backs of hippos (though which are the tick birds and which the hippos in this analogy is open to debate). Or, switching to another colourful image, attributed to Enoch Powell, for politicians to complain about the media is like fishermen complaining about the sea: if they don't like it, they should find another way of earning a living.

I try to treat print, television and radio journalists with respect. I rarely refuse interviews, try to return calls, answer questions as directly and fully as possible, and engage in debate with journalists on topical issues that they are often struggling, as I am, to get on top of. I cannot complain about the resulting coverage. But I am always conscious that any major blunder or indiscretion would be punished as surely as my better contributions are praised. And I could just as easily become a victim of changing fashions as I have recently been a beneficiary. Having built a reputation in part on a successful analysis of economic bubbles, I have become something of a bubble phenomenon myself and have no doubt that there are plenty of pins out there waiting to burst it.

The public has, I think, little appreciation of the way in which a story becomes news and the mechanisms by which parties and individual politicians become part of it. I have become very weary of conversations with party supporters or members of the public who assume that whenever my party is absent from coverage in the main news bulletin or the newspapers, it is due either to laziness or incompetence by the party's spokespeople or to a vast media conspiracy to exclude us. There is certainly a constant battle between the parties for coverage and the output reflects the resources put into it. Television editors and correspondents and, even more, print editors have their political predilections, and exercise them with varying degrees of brazenness. My own party has a small but professional operation and we have to work harder than our competitors to keep in the story and get our views across. But it is not impossible, and I relish accounts of paranoia and jealousy among our rivals. (I have heard it on good authority that whenever my name appears in certain newspapers before those of Tory economic spokesmen, the Conservatives make a formal complaint.)

The focus of activity is the media 'round' whenever there is an important (in my case, economic) story with political implications. Press officers try to secure 'bids' with the BBC, ITN, Channel 4 and Sky to take a live interview or a 'pre-record', reflecting the party line, for a later news bulletin. For the party spokespersons, the first requirement is to be available quickly and to have a sound bite sufficiently important, interesting or distinctive from the other parties for it to be carried forward into the main news bulletin. The Lib Dem will rarely be accommodated as of right, and so has to have something especially memorable to say or to have carved out a reputation as being the effective opposition, as Charles Kennedy did during the Iraq War and I have been trying to do in relation to the financial crisis. The print media are a more complex challenge, requiring a combination of snappy, prompt press releases; the building of relationships with journalists who want political quotes to reinforce their stories; and the carrying out of proactive research, with the help of the party's paid researchers, to create a story and to take ownership of it. Sometimes the rewards from this activity are slow to arrive. I used to put out regular press releases, from 2003 onwards, warning of house-price inflation and burgeoning personal debt, which were regarded at the time as eccentric or scaremongering; but some journalists remembered, notably Evan Davis of the *Today* programme, who was able to tell George Osborne, when he attempted to raise the problem, that he was five years late.

Beyond the world of the sound bite and the 'rent-a-quote', politicians have to prove themselves in one-to-one interviews. Prime ministers and politicians in demand may try to seek out the soft option of friendly interviewers who will not ask awkward questions, will tolerate sloppy or evasive answers and offer an opportunity for the delivery of propaganda, which seems less blatant from a studio couch than from a conference lectern. Anyone in the political world who expects to be taken seriously has, however, to run the gauntlet of less deferential interrogators: John Humphrys, Jeremy Paxman, Andrew Neil, Jeremy Vine, Adam Boulton, among others. Their job is to keep us honest, and it is one of the strengths of British democracy that they have a licence to treat evasive, unprepared and dishonest politicians with disrespect. I have enjoyed torrid arguments with several of the above, but have learned, sometimes the hard way, that clear, brief, honest answers provide a reasonable defence.

Interviewers do not have to be aggressive to be effective. The Marr programme is popular with politicians because the host gives the guest plenty of scope to develop a theme directed at the Sunday late-breakfast audience. But for those who provide enough rope to hang themselves, Andrew Marr will tie the noose. The programme also organizes breakfast afterwards with the non-political guest stars, which in my case included Helen Mirren, Samantha Bond, Kevin Spacey and Richard Dreyfuss, the first two in particular reducing me to open-mouthed, adolescent awe. Kirsty Young of *Desert Island Discs* is utterly charming but, with the help of meticulous prior research, manages painlessly to extract personal intimacies from her interviewees, including me.

For the political aficionados – and there are still some – the biggest draws are still the weekly Dimbleby debates on *Any Questions* and *Question Time*. The public can be reassured that there is no fix. The questions are not revealed to the panellists in advance. With a little common sense and research it is normally possible to work out what most of the questions will be about. But all participants dread being called first to answer some obscure or quirky question that they know nothing about or for which they do not have some prepared repartee. These two programmes, in their different ways, are very testing, since the panellist is trying (or should be trying) to engage with three different audiences: the live and usually lively audience in front of them; the rest of the panel, including the presenter; and the distant millions who are picking up messages from body language or tone of voice. Contemporary politicians are not used to live audiences, except of the party faithful, and these programmes have the salutary effect of exposing ministers to hostile booing, perhaps for the first time in their lives (which is why many ministers decline to appear), and forcing the rest of us to master skills long atrophied, like weighting answers to create a punchline.

But the political aficionado belongs to an increasingly rare species. Learning to wow a Radio 4, *Newsnight* or *Question Time* audience goes far, but leaves untouched the majority of the public who regard politicians as beneath their contempt or above their understanding, or read newspapers only for the sex, horoscopes or football. For this reason, some of us take our political lives in our hands and appear on comedy quiz shows or reality TV, or take up invitations to be interviewed by (in my case) *Esquire*, *Good Housekeeping* or *The Lady*. It is difficult to know where to draw the line. Charles Kennedy won many admirers for his performances on *Have I Got News for You*. But I doubt that George Galloway enhanced his reputation by appearing in a catsuit on *Big Brother*, lapping milk at Rula Lenska's feet.

Have I Got News for You makes *Question Time* seem a doddle: two hours (before editing) of intense concentration, trying to avoid the twin pitfalls of either being marginalized by the witty exchanges between Paul Merton and Ian Hislop – a little like trying to follow high-speed tennis – or else trying too hard, with a clumsy, tactless intervention that is remembered for years afterwards. I just about survived, in part thanks to Ian Hislop's reassurance and the kindness of the editor who left my sillier comments on the cutting-room floor. After my appearance on that and several other shows I have developed a healthy respect for the serious humorist's craft.

It is also to reach a wider audience that I write for the *Mail on Sunday* on a regular basis and, whenever asked, contribute to the *Sun* and the *Star*. I often encounter a purist view that one should only talk to, and write for, 'serious' newspapers with 'progressive' leanings. I take the opposite view: that the real challenge in politics is to find ways of engaging with those who take a different or hostile position or are simply uninterested.

*

Having learned to surf the media, I am now discovering that the waves of mass communications are changing direction radically. I recall with grim amusement that my political career was almost terminated fifteen years ago by a committee of Lib Dem activists who decided that my media skills were hopelessly inadequate, on the basis of my having failed to top and tail a practice local press release. Every weekend ever since, I have bombarded local newspapers with press releases. But having spent a decade and a half developing good links with local journalists, I find that local newspapers are disappearing fast. My local journal of record, the weekly *Richmond and Twickenham Times*, has become part of the Newsquest empire, has lost many of its journalists and struggles to survive as a free sheet; while another local free paper is fighting off the collapse of advertising revenue. The sense of community and local political engagement that went with having a lively local press is now in jeopardy. The media is fragmenting.

Like most politicians, I spend a growing amount of time communicating through the 'blogosphere', email round-robins and websites. Gordon Brown's YouTube adventures demonstrated the perils of the new media as well as the potential. But the Obama campaign brought to the surface the significance of the rapid development of the new media. The USA is unlike the UK in the sense that there is no strong national press and radio and TV are regionally fragmented. It is still possible in the UK to conceive of sustained political debate via the main terrestrial TV channels and the national press. At the time of writing, the BBC's *News at Ten* still represents the best news outlet; the *Today* programme the best forum for a day's agenda setting; and good coverage in the *Mail* the best way to reach a mass readership. But, like other MPs, I am having to learn rapidly about the new world of blogging, the use of Facebook, and contributions to online debates. Just as my correspondence has switched from 5 to 95 percent email in the last decade, I suspect that the balance of old and new media will switch by comparable amounts in the next. I have no problem with learning new tricks. But I worry that the splintering of the media and the cornucopia of choice will have the effect of stifling anything that could be called a national conversation at the heart of our political culture.

The experience of Obama suggests, however, that geographical and medium fragmentation need not dissipate an underlying message. In my more modest way, I have discovered through the response to my book about the credit crunch, *The Storm*, and the extraordinary turnout at public meetings around the country, that there is a hunger for debate on issues of importance and for direct contact with those who seem to have something to say. It is as if the technology of the twenty-first century is producing a reversion to the political styles of the nineteenth and early twentieth centuries: appropriately enough for an economic crisis that seems to have emerged from that era, and which has in turn been subsumed in a deeper political crisis around Westminster MPs.

The expenses scandal of May 2009 has created the biggest political crisis in my lifetime. Within a few weeks, the old certainties about our political institutions, particularly Parliament, were brutally swept away. The reputation of the institution I laboured for so long to join and in which I have spent the best years of my life has been totally shredded. People I have worked with for a decade have been disgraced, and at the time of writing some of the people in Parliament for whom I had – and have – the highest regard were being swept away, while the chancers, the opportunists and the seriously greedy were getting away with a token apology.

As the scandal unfolded, I felt a sense of despair that I was part of a profession and institution that had suddenly become the focus of popular anger and contempt. 'They are all at it' summed up the public mood. I had been, on a much smaller scale, part of a similar storm in Glasgow when several of my colleagues were marched off to Barlinnie prison for fiddling their expenses, and it was generally assumed that councillors were 'on the take' or spent their time and public money on 'fact-finding' trips to Barbados or the Côte d'Azur. At Shell I had been made to feel that I was part of a corporate monster, polluting the planet and engaged in war crimes in Nigeria. But the parliamentary scandal was much worse because it was based not on innuendo and guilt by association but on hard facts about how large numbers of MPs had taken advantage of expenses claims.

On a purely personal level, I escaped criticism. This was gratifying to the extent that those of my constituents who knew and cared did not believe me to be a fraudster and a thief. I also received flattering reviews from, among others, Kelvin MacKenzie in the *Sun* for 'swimming against the tide of sewage'. I was frankly puzzled to find myself in this position, which stemmed, essentially, from a decision – by myself and the other outer London Lib Dems – not to take advantage of the availability of expenses for a second home near Westminster, but to commute from my home in my constituency in the suburbs. Commuting, quite simply, helped me to be a good constituency MP without impairing my work in Parliament.

I think, perhaps, that at a deeper level I still carried around my parents' puritanism and concern for reputation, as well as my own theoretical and academic, rather than practical and personal, interest in making money. On becoming an MP I had given up a better-paid job, but for something that gave me far more satisfaction, and I regularly subsidized rather than profited from my office. So the discovery that large numbers of MPs had managed to turn parliamentary expenses into a supplementary source of income or a means of acquiring a property portfolio and attendant capital gains was a genuine shock. Perhaps I had been naive or simply unobservant. But there was no refuge in self-righteousness. All of us were affected. The two occasions when I appeared on *Question Time* before hostile audiences at the height of the furore were among the most emotionally draining experiences of my years in Parliament.

Standing back from my own role, I could see that what made this such a crisis so damaging was that the public had concluded that a whole generation of parliamentarians, Lords as well as Commoners, had been so corrupted by a culture of greed that it had lost its conscience and any sense of public service it might have had. We were not above but part of, the self-serving, self-interested, greedy world of the City brokers and bankers. Worse, we were the image that the country could see when it looked in the mirror: the ravaged face of a society dominated by the pursuit of money and property at any cost.

Rebuilding a sense of public service and trust in politics and politicians promises to be a Herculean task. My natural optimism that it is achievable is kept well in check by the fact that the main political beneficiaries appear to have been the Conservative leadership. They are steeped in the values that have led to the scandal but they have exploited it with great media skill and total, uncompromising cynicism.

The crisis shone a merciless light not only on the moral

inadequacies of many MPs but on the hollowness of British parliamentary democracy. I have already described the way in which Parliament has become a decorative rather than a useful institution. MPs were not abusing their power: MPs (as opposed to ministers) didn't have any power to abuse. What we saw was the indignity of impotence. Where I, and others, failed was in not noticing, or caring enough about, this decline. The symptoms were all too apparent: the routine absence of MPs from the chamber; the guillotining of debates; the contemptuous leaks of parliamentary statements by ministers to the media; the futility of attempts to amend primary or secondary legislation (in the Commons, if not the Lords); the packing of select committees with government loyalists.

It is clear that simply cleaning up the expenses scandal will not be enough. Honest eunuchs are preferable to dishonest eunuchs, but they are still eunuchs. Parliament will only rediscover its virility and acquire a fresh supply of testosterone if it is radically reformed. That is unlikely to happen without a big shift in the balance of power between executive and legislature, and that is unlikely to occur while under our current voting system unrepresentative governments are elected with large parliamentary majorities. Once governments have reason to be afraid of the power and independence of MPs, then it becomes possible to effect meaningful reforms to procedure. My own particular obsession is that public spending decisions should require parliamentary scrutiny and approval. At present, Westminster is one of the few legislatures in the Western world with no powers in this absolutely crucial area.

One of the more bizarre personal outcomes of the drama was the ousting of the Speaker. I had known Michael Martin a little when we were both Glasgow city councillors. Then he was quiet and uncontroversial, and he stuck very closely to the line of his union and of his mentor, the MP for Springburn, Dick Buchanan, whom in due course he replaced. I always found him perfectly affable and easy to deal with. After Betty Boothroyd, however, he was generally seen as a disappointing Speaker, with a poor grasp of procedure and somewhat slow to react to sudden changes of mood in the House. But he seemed adequate and he built up a sympathetic following because of his being mercilessly patronized by posh public schoolboys on account of his Glasgow accent (he was nicknamed 'Gorbals Mick', which is the equivalent of confusing Lambeth with Leyton). What gradually emerged, however, was that he had tried to block reforms to the expenses system and, when the crisis broke, he publicly rounded on several MPs who were identified with reform. At this point some of us finally gave up on him and suggested his removal. The day when he defied the growing clamour to go and was shouted down in the House ranks as perhaps the most excruciatingly embarrassing in my memory of the place. He resigned the next day.

I was asked by a large number of MPs to stand and there was a press campaign for me to take on the job. *The Times*'s leader column on 20 May 2009 was entitled 'A Cable to Cable', suggesting that it was my patriotic duty to step into the post. I was assured that there was all-party support and I think it was probably true that I had a reputation for being non-partisan, reformist and honest. The attention was enormously flattering, but all my instincts, and my friends, told me to say no. I had no great interest in parliamentary procedure and process and absolutely no ambition to switch from being a player to a referee. I had no great difficulty in declining the invitations. I am sure John Bercow will do the job perfectly well.

I can make a bigger contribution by sticking with my important role in the Lib Dems. I also believe that the expenses scandal has been a sideshow and, regrettably, has distracted attention away from the much bigger scandal and crisis in the banking system and the economy, on which there is still much to do.

Chapter 15

Stormy Waters and Unfinished Business

Such celebrity status as I have enjoyed does not rest on just a few good one-liners or personal anecdotes but also on the way in which the financial and wider economic crisis has thrown a spotlight on party economic spokesmen. This crisis is far from having run its course; there is much pain to come and there could yet be some surprising or shocking outcomes. My own analysis of how the crisis arose and my broad views on the remedies currently being applied are contained in my book *The Storm* and in newspaper columns over the last two years, so they do not require detailed repetition here. It is, however, fair, I think, to claim that my colleagues and I have made the running in the UK in interpreting the growing economic problems and pointing to the most sensible policy responses in a world characterized by new, unfamiliar threats and great uncertainty. My party has yet to harvest the full political credit, but we have, as over the Iraq war, been the effective opposition and if there is any justice in politics we shall emerge significantly stronger.

Unlike the Conservatives, we were not uncritical admirers of the free interplay of financial markets and advocates of owner-occupation for all at any cost, and we were critical of the extremes of income and wealth thrown up by the City, in particular by the bonus culture of the banks. Unlike Gordon Brown and his team, we were not overawed by the bankers and locked into an embrace of mutual dependence and complicity with them.

On the strength of having spotted a few crucially important trends, I am now credited in some commentaries with gifts of foresight that Nostradamus might have envied. In the simple, Manichaean world in which public debate is conducted what matters is to be right rather than wrong. What I had done was to have laboured for a decade and developed some expertise in a field that other politicians had judged to be too complicated, boring and potentially unrewarding.

The journey started shortly after the 1997 election, at the autumn party conference, when my agent Dee Doocey organized a group of friends to help me brainstorm on what issues to pursue in Parliament. I wanted to use my time well and to operate strategically instead of constantly chasing the issue of the day. My professional background meant that I could, and did, contribute confidently to debates about economic policy. But these were somewhat rarefied and removed from the economics of everyday life. The set of issues to pursue, we agreed, was the politics of personal finance. Millions of people cared passionately about their savings and investments (or debts); many, including many of my constituents, were angry about being ripped off by banks, insurance companies and other institutions; journalists had acres of personal finance pages to fill; and few politicians seemed to be interested in or to understand these issues and to articulate consumers' concerns (there were several Tory MPs who had a real understanding, but they mainly saw the issues from the perspective of the institutions they owned or worked in). That hour of conversation was one of the most productive I have ever spent.

I followed my friends' advice and my nose soon started to pick up some unsavoury smells. One case left a lasting impression. An elderly, and rather poor, blind lady in Twickenham had become dependent on a carer who did her shopping and carried out her banking transactions, with the knowledge of the local Halifax branch staff. The bank, however, decided that the arrangement had to be formalized and for a few minutes' work and a signature they charged the customer £100. I protested to the local manager, who passed the problem up the chain of command, where it eventually reached the chief executive, who dismissed my complaint in terms that were so condescending and arrogant that I escalated the issue to the national press. After several more rounds of rather acrimonious correspondence – and bad publicity for the Halifax – the bank eventually agreed to back down, though with very bad grace.

There was a wider issue involving banking, too. Under Conservative legislation, mutually owned building societies were seeking to convert into commercial banks, PLCs. Such conversion promised a cash windfall for depositors should the society demutualize, and offered managers the chance to escape the restraints of mutuality and, in some cases, the opportunity to enrich themselves. I was invited to act as spokesman for a group called Save Our Building Societies, led by a Lib Dem activist called Bob Goodall. We campaigned hard in the media to stop the demutualization of Northern Rock, Birmingham Midshires and Bradford & Bingley. But the long-term financial benefits of mutuality (and the appeal to idealism) proved a hopelessly inadequate inducement alongside the promise of immediate cash windfalls. We were also up against professional 'carpetbaggers': investors who joined building societies specifically in order to profit from the windfalls. The campaigns failed, but there was success in the political field. I helped persuade the Treasury select committee to carry out an investigation and this, together with pressure from an influential group of Labour backbenchers, led ministers to place restrictions on further demutualization. A fuse had, however, been lit, which detonated a decade later when the demutualized building societies, which were at the forefront of expansive and irresponsible lending, imploded in the banking crisis.

I acquired some credibility with consumer groups when I took up cudgels on behalf of Equitable Life policyholders who had lost substantial sums in the collapse of the society following serious failures of both management and regulation. A decade later, the campaign to compensate them continues: the doggedness of the campaigners matched only by the obdurate delaying tactics of the Treasury. I then waded into the controversy over life insurance orphan assets, on the side of policyholders who were being disadvantaged as against shareholders, and had the unusual experience when introducing a debate of being silenced in mid-sentence by the Speaker for trespassing on a court case. Such issues were complex and by mastering them I began to appreciate the force of the old adage that 'in the kingdom of the blind, the one-eyed man is king'.

This useful one eye was particularly helpful with the publication in 2000 of the Cruickshank Report on the banking system. Don Cruickshank was the chairman of the London Stock Exchange. Gordon Brown had commissioned the study following complaints about the cost of business lending by banks Cruickshank argued, in essence, that in pursuit of shareholder value the banks were earning 'excess profits' despite their 'regulatory privileges' (that is, in a crisis the taxpayer would be expected to bale them out as 'lender of last resort'). His conclusion was that the banks should either lose their privileges and be made to compete like other companies (and sometimes go bust), or else keep them but be more closely regulated to curb their profits and protect consumers. I was excited by the force and political significance of this conclusion. Gordon Brown, however, saw little merit in picking a quarrel with the banks. I determined to go where he feared to tread. No one else seemed inclined to follow. I was energized, too, by being able at last to see the wood for the trees, as represented by innumerable consumer complaints about excessive charges, poor service, the aggressive promotion of lending, and the mis-selling of financial services. I was, I think, regarded by the banks as a minor irritant, but I merited a steady flow of visitors from the British Bankers' Association and individual banks explaining to me why I – and Cruickshank – were wrong.

These early skirmishes with the banks brought me to the attention of the financial editors of the daily papers and the correspondents of specialist financial magazines, because few, if any, other politicians seemed interested in these issues. None of the acres of high-profile publicity I have since enjoyed gave me more satisfaction than a headline in the money section of the *Observer* in 2000: 'A lone hero stands up to the big banks', and a similar warm endorsement in the *Mail on Sunday*.

These tentative forays into the politics of finance also taught me about time management. Olympia was very ill at this stage and I had to economize on time elsewhere. I realized that it was possible to make an impact as a member of the Treasury select committee and also as a campaigner on behalf of consumers, using Parliament to amplify press initiatives. What did not make any impact was legislative scrutiny in Parliament, debating the minutiae of legislation rendered largely incomprehensible by the recondite language of parliamentary draftsmen, and in any case unamendable because of the government's in-built majority. At this time an enormously long piece of legislation setting up the Financial Services Authority was winding its way through Parliament. I went to one or two of the meetings of the committee in charge of scrutinizing it. I sat through hours of speeches by Tories filling out time but essentially representing City interests, and by a nice but hopeless minister who clearly did not understand the notes passed to her by officials, which she dutifully read out. Many amendments were put forward to improve the legislation but were routinely rejected. I made a few points about the principles of regulation on consumer-related issues, but then abandoned the committee, never to return. My absence attracted critical resolutions in Parliament, but I felt that my time was better spent elsewhere. We now know that the model of regulation and supervision encapsulated in that legislation was dangerously flawed, but nowhere in the interminable, rambling discussions about clause X and sub-clause Y was there ever a satisfactory discussion of the real nature of systemic risk and how a banking collapse might be averted or managed. I confess to being absent without leave while this opportunity passed Parliament by.

Following the 2001 election were the boom years of big government spending increases and debt-driven consumer binge. Both, but especially the latter, incubated the seeds of future disaster. Bodies like the Citizens Advice Bureau began to pick up signs of extreme indebtedness among, at that stage, relatively small numbers of businesses, and I publicized some very questionable lending practices by the banks, which were aggressively promoting overdrafts and credit cards and mortgages at impossible multiples of income. Early in 2003 the Daily Express published a full-page feature on a 'ten-point' plan that I had drawn up to provide practical solutions to a growing debt problem. When Charles Kennedy promoted me to be our shadow Chancellor in autumn 2003 I decided to focus on this set of issues, leading shortly afterwards to my much-quoted exchange with Gordon Brown in which he swatted aside my concerns about debt and the linked issue of the 'bubble' in house prices.

More and more worrying signs appeared of dangerous or questionable practices in the banking sector and I started to be inundated with requests to take up consumer issues: dodgy equity release products; biased financial advice; expensive payments protection; non-verified mortgages; credit card charges. At this stage the personal debt issue had not penetrated the mainstream political debate and my small team and I tried to invent gimmicks to capture the public imagination. We had a demonstration outside the Treasury when personal debt reached £1 trillion, and my first televised response to the 2004 budget featured a graphical representation of billions of McDonald's beefburgers stretching to the moon and back to illustrate the vast sums involved.

How much of all this got through to the public I do not know, but the UK financial establishment was sufficiently concerned, or irritated, to invest resources in trying to neutralize and re-educate me. There were good lunches in the leading banks' boardrooms. After I had been especially rude about HBOS, I was invited to a one-to-one with James (later Sir James) Crosby, who, unlike the other bankers I met, clearly understood the issues and the dangers of systemic risk and the volatility of the housing market. He was a highly intelligent mathematician and the first banker I had met who grasped (and sympathized with) the need for counter-cyclical capital requirements for banks in order to counter boom and bust cycles. But he explained that he was obliged by his board and shareholders to pursue an aggressive lending strategy to build up the bank's market share. My former Shell colleague, Maarten van den Bergh, chairman of Lloyds, explained separately how Lloyds had once been conservative and responsible in its lending policies but was in danger of being left behind without a major acquisition: thinking that led in due course to the disastrous marriage with HBOS under his successor.

I felt I had scaled a small peak of recognition when I was invited to lunch with Mervyn King and several of his colleagues from the Bank of England's Monetary Policy Committee to debate the issues around debt and the housing market. There was a certain defensiveness over the issue around the table and I was assured that there wasn't really a problem because household assets well exceeded household debt (though the assets consisted overwhelmingly of inflated house prices). It was also clear that, under the surface, there was a worry. The Governor himself warned of housing inflation in 2004 but, mystifyingly, didn't return to the subject as the problem subsequently grew. The Bank had no direct responsibility for house price inflation and he was perhaps nervous about being accused of exceeding his mandate. Fortunately, I had no such inhibitions.

There were other signs, too, that the boom in economic growth, which was global and not just Britain's alone, was heading into dangerous territory. One was the surge in oil prices that started to become apparent in 2004, as rising demand met fixed supply and dwindling spare capacity. I was considered to be an 'expert', having worked for an oil company, and was frequently interviewed. Rachel will never allow me to forget my *Today* programme interview on oil prices from the marital bed on the second day of our honeymoon in Wales. But much of the next year was given over to general election preparations in which the debate centred on taxation and public spending. Before and after the election I continued to pump out a relentless barrage of press releases on banks, bank lending and the housing market. But nobody appeared to be listening. I was the little boy who had cried wolf too often, and there were no wolves in sight. In particular, I made myself seriously unpopular whenever I was quoted in the papers as saying that the housing market was overvalued and that banks like Northern Rock which were lending at 100 per cent or more of the value of property were being especially reckless.

The wolf pack finally arrived in the late summer of 2007 while the lambs were still frolicking in the sun. Rachel and I were on holiday with friends in the Lake District when I received a mobile call at the top of a mountain from Sam Fleming, a financial reporter on the *Daily Mail*. He had been happy to carry my apocalyptic warnings about the banks and the housing market, which conveniently dovetailed with the line of the *Mail*. The *Mail*'s financial editor, Alex Brummer, whom I had got to know a little from annual encounters at the Remembrance Day service at Richmond synagogue, had been warning for years about Northern Rock's dangerous business model and the questionable activities of Mr Adam Applegarth, the chief executive. There were now ugly rumours swirling around Northern Rock, which appeared to be having trouble raising funding, and what did I think? The bank was in difficulty because rapid expansion of lending at the peak of the housing boom had exposed it to excessive dependence on funding through mortgage-backed securities, which were increasingly distrusted in the wake of difficulties in the US sub-prime lending market. My own comments from the mountain top, reiterating innumerable past criticisms of irresponsible lending, no doubt contributed to anxiety around the bank, though I suspect that Robert Peston's reporting on the BBC had far more impact on the public.

When I returned to London for a few days before the party conference in Brighton, public worries about Northern Rock had reached a tipping point and queues started to form outside branches as Britain began to experience its first run on a bank for almost 150 years. In between media interviews I was called on my mobile phone by Callum McCarthy, the chair of the FSA, who tried to tell me that I was at least partly responsible for the run; that the FSA believed Northern Rock to be a perfectly sound and well-run bank; and that it had a very good loan book, contrary to my assertions. Its problems were to do with irrational worries over access to international borrowing and were not due to mismanagement. It was to be many months before the extent of the FSA's misreading of the situation became fully apparent, but I kept repeating my rather simple point that any bank lending more than the value of property at what seemed to be the peak of the market was living dangerously. Since it was clear that there was a panic developing, and also that I was being listened to, I was conscious that I was potentially skating on thin ice and so I established a close network of friends with financial knowledge and experience – in particular, Lord (Matthew) Oakeshott – to bounce ideas off and to check facts with before launching into the media. That advice has been absolutely essential as the financial crisis has escalated and grown in complexity. I have been fortunate, too, in having a strong back-up team and a succession of very capable deputies – Chris Huhne, Julia Goldsworthy and most recently Jeremy Browne – who have done the unglamorous heavy lifting in parliament, creating time and space for me to concentrate on the high profile and topical issues.

While it was gratifying to have been able to make what, in retrospect, were good and influential interventions, the political agenda at the three party conferences that year (2007) was dominated by uncertainty over the timing of a general election and, in particular, by the issue of tax. The launch of Lib Dem tax policy was well received: cutting taxes for those on low incomes and financing the cuts by closing tax loopholes and reducing reliefs for the well-off. My team and I, with the help of a specially commissioned public opinion survey, were able to break the taboo on criticizing the tax privileges of the non-doms. Two weeks later, in a remarkable act of chutzpah, George Osborne pinched the policy for the Tories and used an improbably large estimate of tax yield to finance a big cut in inheritance tax, which had become a major issue in the dying frenzy of the housing bubble. I have never rated George's understanding of financial and economic matters, but he is a political operator of some substance and this was a brilliant move. Together with Cameron's unremarkable but lionized speech, it changed the whole political dynamic and frightened off Gordon Brown from an early election: a disastrous error from which he never recovered.

It was soon clear that the banking system was the serious battleground, not inheritance tax. In the confused days and weeks that followed the collapse of Northern Rock, few of the key actors seemed to have a clear idea of what was needed: not surprisingly, nobody this side of 1866 had had experience of managing a bank run. The Chancellor, Alistair Darling, had been in the job only a few weeks and was a lawyer without any economic hinterland. After a damaging period of indecision, the government offered a large loan to rescue the bank so as to stop the panic from spreading. It guaranteed the bank's depositors, apparently without conditions, and also entrusted the management of the bank to Adam Applegarth, whose behaviour had precipitated the collapse. The Governor of the Bank of England, Mervyn King, was clearly uncomfortable with events and upset the banking community by lecturing it on moral hazard – the (entirely sensible) idea that bank bail-outs encourage irresponsible bankers to continue to behave irresponsibly. But he was then required to perform a U-turn and lead the rescue operation. Rushing between fringe meetings in Brighton, I got a strong sense, bumping into journalists, that there was an appetite for a politician who could explain what was going on and offer an alternative to the idea of pouring billions of pounds of taxpayers' money into a badly run bank. The Conservatives were preoccupied with blaming Gordon Brown for having split the Bank of England and the FSA and, while this criticism had some validity, it was backward-looking and did not address the central issue of what to do next. There was a vacuum waiting to be filled.

I argued that Mervyn King was right about moral hazard but, since a rescue had been launched, it could not possibly proceed on the basis of the taxpayer taking on the risks and losses while the shareholders and managers privatized the profits. The taxpayer must receive any profits in return for the rescue; the shareholders could not expect to have their equity investment protected; and the managers should be sacked. In effect, the bank should be nationalized. Matthew Oakeshott and I debated the pros and cons of embracing full nationalization and I was encouraged to use the 'N' word without embarrassment, which became a telling point in the national news coverage.

The first reactions were not encouraging. I had a flood of angry emails and telephone calls from shareholders who blamed me for the collapse in the share price. I became public enemy number one in the North-East for casting aspersions on the competence and integrity of Mr Applegarth and his team. They were civic heroes in Newcastle and were shortly to be given the freedom of the city by the council. Geordie pride was deeply offended. The problem was made worse by the fact that Newcastle was a flagship Lib Dem council which was doing well under an impressive group leader, John Shipley. Council leaders are important people, running big budgets, and normally do not take kindly to MPs parking tanks on their lawn. But John understood the wider picture and skilfully defused any conflict. Then I was contacted by an old friend from my days in East Africa, Alistair Balls, who ran the Northern Rock Foundation, which had done a great deal to support the arts and other good causes in the region but which was now threatened. Somehow, the Foundation had to be protected.

There was also, however, strong and encouraging support. Some was from old lefties who were bowled over to see the Liberal Democrats arguing for nationalization. A lot of Labour MPs could not understand why we were making the case rather than their own ministers. The case for public ownership in this rather special set of circumstances was also taken up by the *Economist*, the *FT* and the *Evening Standard* – none of them obviously lefty – and it was the Conservatives, who opposed the idea, who seemed excessively ideological and irrelevant. My own party activists and MPs were delighted that I had got us on to the front foot after months of painful coverage at the end of the Ming dynasty.

But the government was determined to press ahead with a 'private sector solution', and among the front runners was a pro-posal to let Richard Branson buy the bank, albeit with government loan guarantees. My team and I opposed this proposed sell-off as the privatization of profits and the socialization of losses. In the process, I seriously antagonized Richard Branson, whom I had hitherto rather admired as a buccaneering entrepreneur. But our questioning of his suitability to run a high-street bank and criti-cism of his recourse to Caribbean tax havens provoked a stream of angry, threatening faxes. The doubts that we raised about the Branson bid contributed, I am sure, to its eventual demise.

The government was extraordinarily maladroit and appeared to have neither political antennae nor economic sense, but a rather ludicrously optimistic faith in the expensive advice of investment bankers, self-interested sharks masquerading as national saviours, and the failed managers and directors of Northern Rock, who were prised out far too late. When Matthew Oakeshott asked Northern Rock about the availability of 125 per cent mortgages and was offered one without conditions, we were able to demonstrate that, three months after the bank had col-lapsed, its managers had apparently learned nothing and were building up big future losses for the taxpayer. Eventually, after several months of fruitless and expensive negotiations for a private sector solution, the government announced in February 2008 that the bank had to be nationalized.

The next few days were among the most frantic in a very frantic year. The drama started with a weekend in Twickenham at a local Lib Dem fund-raiser being interrupted by a Sky camera crew and Five Live radio car wanting comments on fat cats' pay.

No mention of Northern Rock. On Sunday morning, my wife and I were supervising the preparations for an onslaught by builders on the lounge wall and my grandson Charlie was playing in my Aladdin's cave of toy cars. A call from the press office alerted me to the decision and I was summoned to the BBC studios in west London, while other media outlets sent crews to Twickenham. The drama continued long into the night and at 6 a.m. next morning it was −5°C and GMTV was outside the front door for an interview with Kate Garraway. Then, after another round of interviews, a visit to the Chancellor, and a parliamentary statement, the government decided that it planned to pass the nationalization legislation in a day. We supported the government and the Commons debate went well until, about 11 p.m., it became clear that ministers did not understand the significance of Granite, an offshore entity originally set up as part of the complex securitization process.

I finally arrived home at around 2 a.m. The media frenzy continued and I was drafted in to Question Time in Newcastle to confront confused and angry Geordies. But, as became clear from the press coverage, in the space of a few days there had been a quantum leap in the Lib Dems' and my own economic credibility. The government had been forced under pressure of events to accede to a radical policy that we had advocated. We had to defend Alistair Darling against criticism from the Conservative side that there were other viable options, and I had the satisfaction of being credited with having got the issue right: the first time since the start of the Iraq War that the Lib Dems had successfully led the public debate on a major issue.

In the months after the nationalization of Northern Rock my team continued to worry that there were dangers from bank lending practices, particularly in the domestic and commercial property markets, where it was clear that there was a market downturn already under way. The global financial crisis was also building up in intensity with the collapse and rescue of Bear Sterns and large-scale intervention by the Bush administration in saving the US mortgage-lending industry. The Bear Stearns crisis occurred when Rachel and I were enjoying a week's skiing with the Oakeshott family, with whom I had learned to ski the year before. I was able to piece together only fragments of the drama in France and returned with a sense of foreboding not dissimilar to that which I had brought back from holiday in India after 9/11. A financial crash was on the way.

In May, with Nick Clegg, I launched a New Deal for the City which set out some proposed reforms – to curb the bonus culture, reduce boom and bust cycles through bank capital requirements, and regulate the shadow banking system. The recommendations were not wildly revolutionary. But we received some credit in the City for addressing these issues ahead of, rather than after, the main crisis broke and in terms that were moderate and liberal, though very firmly directed towards stopping abuses in the Square Mile.

In the same month I and my colleagues launched an opposition day debate in the House, which would have been unremarkable but for the minister's responses, which are now something of a collector's item. I warned, I think in guarded terms, of the consequences of a falling housing market combined with an economic slowdown, probably a recession: that is, negative equity and growing repossessions. The two ministers, Angela Eagle and Jane Kennedy, had been briefed by the Treasury to swat aside these ridiculous, hysterical assertions and absurd Lib Dem fantasies about recession. I have long since learned to enjoy jokes at my expense and not to be fazed by parliamentary banter. But I was truly alarmed to see that the Treasury apparently believed in its fairy tale of booms without busts and ever-rising house prices. Outside, in the real world, there was growing alarm about the economy.

But at this stage of the economic crisis, economic policy thinking was still located within the framework of monetary independence and Gordon Brown's fiscal rules (however fractured). I had been asked to give the Institute of Fiscal Studies' annual lecture in June and devoted a lot of time to it as a means of thinking through new approaches to economic policy, and in particular how to incorporate asset prices into inflation targeting. I was conscious, too, that a decade of constituency surgeries and press releases had not done much for my professional skills and reputation as an economist, and was determined to get up to speed (and to impress).

The daily news from the financial markets, and especially from the USA, spoke of a gathering storm, perhaps a hurricane. But as the summer advanced, there was a strange feeling: a sulphurous, threatening gloom, but only a few spots of rain. I took up an invitation from Toby Mundy of Atlantic Books to produce a book on the crisis and Rachel offered to help me by forgoing a summer holiday and instead bashing out typed drafts as I wrote, and rewrote. August was spent on a mixture of constituency duties and writing in Rachel's luxurious garden shed. My task was to make myself understand a complex, multi-layered, global and still evolving crisis, absorbing a large amount of contemporary and historical literature. I had learned to write long scripts very quickly. But this exercise also involved some difficult practical and theoretical issues: like putting together a big jigsaw puzzle and with only half the pieces. I had assembled a rough draft a few days before our party conference started in September, and as the conference gathered the storm finally burst with Lehman Brothers facing collapse and shares in British banks falling through the floor. As with Northern Rock the year before, the party conference coincided with a major financial drama. My job, as in 2007, was to try to compose a distinctive, audible Liberal Democrat response to the crisis, rather than letting ourselves be drowned out by it.

I realized that, in the wake of Northern Rock and my wider comments on the banking crisis, the media were coming to me rather than the Tories for comment. It was important to maintain credibility and to have a distinct, forward-looking line. When Bradford & Bingley collapsed the government did not prevaricate but decided on a partial disposal and nationalization of the rest. I did not demur. What I and my team did was to focus on short-selling of bank shares by hedge funds. I called for a ban and a few days later the government introduced one, temporarily as it transpired. The call for a short-selling ban was controversial and I seriously alienated people in the City, including prospective party donors. But the case had to be made. The problem related to the way in which short-selling had destabilized banks that depend on government guarantees, implicit and explicit. And while there is an entirely legitimate role for speculative activity in markets, there are good reasons to question it when speculators are using borrowed money rather than their own.

With the banking system in a tailspin and the prospect looming of a serious recession – perhaps a slump – there was a cross-cutting issue that led to considerable confusion over the direction of economic policy. Oil prices had been rising steadily since before the Iraq War, from a low of $25 per barrel to an astronomic $140 at the end of last summer. There was inexorable pressure from rising demand in China and India on the one hand, and rigidity of supply on the other, caused by underinvestment by state-owned and private-sector oil companies, deepening economic nationalism (in Iran, Russia, Mexico and Venezuela), and disruption due to violence (in Nigeria and Iraq). Spare capacity had dwindled to virtually nil and speculative pressures pushed the price up to extraordinary levels. Headlines were dominated by the oil price spike, and on a short visit to Shetland I saw the crisis graphically illustrated, with unleaded petrol costing £1.40 per litre and cars being parked at country crossroads so that drivers could share.

Economically, the oil shock had the disastrous effect of diverting the Monetary Policy Committee from the consequences of the market crash and causing it to stall over interest rates when the rapidly deteriorating economy demanded a deep cut. At the end of September the position of the banks was critical and this threatened to spill over into the wider economy. I wrote an article for the *Sunday Times* calling for a deep, 2 per cent interest rate cut as well as recapitalization of the banks. I did so with some heart-searching because I had been a strong supporter and advocate of Bank of England policy independence and had made my maiden speech on the subject in 1997. I was compromising that independence, albeit from the opposition benches, by shouting at the Monetary Policy Committee to wake up to the gravity of the crisis. A former member of the MPC, 'Danny' Blanchflower, has since confirmed that serious tensions existed within the committee at that time, the first time in its ten-year history that a deep division over strategy had arisen. In the event, the 2 per cent cut occurred at the following meeting.

It became clear over that weekend that a major banking collapse was imminent. On the Sunday morning I was invited on to the Andrew Marr programme to discuss the *Sunday Times* article and it emerged for the first time that our suggestion of partial nationalization was now under active consideration. RBS, then the world's biggest bank in balance sheet terms, and HBOS were close to collapse, with worthless shares and extreme difficulties in raising inter-bank lending. I learned a few days later, in a meeting with the Governor, that the banks had collectively reached the point of being unable to borrow overnight. They were twenty-four hours from collapse, such was the loss of confidence and trust in them. The next twenty-four hours involved a constant round of media interviews, on the one hand stressing the need for decisive government intervention, with de facto nationalization, while on the other trying to help calm people's panic about their own bank accounts. In the event the government and the Bank of England acted decisively, with guarantees for inter-bank lending and recapitalization through the acquisition of shares to replenish capital. RBS was in urgent need of capital, as was HBOS, and via a hastily arranged shotgun marriage between the relatively healthy Lloyds and HBOS, Lloyds was also drawn in.

I was called in by the Chancellor on Monday morning, separately from George Osborne, to have the policy explained. This seemed cosmetic because the details were in the morning newspapers and I had been touring the television studios and carrying out pavement interviews in the City since 7 a.m. But there was more to the meeting than formality: Darling was anxious to have cross-party agreement since this was a national emergency. I had no problem in principle but, since I and my party were often accused by the right-wing press of being in bed with Labour, it was important to be sure that the Conservatives were also on board. They were, at least for the next few days, until they sensed that cross-party unity was helping Labour.

That afternoon I publicly endorsed the package in Parliament, stressing that the rescued banks could not be left to act in the interests of failed management and the remaining private share-holders but must act in the taxpayer's interests. The government had some suspiciously vague agreements on new lending and bonuses which would emerge later as a major weakness. But in the short run our role was to help make the case that lead-ing banks could not be allowed to collapse and that de facto temporary nationalization was the correct response to such a banking crisis, as had been deployed earlier in Sweden, Korea and Israel. The Tories agreed, uncomfortably, and only John Redwood seemed to have a coherent alternative view.

Drafting *The Storm* over the summer had already given me a crash course in the subject matter and this helped to elevate me – sometimes to my alarm – as one of the leading 'experts' of the crisis, alongside Robert Peston of the BBC. Nick Clegg delegated to me the response to the crisis and I had the satisfaction of seeing the Lib Dem line holding its own in the news bulletins and press comments.

There was a succession of complex sub-plots, each of which dominated the agenda for a while. Ideally, a considered response was needed, but an almost immediate media reaction was required in order to be, and to stay, in the story. There was a lot of skating on thin ice. I had broadly endorsed the HBOS–Lloyds merger on national interest grounds, though it was clearly a questionable deal for Lloyds (which they nonetheless snapped up gladly). Going back to my lunch with Sir James Crosby five years earlier, and even before, I had sensed, and occasionally said, that HBOS was a bad bank in the style of Northern Rock. I was therefore seriously thrown when a Scottish campaign was launched to rescue HBOS from the clutches of the Sassenachs and to avert the threat to jobs in Edinburgh. As with RBS, which had, however implausibly, marketed itself as a great advertisement for Scottish banking, there was a nationalistic prickliness about the threat to 'Scotland's banks' (even though the RBS balance sheet was fifteen times the size of the Scottish economy – a small country with a big bank attached to it). The able new leader of the Scottish Lib Dems, Tavish Scott, wanted to run with the issue by pursuing a separate, Scottish buyer for HBOS and I felt politically obliged to back him. There were also genuine concerns at a UK level about the competition policy implications for the mortgage market and among Lloyds' shareholders about the way in which they had been shafted. I organized a U-turn and led the troops in Parliament to vote against the merger. Such is the difference between a commentator and academic, and a politician.

The minutiae of the banking crisis were rendered less important by the growing debate about macroeconomic effects and the growing recession. The government had been very slow to acknowledge the risks of recession and the consequences of rising unemployment for policy and for the budget deficit. The 2008 Autumn Statement was a masterpiece of self-deception (or deceit). My team and I argued strongly for an active policy response to fight the risks of deflation and rising unemployment. We defended the aggressive monetarism of the Bank of England's policy of lowering interest rates, followed later by quantitative easing. We also supported the government's willingness in principle to provide a modest fiscal stimulus – albeit in a way, the VAT cut, that was unconvincing and wasteful.

We had been concerned from the outset of the crisis about the collapse of the construction industry. Having spoken at several property industry conferences, I was left in no doubt as to the scale of the crisis in commercial property, private construction companies and housing associations, with a big overhang of unsold property and mounting construction industry unemployment. Our response had been to advocate the acquisition of unsaleable new dwellings for rental, a large-scale programme of social housebuilding to replace the failed model of quotas of social housing on private development sites, and emergency action to head off large-scale repossession. The government acknowledged the pressure to act on these fronts but was infuriatingly slow in implementing decisions. It was only a year after we had urged action, and six months after a commitment had been made to new social housing, that serious money began to flow into the sector.

As Britain, like America, developed an aggressive monetary and fiscal response to the crisis, I found myself agreeing with the broad thrust of government policy while disagreeing on a lot of specifics. The Conservatives' response to the crisis was poor by any standard: unremittingly negative, frequently changing, and seemingly devoid of any economic content. But I had already learned to appreciate that Osborne and Cameron were politically smart. They were quick to pick up the anxiety and resentment of elderly savers about low interest rates and managed to bury their earlier failure to spot the dangers of mounting household debt, deliberately confusing the issue with the emerging problem of government debt. I heard at second or third hand that George

Osborne was relaxed about being a poor shadow Chancellor if he was going to become the real one on the back of the government's unpopularity.

Our own dividing line with the government was over its passive approach to the banks. It became increasingly clear that the Treasury (though probably not No. 10) wanted an arm's length relationship, as far removed from nationalization as was possible given the large injection of taxpayers' money. The senior management of the semi-nationalized RBS and Lloyds were getting contradictory signals from the regulator – to build up capital – and the government – to lend more to solvent companies – and their instincts were to go with the former. Corporate Britain was being starved of capital.

Christmas 2008 was a victim of the need to get *The Storm* to the publishers on time for a launch in April. A lot had happened since the summer and there was a lot of writing and rewriting to be done. Rachel, as in the summer, was extraordinarily patient and typed up the later chapters as I wrote them.

The next six months involved more intense, relentless activity than I had ever previously known and I learned to appreciate the advantages of a strong constitution and a loving wife and family. I had begun to achieve serious celebrity status on the back of the economic crisis, even more than at the end of my period as acting leader. Desert Island Discs, which went out in January 2009, was a success, reinforcing the idea that I was a human being instead of (or as well as) an economic nerd. There was a stream of honours: Parliamentarian of the Year from Channel 4, together with similar recognition from *The House Magazine*, *Oldie* magazine, *GQ*, the *CAB* and others. Flattering as these occasions were, what mattered to me more was the hard graft of business conferences, provincial tours, parliamentary speeches and media interviews, slowly building up credibility for myself and my party through a network of contacts and feedback from the grass roots.

I was conscious at this stage of receiving considerably more publicity and favourable comment than my party leader. With a lesser person this would have caused considerable tension. But Nick recognized that issues would arise later – as happened with the Gurkhas and the expenses scandal – when he could find his own voice and popularity.

The publication of *The Storm* in March 2009 was well timed, coinciding with a surge in both public interest and public anxiety, as well as Gordon Brown's successful G20 summit. The book attracted extensive and broadly favourable reviews, even from those, like Dominic Lawson and Simon Jenkins, who were not instinctively well disposed to my politics. The book achieved my objective of providing a clear, easily accessible guide to the different dimensions of the financial and economic crisis: global and local; past, present and future; economic and political. My greatest satisfaction was that after publishing, I estimated, two million words in my lifetime so far, which had languished in almost total obscurity, I had at last produced a few thousand words that people wanted to read. My self-confidence as a writer grew when I was asked to write a weekly column for the *Mail on Sunday*. My late father must be chuckling in his grave that I am writing for the Sunday sister of his favourite newspaper.

On the back of the book was a degree of public interest in serious discussion beyond my wildest imaginings. Having spent a lifetime struggling to attract a free audience of a few dozen, I was amazed to discover that hundreds would come to a forty-minute talk, plus Q&As, as happened in Oxford, Bristol, Ely and London and at the Yvonne Arnaud Theatre in Guildford. I was treated to a full and appreciative house of almost a thousand at a lecture in the City Guildhall, attended by bankers about whom I had been less than complimentary. At the Hay Festival, 1300 people were packed into the big tent. But it was good, and necessary, to be brought down to earth occasionally, as when I spoke to a multi-ethnic audience of 200 teenagers at a college in Uxbridge, who patiently waited when I was forty-five minutes late, listened politely, and then peppered me with numerous questions centring on the two main political questions: 'why should we vote at all?' and 'why should we vote for your lot?'. It was also good and necessary to be forced out of my economic comfort zone to deal with public wrath over MPs' expenses, and in particular to face those two heated *Question Time* audiences in Ealing and Salisbury.

With celebrity status came, I was told, an ability to move markets. I found this difficult to credit, but was assured by those on the receiving end that my comments had come close to bringing down leading banks, particularly Barclays. I had calls from Stephen Hester of RBS and an especially agitated John Varley at Barclays who worried that my critical remarks about Barclays Capital's lavish bonuses and tax avoidance activities were destabilizing the share price, which was then highly febrile. The calls were followed by a fraught discussion in a parliamentary committee room in which Mr Varley and his team ran into a stream of tough but fair questioning led by Matthew Oakeshott.

A stream of whistleblowers also came to me to expose past goings-on in Barclays, RBS, HBOS and the FSA. After satisfying myself that they were genuine (we had one hoax) and not simply settling old scores, we released their testimony to the press.

It was clear that there had been some appalling abuses taking place in the banks. But with the unrolling of the MPs' expenses scandal, there was a sharp fall in the market for MPs, even those untouched by the scandal, chiding the banks for their past excesses. As the *City A.M.* newspaper proclaimed in its headline: 'Now THEY can't lecture US'.

After the distraction of being almost dragged to the Speaker's chair in the wake of the expenses scandal, I have returned to the task of defining an economic vision, and wider policy framework, for a centre-left party which is no longer on the periphery or a source of ridicule but now has a sporting chance of breaking through and becoming a major force. The most obvious way in which a breakthrough would occur is that at the next General Election, or the one after it, it will become apparent that the traditional binary, two party, system has largely broken down.

There is already a fragmentation of political loyalties occurring and the Liberal Democrats are an important fragment but not the only one. The much debated 'hung parliament' could bring this process to a head; or perhaps the realisation that 'elective dictatorships' based on minority, and lukewarm, public support cannot any longer function effectively, particularly at times of serious economic stress. There are numerous sub-scenarios as to how these stories could play out but the upshot could well be some form of electoral reform and the acceptance that – as is commonplace in local government already – parties can and should work together rather than perpetuate tribal apartheid.

On a personal level I would like to be in a position to translate ideas into practice in government: to do things rather than talk about them. But I have no compulsive need for the status of office or the temporary glories of being welcomed into someone else's 'big tent' and I recognise that the Liberal Democrats may have to be patient and play a long game.

A breakthrough could occur in a different way, if the internal and external disillusionment with Labour were to reach such a point that it faces an existential crisis of the kind experienced by the Liberals in the 1920s and 1930s. Parties do rediscover their sense of purpose and will to win and my own party has recovered from near-death experiences, notably in the late 1980s. I also had a ringside seat in government in 1979 when there was a similar sense of political failure and surrender. I and others in the SDP wrongly judged the condition to be terminal. But I have a hunch, if no more, that this time we are heading for a serious realignment. If this occurs there will be an opportunity to complete the work I first embarked upon as a student politician trying to bring together and reconcile the different strands of what is loosely called progressive politics.

Even as I use this political jargon however, I am conscious of its limitations. And although I subscribe to what can be called the 'progressive agenda' – a sympathy for the underdog; a distaste for gross inequalities of opportunity, wealth and income; a support for properly provisioned public goods – it is far from representing the totality of what I believe and am in politics for. Deep down I am an old fashioned liberal. What makes our society fundamentally different from either the totalitarian horrors of the 20th Century (whether perpetrated by the Nazis or the Communism of Stalin and Mao) or such evils as apartheid or theological autocracy, is respect for individuals in all their variety and quirkiness. I was educated out of the racial and cultural stereotypes with which I was brought up and I was never a very convincing class warrior. I now recognise kindred spirits across the main political parties and outside them.

Fascinating though it is to speculate about future political scenarios and alignments, the more urgent need, for both party and country, is to work on a route map out of the current economic and political crisis. The daily feverishness of the stock exchange and fluctuations in the public mood disguise some troubling long term weaknesses which have been brutally exposed in the last two years. For three decades there had been a gradual revival of national self-confidence from the pessimism and sense of decay which prevailed in the 1970s. But much of that revival has been exposed as hollow.

There was Britain's great success story – the financial services industry, the City – which we now realise was incubating self-destructive folly and greed and has inflicted great damage on the economy. There was a passionate attachment to property ownership as the basis of personal wealth and self-esteem which has been shown to be just as vulnerable to boom and bust as any other speculative mania. There was a long consumer boom with rising expectations of physical comfort, more leisure and more travel which was underpinned by excessive household debt and the depletion of environmental resources. There were morale boosting military achievements but they were based on overstretched resources.

Some of these illusions will be self-correcting as expectations adjust to a more challenging reality. But I sense that the political parties are reluctant to face up to the scale of the problems. There is a public appetite for politicians to 'tell it like it is'; but the appetite goes largely unsatisfied. The winner-takes-all system imposes a stranglehold leading to positioning, triangulation and political manoeuvrings in a very limited political space. Truth risks political suicide. But it has to be tried.

The first issue which has to be faced, and will dominate political life for years to come, is the fiscal problem: chronic, structural, deficits. The immediate cause has been collapse of revenue and increased financial constraints in the wake of the banking collapse. Massive losses have been temporarily absorbed by the state. A more longstanding problem is the Labour government's ambition to create Scandinavian levels of social provision and welfare without Scandinavian levels of taxation and without the political and administrative structures – decentralised decision making and cross party consensus – necessary to support them. Even as these problems are addressed there are looming issues of increased health and care demands from an ageing population.

In the crisis conditions of 2009 these problems can be concealed in very high levels of deficit financing and government borrowing – and that is the right policy in recession – but this cannot be sustained for long. We could easily descend into a vicious downward spiral of rising costs of borrowing, and rising government debt, leading in due course to high inflation or penal taxation or both. The next five to ten years will be dominated by the politics of fiscal correction, and in particular by austerity in public spending. There are fiscal conservatives (and Conservatives) who will approach this task with relish having long wished to complete the unfinished revolution of the 1980s and take an axe to the NHS, state education and the welfare state. I certainly do not relish such a task; nor, I suspect, do large swathes of the public who nonetheless recognise the need for financial discipline. My personal and constituency experience has taught me that there are public services which are under-supported: mental health, adult part-time education, scientific research, training and rehabilitation of young offenders, social housing, respite and support for carers. These are the unfashionable bits of public spending that will not survive - nor will genuine public investment - unless there is a careful review of priorities elsewhere. Such prioritisation will not be comfortable.

But I see my party's role and my own as leading the public debate on how to achieve it. It is tempting to take refuge in 'greater efficiency' and 'reduced bureaucracy' and, while these things are necessary and desirable, the capacity of politicians to deliver them is far less than they claim. What has to be faced is the need for severe restraint on public sector pay and future pensions, especially at the bloated top end of the scale; a willingness to tackle middle class welfare entitlements as in the tax credit system; a downgrading of the country's global defence role; and a willingness to extend personal co-financing in fields such as social care and higher education.

There is a danger that a period of austerity in the public sector is achieved by damaging the country's long term future, allowing school standards and physical infrastructure to degenerate and abandoning some of the visionary investments – in high speed rail or harnessing tidal power – which are desirable for environmental sustainability. While it is easy to spout rhetoric about investment for future generations, mobilising the resources to achieve it will be a difficult sell.

Taxation is a political minefield and fine, radical politicians from John Smith to Charles Kennedy have suffered the effects of detonating hidden bombs. I have worked hard to change my own party's thinking away from an instinctive approval of higher taxes and in particular high rates of income tax on low and middle earners. Even at a time of fiscal difficulty, there is a powerful economic and moral case for lifting low earners out of direct tax. But I do value my party's continued commitment to redistributive taxation and for closing off, as far as possible, the loopholes and generous tax allowances which favour the wealthy. 'Fairer not higher taxes' is the right mantra. In a prolonged fiscal crisis, however, some further taxation may be unavoidable and, if that is to happen, the least damaging way of proceeding is through taxation of consumption and land, the latter an obvious if technically challenging way to combat the national obsession with property speculation. A century on from Lloyd George's 1909 budget there is an urgent need for an approach to fiscal management which is honest, disciplined, radical and redistributive.

Alongside the management of the fiscal crisis the other central economic issue is radical reform of the financial system, domestically, in Europe and globally, to prevent a recurrence of the financial collapse. A disproportionately large financial sector is dangerous because of its capacity to inflict enormous costs on the rest of the economy when a collapse occurs. I have used the analogy with Chernobyl. After such a disaster, it is imperative to adopt higher safety standards. I have written extensively on what I believe has to be done and this is not the place to rehearse the arguments in detail. But what alarms me is the way in which vested interests, political cowardice and inertia are blocking serious and necessary reform. Lazy arguments about promoting the 'competitiveness' of the City and encouraging financial 'innovation' are winning the day. It is hardly surprising that Conservative politicians whose predecessors deregulated the financial sector and demutualised building societies should have a political and intellectual investment in the status quo; but the subservience of the Labour Party to the same interests is genuinely shocking and one of the reasons why I believe the Labour Party has outlived its usefulness. There is a similar conservatism in the Obama administration but they have less at stake since the UK banking sector is many times larger in relation to the economy than the US equivalent. The UK debate has been shunted into a siding by the Conservatives with a second-order argument about which quango should do the regulating, thereby avoiding the central issues.

The case must continue to be made that banks cannot be allowed to pursue short term profit and bonus-maximising objectives if this puts the rest of the economy in peril. The sector and the large banks are currently too big for any British government to guarantee. There is plenty of scope for debating the techniques for regulating these institutions but breaking them up seems to me an essential step to managing the systemic risk they pose and for competitive purposes. As for the nationalised and semi-nationalised banks, the government is in too much of a hurry to re-privatise them. Experience of other countries which have been forced to nationalise their banks in a crisis is that it may take a decade or more to restructure them, manage their bad assets and to pave the way for asset sales which are profitable for the taxpayer. In the meantime, they have a role in supporting economic recovery which the government is failing to realise in a misguided attempt to prove to the City that it will not interfere, even in strategic lending and remuneration policy. As the Labour government shuffles lamely towards the exit door, its failure to build on and develop a timely crisis intervention in October 2008 will come to be seen as a major missed opportunity. But it is not too late to change course.

*

The fiscal crisis and the toxic legacy of the banking crash will dominate economic policy debate for a long time to come. Whether in opposition or government I expect to be centrally engaged in that debate. But these are not just issues for economic nerds. They are political. And looming over the country's economic crisis is a political crisis: the shaming and discrediting of the political class, and specifically of parliament.

Yet there was never a time when strong and healthy democracy was more needed and for the progressive tradition of politics to be championed. There is a likelihood that, on the 'Buggins' Turn' principle, the Conservatives could slide back into power on the strength of a public appetite for 'change'. Having studied at the Blair academy, they have brilliant public relations and tactical skill but little conviction or purpose beyond personal ambition, rewarding their friends and indulging a nostalgia for the 1980s. The contrast with the United States, which produced inspirational politics in response to crisis and previous failures of leadership, is palpable and painful. The country desperately needs the courage and energy of the 1906 Liberals or the 1945 Attlee government or, for that matter, Mrs Thatcher. But we face the prospect of rule by charming but utterly inexperienced young men armed with only a sense of entitlement to run the family estate. There is a risk that the idealism and energy of the politically committed, especially young people, will be siphoned off into single issue campaigns and fragmented protests which are dissipated in a political vacuum. There is a risk too that a sense of political failure could mutate into nationalism and racism. The United Kingdom could fracture along Hadrian's Wall and England along cultural and class lines.

This sense I have of unfinished business and of difficult times ahead helps to explain why I have no intention of quitting the political scene any time soon, unless of course my local constituents decide to get rid of me. Goodness knows, it is tempting to walk away. There are those endless conversations with people which have to start with mumbled explanations that I am not actually stealing their taxes or spending half the year on holiday. Even the nice people, and there are many – strangers who come up to me in the street and on the underground with words of encouragement – often suggest that I should be doing something else. I have plenty to fall back on. I have a family I am very proud of – children and grandchildren – and do not spend enough time with them. I have a blissfully happy marriage and an opportunity to spend more time with my wife in idyllic rural surroundings. I could spend a comfortable retirement addressing approving audiences, saying 'I told you so'. Such humility as I still possess tells me that I am not indispensable and certainly not immortal.

Yet I believe it would be wrong to walk away: indeed, a betrayal of the family, friends and political supporters who helped me to get where I am. There is an enormous job to be done for my party and as part of a wider national debate. I believe that there is a duty, now more than ever, to defend the idea that politics is an honourable and important activity and that the country would be greatly diminished if we gave up on parliament and other democratic institutions.

I draw encouragement from the fact that some of our greatest leaders came into their political prime in their sixties or seventies. And I cannot be the only pensioner in the country to have discovered deep reserves of energy, curiosity and ambition when convention suggests that we are 'too old'. This is no time to quit.

Index

Afghanistan 155, 273
Airlie, Jimmy 120
Al Yamamah arms
   contract 293–4
Alexander, Gavin 213
Alfonso, Juan Pablo Pérez
   142
Ali, Anthony 198
Ali, Tariq 204
Allende, Salvador 139
Angola 148–9
Applegarth, Adam 326,
   329, 330
Ashdown, Paddy 227,
   248–51, 272, 290
Audrey (girlfriend) 24–5
Aylmer, Gerald 60

BAe Systems 92, 210,
   293–4
Balassa, Béla 168
Balls, Alistair 330
Bank of England,
   Monetary Policy
   Committee 325
banking crisis 320–44,
   350
Barclays 343
Bayley, Hugh 223
Baylis, Trevor 269
Bear Stearns 333
Benn, Tony 121, 128
Bennett, Joan 233–4, 298
Bercow, John 317
Bergh, Maarten van den
   186, 325
Birmingham Midshires
   building society 320

Blair, Tony 193, 208, 211,
   245, 248, 262, 273, 290–1,
   302, 351
Blanchflower, Danny
   336–7
Blunkett, David 249, 302
Boothroyd, Betty 316
Botswana 93
Boulton, Adam 280, 308
Bovey, Keith 134
Boyle, Sir Edward 40
BP 199
Bradford & Bingley 320,
   335
Brandt Commission, the
   177
Branson, Richard 295, 331
Brennan, Norman 241
British Bankers'
   Association 321
Brittan, Leon 47
Brooking, Trevor 240
Brown, Gordon 127–8, 131,
   175, 274–6, 281, 288,
   291–2, 295, 302–3, 311,
   319–21, 328, 329, 334,
   342
Browne, Jeremy 328
Browne, John 199
Bruce, Malcolm 249, 251
Brummer, Alex 326
Brundtland Commission,
   the 177–9
Buchan, Janey 116
Buchan, Norman 116
Buchanan, Colin 124–5
Buchanan, Dick 316
Bulger, Denise 241

Burke, Bill 3
Byers, Stephen 269

Cable, Annie 3, 8, 24
Cable, Edith (nee Pinkney)
   2, 3, 7, 10–11, 14, 20, 24,
   29, 32–3, 54, 70, 278–80
Cable, Evie 8, 220
Cable, Hugo 224, 229,
   258–9, 263–4, 266
Cable, John 8
Cable, Keith 10–12, 28–9,
   32, 70, 72–4, 279–80
Cable, Len 2–3, 7, 9, 11,
   14–17, 22, 25–6, 28, 31–3,
   54, 63–4, 70–5, 216
Cable, Olympia (nee
   Rebelo)
   arrival in Britain 53,
      59–60
   courtship 54–62
   family and
      background 56–61,
      73
   education 57
   life in Kenya 62–8
   marriage to VC 66–8
   honeymoon 68–9
   LC's acceptance of
      74–5
   life in Glasgow 106–8,
      130–1
   visit to India 158–65
   life in Twickenham
      204–5, 208, 212–13,
      238–9
   breast cancer 223–5,
      228–9, 230–1

(*nee* Rebelo) *contd.*
  1992 election campaign
    226, 227–8
  constituency work 233,
    242
  health deteriorates
    251–62
  achievements and
    ambitions 252–8
  death 261–2
Cable, Paul 69, 72, 117, 121,
  206, 212–13, 224, 254–6,
  279
Cable, Rachel (*nee* Wenban-
  Smith) 101, 165, 264–8,
  279–80, 298, 334, 341
Cable, Reg 3, 8
Cable, Vince
  childhood 1–12, 31–3
  family backgrounds 2–4
  education 4–7, 11–12,
    22–9
  adolescence 13–31
  political education 15–
    17, 18, 22, 202–3, 345–6
  Oxbridge place 27–9
  university education
    34–52
  university political
    education 39–49
  eastern bloc visit 51–2
  Overseas Development
    Institute fellowship
    52, 78–9
  courtship of Olympia
    54–62
  life in Kenya 61–2, 62–8,
    76–102
  marriage to Olympia
    66–8
  honeymoon 68–9
  estrangement from
    parents 69–70
  life in Glasgow 103–34
  PhD 106
  political campaigning in
    Glasgow 108–17
  service on Glasgow
    council 113–31
  diplomatic service
    135–51
  visit to Soviet Union
    153–4
  visits to India 155–66

  at the ODI 166–72
  Commonwealth
    secretariat post 172–7,
    221
  on Shell's group
    planning team 180–92
  as Shell chief economist
    193–201
  life in Twickenham
    203–15, 210
  as special adviser to
    John Smith 208–11
  move to the SDP 213–21
  York candidacies 215–23
  elected MP for
    Twickenham 225–31,
    232–4
  constituency work
    234–44
  maiden speech 245
  joins shadow cabinet
    251, 270–1
  bereavement 261–2,
    263–4
  courtship and marriage
    to Rachel 264–8
  parliamentary career,
    2001-5 268–78
  and the leadership crisis
    283–5
  elected party deputy
    leader 285
  leadership of party
    289–96, 298–9
  celebrity 297–8, 341–3
  Parliamentarian of the
    Year award 301
  media relations 305–12
  asked to be Speaker
    315–17
  investigation of
    economic crisis
    318–44
  future plans 344–52
Cairn Energy 191
Callaghan, James 71, 139,
  147, 150, 209–10, 216
Calton, Patsy 282
Cambridge, University of
  37–8, 40–9, 54, 61
  Fitzwilliam House 28,
    34–8
Cameron, David 282, 291–2,
  295–6, 328, 340

Campaign for Democratic
  Socialism 43–4
Campbell, Menzies 104,
  280, 284, 284–5, 287–9,
  290, 302
carbon taxes 185
Caribbean states 171–2
Carless, Hugh 137–9, 141
Carmichael, Neil 109, 114
Casey, Terry 15
Cash, Bill 246, 304
Castro, Fidel 146
Chatham House 192–3
Chávez, Hugo 143
Cheadle 282
China 181, 187, 189–90, 336
Ciano, Dr 83
Citizens Advice Bureau 322
Clark, William 78
Clarke, Charles 302
Clarke, Kenneth 47, 49, 273
Clegg, Nick 288, 298, 300,
  333, 338, 342
Clwyd, Ann 273
Comerford, Father 58–9
Commerce of Culture, The
  (Cable, Jain and Weston)
  170
Common Market, the
  129–30
Commonwealth secretariat
  172–7, 221
Communist Party 121–2
Conservative Party 40, 45,
  109–10, 218, 241, 271–2,
  277, 281–2, 286–7, 307, 318,
  320, 328–9, 340–1, 350–1
Cook, Robin 114, 119, 127,
  129, 131
Corbin, Jeremy 304
Costello, John 35–6
Coward, Michael 35
Cox, James 118
Craigen, Jim 131–3
Crosby, Sir James 324–5,
  339
Crosland, Anthony 44,
  149–50, 213
Crossman, Richard 46
Cruickshank, Don 320–1
Cuba 141, 146–9
Cuban missile crisis 38
Cunningham, George 214
Cunningham, Mavis 205

Darbari, Puja 293
Darling, Alistair 303–4,
  329, 332, 337–8
Davey, Ed 230–1
David (childhood friend)
  18–20, 41
Davies, Christie 48
Davis, Ewan 308
de Geus, Ari 181
Demos 193
Deng Xiaoping 169
Denham, John 273
Derek (HF 'Host') 30
Desai, Nitin 177
Deterding, Henri 183
devolution 127–9
Dewar, Donald 104, 133
Dimbleby, David 281, 309
Dixon, Alesha 296
Dobb, Maurice 37, 51
Doherty, Dan 115
Donnelly, Dan 115
Doocey, Dee 227, 230–1,
  234, 319
Doss, Alan 66
Douglas, Dick 128
Douglas-Home, Sir Alec
  45
Dumont, René 87
Duncan (childhood
  friend) 13–14, 17–18
Duncan Smith, Iain 271,
  277, 286, 299, 302
Dunne, John 133–4

Eagle, Angela 333–4
Ealing Southall 287–9
East African Union, the 85
economic crisis 318–44,
  347–50
Economist Intelligence
  Unit 166, 171
Ecuador 141, 145
Edinburgh University
  126–7
elections
  1959 19–20
  1974 205
  1979 207–8
  1983 215–21
  1987 221–3, 226
  1992 192, 211, 225–8
  1997 229–31, 232–3, 241
  2001 251, 262

  2005 278, 280–2
Ennals, James 139
environmental issues
  177–9
Equitable Life 320
European Commission
  166–8
European Union 166–8,
  244, 276
Eustace, Elmo 206
Evans, Neil 261
expenses scandal, the
  301, 305, 312–17

Fabian Society, the 207
Facing Mount Kenya
  (Kenyatta) 77
Falklands War 138, 219
False Start in Africa
  (Dumont) 87
Feinstein, Ann 217, 222
Feinstein, Charles 217
Feltham young offenders'
  institution 242
Fernandes, George 159
Field, Frank 304
Financial Services
  Authority 322, 327, 343
Fisher, Mark 304
Fleming, Sam 326
Flight, Howard 281
Foot, Michael 219
Foot, Paul 109, 204
foreign aid 87–9
Foreign Office, the 137–51
  Information
    and Research
    Department 149–50
Foulkes, George 129
Foyle, Snadra 234
Fulton, Tom 115
Future of Socialism
  (Crosland) 150

Galbraith, J. K. 44
Galbraith, Tam 111–12
Galloway, George 304, 310
Galloway, Steve 218–19,
  221–2
Gandhi, Indira 159, 161,
  173
Gandhi, Sanjay 159
Garraway, Kate 332
Gheewala, Ramesh 99

Gichuru, Mr (Kenyan
  finance minister) 80–1,
  90
Gillings, Guy 199
Giscard d'Estaing, Valéry
  167
Glasgow 72, 74–5, 103–34,
  135, 204, 313
  council 113–31
  Labour Party 108–34
Glasgow Trades Council
  116
Glasgow University 68,
  104–6
Glass, the Reverend Jack
  117
Glazer, Tom 35
Goa 56, 158, 161–6, 263–4,
  265, 284
Goldsworthy, Julia 328
Goodall, Bob 320
Gordon, John aka John
  Junor 17
Gray, Sir William 115, 119
Greaves, Bernard 44
Greer, Germaine 48
Gregory, Conal 217, 219,
  221, 223
Grimond, Jo 39, 41–3
Guest, George 255
Gunn, Jimmy 110–11, 115

Hague, William 245, 286,
  299, 302
Hain, Peter 205
Halifax (bank) 320
Hampstead 207–8
Hannan, Willie 114, 131
Hargreaves, Andrew 128
Harley, Bill 121
Harris, Evan 251
Hart, Judith 138, 146, 209
Have I Got News for You
  310
Hawke, Bob 173
HBOS 324–5, 337, 339, 343
Heal, Geoff 152, 156
Healey, Denis 214
Heath, Edward 120
Herron, Frank 120
Hester, Stephen 343
Hewitt, Patricia 269
Heyer, Surjit 99
Hislop, Ian 310

Hodge, David 132
Hodge, Margaret 214
Hoey, Kate 240, 304
Hogg, Douglas 304
Holdgate, Sir Martin 178
Holiday Fellowship, the
  30–1
Holland, Stuart 128
Hoon, Geoff 274
Hope, Sir Peter 142
Hornsey 208
House of Commons 45
Howard, Michael 46–7,
  241, 274, 277, 280, 286,
  302
Hughes, Helen 168
Hughes, Simon 247, 251,
  285
Huhne, Chris 174–5, 215,
  285, 288, 298–9, 328
Hume, David 104
Humphrys, John 308
Hun (OC's friend) 60
Hunter, Mark 282
Hurst, Greg 283
Hylton-Foster, Sir Harry
  16

Ibrox Park disaster (1971)
  108
immigration 38
Immigration Bill (1968) 72
India 35, 71, 151–3, 155–71,
  187, 189, 190–1, 251–2,
  263–4, 336
Institute of Fiscal Studies
  334
Intelligent Radical's Guide
  to Economic Policy, The
  (Meade) 50–1
International Finance
  Corporation 176
International Monetary
  Fund 175
Internet, the 311–12
Iraq War, 2001 272–4, 283,
  292, 302, 307
Ison, John 215

Jacques, Martin 193
Jain, L. C. 169–70
James, Eric 59
Jenkins, Roy 111, 150, 214,
  219

Jenkins, Simon 342
Jenny (OC's friend) 60
Jessel, Toby 205, 226, 231
Jetha, Nizar 99
Jewell, Mr (teacher) 22–3,
  28
John (childhood friend)
  18
Johnson, Martha 114
Jones, Digby 270
Jones, Jack 116, 121
Jowell, Tessa 207
Julius, DeAnne 185

Kane, Gordon 113
Kaunda, Kenneth 173
Kelly, Miss 145–6
Kelly, Sir Michael 114
Kelly, Ruth 245
Kennedy, Charles 250–1,
  270, 273–4, 276–7, 280–5,
  287, 290, 292, 307, 310,
  348
Kennedy, Jane 333–4
Kenny, Aida (nee Cable)
  72, 213, 224, 228, 255–8,
  279
Kenny, Stephen 258–9
Kenya 57–9, 61–8, 76–102,
  158, 265
  expulsion of Asians
    70–2, 85, 98–9
  population 76–7, 97
  the Treasury 79–89
  corruption 83–5, 87,
    90–3
  foreign aid 87–9
Kenyatta, Jomo 77, 85, 88,
  89–92
Keynes, J. M. 50
Kibaki, Mwai 90–1
Kibe, Joe 80–1
King, Mervyn 325, 329
Kinnock, Neil 225
Kirkwood, Archy 289
Kissinger, Henry 147
Knight, Ted 208
Kreuger, Ann 168

Labour Party 44–5, 72,
  108–34, 203–13, 218–19,
  221, 226, 286, 300, 345,
  349–50. see also New
  Labour

Lall, K. B. 167
Lally, Pat 121
Lamont, Norman 47, 175,
  232
Lateef, Sarwar 35, 166
Latin America 136–52,
  158, 174
Lawrence, Stephen 247
Lawson, Dominic 342
Leavis, F. R. 37
Lee Kuan Yew 173
Lestor, Joan 138–9
Letwin, Oliver 275
Lever, Lord 174
Lewis, John 156
Libby, Terry 78–9, 100
Liberal Democratic Party
  218, 225–32, 248–51, 270–
  2, 277, 280–5, 287–96,
  298–300, 307–8, 318–19,
  328, 344–5, 348
Liberal Party 41–3, 205–7,
  214–15, 218–19, 225
Liddell, Helen 128
Liddle, Roger 215
Littlejohn, Richard 270
Livingstone, Ken 207–8
Lloyd, Lord 258
Lloyds 325, 337, 339, 341
Long, Albert 115
Lords, House of 305
Ludford, Sarah 230
Lynde House 243–4
Lyon, Alex 45, 216–17,
  219, 221

McCarthy, Callum 327
McCrory, Mrs 109
McDonnell, John 303–4
McFadden, Jean 108, 114,
  121
McFadden, John 108–9
McGrath, Gerry 131–3
McGuire, Anne 115–16
McInespie, John 113
Mackenzie, Bruce 90
MacKenzie, Kelvin 313
Mackintosh, John 128
McLean, Malinda 225–7,
  230, 234
Maclennan, Bob 129
McLeod, Iain 40, 46
McNulty, Tony 269
MacPherson, Duncan 206

Mahathir, Datuk Seri 173
Mains, John 113, 115, 118, 119
Major, John 175, 228, 286
Mallalieu, Ann 48–9
Mandela, Nelson 38, 89
Mandelson, Peter 269–70
Mann, Bashir 130
Marion (girlfriend) 25–6
Marr, Andrew 280, 308–9, 337
Marshall, David 115
Marshall-Andrews, Bob 304
Martin, Michael 114–15, 314–15
Mason, Chris 42, 135
Mathieson, Sheena 48
Matiba, Kenneth 85
Maxton, Jimmy 119
May, Teresa 271–2
Maysoon (OC's friend) 60
Mboya, Tom 62, 81–2, 90–1
Meacher, Michael 209
Meade, James 50–1
media, the 305–12
Merton, Paul 310
Michuki, John 80, 84–5, 91
Middle East 188
Militant 122, 204, 208
Millan, Bruce 128, 129
Miller, Maurice 72
Moi, Daniel carap 90–2
Monetary Policy Committee 336–7
Monks, John 270
Montreal Protocol, the 179
Moore, Henry 26–8
Mothersdill, Irene (nee Pinkney) 3, 10
Mothersdill, Reg 3, 10
Mothersdill, Susan 10
Mubia (Kenyan servent) 78–9, 97
Mugabe, Robert 148, 173
Mulgan, Geoff 193
Mundy, Tom 334
Murumbi, Joe 91
Mwangale, John 97

Nairobi 54, 56, 65–6, 76, 78
Narain, Lisette 230
National Front, the 205
Ndero, John 96
Neil, Andrew 280, 296, 308
New Deal for the City 333
New Labour 232–45, 248–9, 268, 271, 281
New Society 125
Newby, Dick, Lord 230
Newcastle upon Tyne 330, 332
News at Ten 311
Newsnight 201
Ngala, Ronald 90–1
Ngei, Paul 83
Ngeny, Arap 81
Nigeria 174, 186, 194–9, 336
1922 Committee 43
Nioni 99
No Entry (Steel) 72
Northern Rock 294–5, 320, 326–33, 339
Norway 129–30
Nove, Alec 104, 191
Nyerere, Julius 173

Oakeshott, Matthew 294, 327, 329–30, 343
Oaten, Mark 284–5
Obama, Barack 311–12, 350
Odinga, Oginga 91
Odongo, Okello 88
O'Donnell, Gus 104
Ogot, Grace 62
Ogot, Pamela 61–2, 65–6, 94–5, 102
oil 142–3, 181–2, 188–92, 193–201, 325–6, 336
Ojwang, Gilbert 96
OPEC 142–3
Osborne, George 308, 328, 337, 340–1
Ouko, Robert 84
Overseas Development Institute 52, 78–9, 166–72
Owen, David 150–1, 209, 214, 222, 225

Pakistan 156, 158
Palme Commission, the 177
Papp, Susan 74
Parliament 244–8, 290–2, 301–5
Parry, Martin 178
Patel, Dr Chai 243–4
Paxman, Jeremy 201, 308
Payne, Sara 241
Peacock, Alan 59
Pérez, Carlos Andrés 143, 145
Persaud, Vishnu 175–6
Peston, Robert 327, 338
Pinkney, Annie 3
Pinto, Pio Gama 59
Pliatzky, Leo 209
Politics of Harold Wilson, The (Foot) 109
Pollitt, Brian 46
Pond, Chris 246
Potter, Jim 152
Powell, Enoch 40, 130
Protectionism and Industrial Decline (Cable) 168
Putin, Vladimir 192

Question Time 309–10, 314, 332, 343
Quiet Crisis in India (Lewis) 156

Race, Reg 207–8
racial discrimination 38
Ramphal, Sir Sonny 172–7, 221
Razzall, Tim, Lord 214–15, 280
Rebelo, Amata 73, 252
Rebelo, Aurelio 73
Rebelo, Celso 72, 158, 160–1, 163–5, 251–2, 265
Rebelo, Mr 57, 58, 62–4, 66, 71, 73, 158, 162–3
Rebelo, Mrs 57, 67, 265
Rebelo, Selina 73
Rebelo, Vanita 165
Red Papers for Scotland (Brown) 127–8, 303
Redwood, John 246
Ree, Harry 59
Reeves, Andrew 262

Reid, Jimmy 120
Reid, John 116
Rennard, Chris 282
Rich, Walter 222
Ridley, Nicholas 120–1
Rifkind, Malcolm 110
Robertson, George 128, 131
Robinson, Joan 50–1
Robinson, Nick 280
Roddick, Anita 195
Rodgers, Bill 43, 219
Ross, Willie 127–8
Rothschild, Lord 140
Royal Bank of Scotland
  337, 339, 341, 343
Russia 188–9, 191–2, 199,
  336

Samuel, Geoffrey 206–7
Samuel, Marcus 182
Saro-Wiwa, Ken 194
Saudi Arabia 92, 293–4
Save Our Building
  Societies 320
Savosnik, Kurt 81–4, 87
Scanlon, Hugh 116
Schwarz, Peter 181
Scotland, devolution
  127–9
Scott, Derek 215
Scott, Tavish 339
Scottish Development
  Agency 129
Scottish Enterprise 129
Scottish National Party
  109–10, 114, 128
SDP 213–21, 225
Sedgemore, Brian 281
Sharma, Reeti 66
Shaw, Geoff 116, 121
Shaw, Pat 113
Shell 179–201
Shepherd, Richard 304
Sherlock, Neil 230
Shipley, John 330
Short, Clare 216–17, 304
Sillars, Jim 128
Singh, Manmohan 168–9
Singh, Parmeet 99
Sinha, Radha 105
Sirc, Ljubo 104–5
Skinner, Dennis 290, 304

Smith, Adam 50, 84,
  104–5
Smith, Sir Arnold 143–4
Smith, Ian 148, 173
Smith, John 104, 128, 131,
  208–9, 214, 348
Society of Friends (the
  Quakers) 20–2
Soviet Union 52, 88,
  153–4, 181, 191–2
Spicer, Sir Michael 43
Steel, David 72
Stewart, Mark Moody 190
Stimson, Phil 114
Storm, The (Cable) 312,
  318, 334–5, 338, 341–2
Straw, Jack 274
Stuart, Mark Moody 199
Suan (OC's friend) 60
Sweetman, Trevor 66
Sykes, Manuela 42

Tanya (girlfriend) 36–7
Tanzania 92–3
Tapsell, Sir Peter 304
Taverne, Dick 43
taxation 348–9
Taylor, Ian 273
Taylor, Matthew 270, 280
Taylor, Teddy 110, 130
Teather, Sarah 277
Thatcher, Margaret 16, 75,
  118, 120, 129, 173–4, 179,
  213, 218, 219, 225, 227, 239,
  286, 351
Theory of Moral
  Sentiments, The (Smith)
  105
Thomson, George 129
Thorpe, Jeremy 41–2
Tickell, Sir Crispin 179
Today 308, 311, 326
Tonge, Jenny 274
Tothova, Agnesa 255–6
Toynbee, Polly 215
Tranh 167
Tugendhat, Michael 47
Turner, Kate 240
Turpie, Len 110
Twickenham 192, 202–16,
  225–44, 271–2, 331–2
Tyrrell, Joan 80, 87

Uganda 72, 130
Unilever 183
United National
  Economic Programme
  (UNEP) 177
United Nations 175–6
United States of America
  88–9, 311, 333–4, 340, 351

Varley, John 343
Vassall, John 111
Veeren, Jeroen van der
  186
Venezuela 141–4, 189, 336
Victims of Crime Trust
  241–2
Vine, Jeremy 308

Wachem, Loew van 183,
  199
Wack, Pierre 181
Wainwright, Richard 42
Waller, John 226
Ward, Dame Barbara 177
Watson, Alan (Lord) 42
Watts, Phil 199–200
Wealth of Nations, The
  (Smith) 105
Webb, Steve 251
Wells, Jill 66
Weston, Ann 170
Whelan, Father 67–8
Whitney, Ray 149
Wight, Robin 35
Williams, David 271
Williams, Gwyn 59–60
Williams, Shirley 219
Williams, Sir William
  214–15
Willis, Phil 251
Wilson, Harold 44–5, 109,
  139
Wilson, Tom 105
Woodriffe, Maureen 215
World Bank 168, 175
Wright, David 43

York 1–2, 4, 9–10, 42, 45,
  53–6, 69–70, 215–23, 227
  University of 53–4,
  59–60
Young, Kirsty 309